Methodological Issues
in Aging Research

The Notre Dame Series on Quantitative Methodologies

Building on the strength of Notre Dame as a center for training in quantitative psychology, the Notre Dame Series on Quantitative Methodologies (NDSQM) offers advanced training in quantitative methods for social and behavioral research. Leading experts in data analytic techniques provide instruction in state–of–the–art methods designed to enhance quantitative skills in a selected substantive domain.

Each volume evolved from an annual conference that brings together expert methodologists and a workshop audience of substantive researchers. The substantive researchers are challenged with innovative techniques and the methodologists are challenged by innovative applications. The goal of each conference is to stimulate an emergent substantive and methodological synthesis, enabling the solution of existing problems and bringing forth the realization of new questions that need to be asked. The resulting volumes are targeted towards researchers in a specific substantive area, but also contain innovative techniques of interest to pure methodologists.

The books in the series are:

- *Methodological issues in aging research*, co-edited by Cindy S. Bergeman and Steven M. Boker (2006)

Methodological Issues
in Aging Research

Edited by

Cindy S. Bergeman
Steven M. Boker
University of Notre Dame

2006

LAWRENCE ERLBAUM ASSOCIATES, PUBLISHERS
Mahwah, New Jersey   London

Senior Editor:	Debra Riegert
Editorial Assistant:	Kerry Breen
Cover Design:	Steven M. Boker
Cover Layout:	Kathryn Houghtaling Lacey
Text and Cover Printer:	Book-mart Press, Inc.

Lawrence Erlbaum Associates, Inc., Publishers
10 Industrial Avenue
Mahwah, New Jersey 07430
www.erlbaum.com

CIP information for this volume can be obtained by contacting the Library of Congress.

ISBN 0-8058-4378-7 (cloth : alk. paper)
ISBN 0-8058-4379-5 (pbk. : alk. paper)

Books published by Lawrence Erlbaum Associates are printed on acid-free paper, and their bindings are chosen for strength and durability.

Printed in the United States of America
10 9 8 7 6 5 4 3 2 1

Contents

Preface

Cindy S. Bergeman and Steven M. Boker
University of Notre Dame

This volume resulted from the inaugural conference in the Notre Dame Series on Quantitative Methodologies (NDSQM) held at the University of Notre Dame in 2002. Building on the strength of Notre Dame as a center for training in quantitative study, the Notre Dame Series on Quantitative Methodologies offers advanced training for early career scholars and young researchers from around the nation. Leading scholars in the field provide instruction in state of the art methods designed to enhance the quantitative training in a variety of substantive domains. Although the approaches discussed in this volume are applicable to diverse populations, the focus of the first conference was methodological issues that are especially relevant to aging research.

The goal of this volume is to provide researchers with innovative techniques for the collection and analysis of data focusing on the dynamic nature of aging. To accomplish this goal, we assembled a premier group of scholars in the field of methodology and aging to describe and discuss the application of a variety of techniques, such as structural equation modeling, latent class analysis, hierarchical linear growth curve modeling, dynamical systems analysis, multivariate, multilevel Rasch models, survival analysis, and quantitative genetic methodologies. These new techniques provide better estimates of the direct effect of environmental or treatment effects; more precise predictions of outcomes which in turn increase the diagnostic power of test instruments; the potential for developing new treatments that take advantage of the intrinsic dynamics of the course of a disease or age–related change to enhance treatment; and better estimates of the dynamic pattern of genetic and environmental influences on development in later life.

Nesselroade opens the book with a discussion of the challenge posed by the convergence of theory and method and the impact that this may have on the future of aging research. A well thought out and executed program of study, integrating the techniques discussed in this volume, will contribute to theory development and advance powerful insights into the determinants of the aging process.

Bergeman & Wallace (Chapter 2) set the stage for the data analytic contributions by highlighting fundamental methodological issues for the study of older population and the importance of integrating theory into studies of later life. Chapters 3 through 9 focus on specific techniques that can be applied to a variety of types of data to help elucidate the complex and dynamic relations among important variables of study.

Structural equation modeling (SEM) allows researchers to examine constancy and change on the underlying, or latent, level (i.e., for the construct of interest, not just a measured scale), and to deal with complex issues of measurement error. Extensions of these models have focused on incorporating growth trajectories that allow for the assessment of underlying growth/decline as a function of latent changes. The chapter by McArdle & Hamagami (Chapter 3) extends the application of this technique by incorporating model-based dynamics. Using assessments of intellectual abilities collected over a 60–year period, they demonstrate the use of models that not only address measurement issues and latent growth curves, but also include multiple variables and multiple groups in dynamic analysis.

Hierarchical linear modeling (HLM) provides a potent, but flexible technique for assessing a variety of theoretical questions about individual differences in developmental trajectories over time. In this volume, Curran, Bauer, & Willoughby (Chapter 4) demonstrate how techniques for testing and probing higher-order interactions, which are traditionally used in ordinary least squares regression, can be used in hierarchical linear models as well. To illustrate this technique, the components of health trajectories (i.e., intercepts, slopes) of older adults were predicted from a measure of social support, gender, and their interaction. The results indicated that the inclusion (and probing) of higher-order interactions provides a more complete and theoretically-rich analysis. Johnson & Raudenbush (Chapter 5) examined the application of a multivariate, multilevel Rasch model to self-reported behavior, a procedure that has multiple applications in aging research. Although the example used in their chapter did not utilize data from an older population, it illustrates how Item Response Theory can be used to create and assess the metric used in measuring change, at multiple levels, using multiple measures (items). They demonstrate that assessing participant demography in conjunction with repeated data from multiple cohorts allows for the possibility of separating age, cohort and history effects in longitudinal data.

Without valid and reliable measurement, the application of ones method in terms of the assessment of the constructs of interest is problematic and thus the ability to test, advance, and refine theory is jeopardized. Much research has focused on measurement issues using interval-scale data, but less is know about nominal scale reliability (e.g., classification). Schuster (Chapter 6) overviews latent class analysis approaches to the determination of the reliability of nominal classifications comparing the target–type approach to the response error approach to assessing rating quality. This chapter provides a comparison of these approaches based on parsimony, sensitivity, rater–specific error rates, category–specific error rates and the overall reliability index.

Boker & Bisconti (Chapter 7), apply linear differential equations models of short and long-term dynamics to a longitudinal "burst" of data in a sample of recent widows. The results not only illustrate the components of emotion regulation following a major life stressor, but also identify resilience mechanisms that relate to individual differences in these trajectories.

Wenger, Schuster, Petersen, & Petersen (Chapter 8) investigate the application of proportional hazards models and frailty models to response time data to explicate the viability of the technique for studies assessing real-time information processing capacity. These authors argue that response time data are used extensively for the study of cognitive processes, and that the hazard function is a more appropriate indicator of processing capacity than are the mean or median response times. Data on a free– and cued–recall task in normal and mildly impaired elders is used to illustrate these points.

Neale, Boker, Bergeman, & Maes (Chapter 9) apply state of the art behavioral genetic techniques to longitudinal data to identify the etiology of individual differences in behaviors of interest. This chapter provides a brief background in behavioral genetic methodology as well as a description of innovative extensions of these methods to growth curve and dynamic systems analysis. Systolic and diastolic blood pressure measures from twins participating in the Medical College of

Virginia Study of Cardiovascular Health illustrate the applicability of these techniques.

It was certainly a privilege to work with this dynamic group of presenters who generously gave of their time to develop and present their talks, inform the discussions of issues relevant to methodology and aging, and meet one–on–one or in small groups with interested conference participants. It is in the confluence of these approaches that we all learn more about the complexities of conducting research with older populations.

This volume would not have come about without the encouragement, support and guidance of our keynote speaker, John Nesselroade. His theoretical work delineating the need for focusing on intraindividual change underpins many if not most of the methodological and statistical approaches found in this volume. We were honored that he was the inaugural speaker at NDSQM and that his chapter introduces the first of this edited series.

We gratefully acknowledge the financial support from the Institute for Scholarship in the Liberal Arts in the College of Arts and Letters, the Office of Research in the Graduate School, and the Department of Psychology at the University of Notre Dame. With out this initial support, we would not have made the series a reality. Funding for the work was provided in part by grants from the National Institutes of Health (NIA 1R29 AG14983) to Steve Boker and (NIA 1 RO3 AG18570–01) to Cindy Bergeman.

We also want to thank faculty, students and staff who helped to make this conference a reality. In particular, Drs. Scott Maxwell and Ke–Hai Yuan of the Psychology Department who participated in the conference as discussants. Graduate students from our Quanitative Program, Eric Covey, Ken Kelley, and Joe Rausch were incredibly helpful during the conference. A special thank you is also due to Pascal Deboeck and Stacey Tiberio, without whose diligent help in converting all of the manuscripts to a consistent LaTeX style this volume would not exist.

We appreciate the thoughtful comments from Lisa Harlow, Ph.D. (University of Rhode Island), Keith G. Widaman, Ph.D. (University of California–Davis) and Barbara M. Byrne, Ph.D. (University of Ottawa) who review an earlier draft of this volume. In addition, the guidance and persistence of the editorial staff at LEA, in particular Debra Riegert and Kerry Breen has been invaluable.

Correspondence may be directed to Cindy S. Bergeman or Steven M. Boker, Department of Psychology, University of Notre Dame, Notre Dame, IN 46556, USA; email sent to cbergema@nd.edu or sboker@nd.edu; or browsers pointed to http://www.nd.edu/~sboker.

Methodological Issues
in Aging Research

Quantitative Modeling in Adult Development and Aging: Reflections and Projections

John R. Nesselroade
University of Virginia

Quantitative research in aging is at an important crossroads. Theorists in a variety of substantive areas (e.g., cognition, memory, emotion) have tried to make important advances in the past few years, but the necessary empirical underpinnings tend to rely primarily on the methodological tools that have dominated the study of behavior, development, and change for the past several decades — the restrictive conceptions of static equilibrium, linearity, and additivity. It is time to push for the further development and adoption of alternative methodological approaches that embrace more dynamical and, when appropriate, nonlinear conceptions. It is also not amiss for methodologists to challenge the theorists to foster more dynamical concepts regarding the nature of aging. Looming in the interface of the method–theory collaboration is the fact that idiosyncrasies in stimulus perceptions and response patterns jeopardize analyses depending on the traditionally casual aggregation of data over experimental units. This matter will have to be addressed before the high levels of validity and precision we seek for lawful relationships can be attained.

1.1 Reflections

I am honored to participate in this inaugural conference of the Notre Dame Series on Quantitative Methodology with its focus on adult development and aging.[1] In psychology, in general, we have a very long history of concern with change and how to quantify it. Some of us are concerned primarily with developmental change, some with the outcome of structured interventions, and still others with processual change such as in the likely voting behavior during the waning days of political campaigns. I have been laboring in the vineyard of change measurement, primarily in personality and ability attributes, for over 40 years and I can still vividly recall how impressed I was by the magnitude, thoughtfulness, and no small amount of passion characterizing the literature on the topic that was already available back in the early 1960s when, as a graduate student in Raymond B. Cattell's laboratory, I first started examining it. For example, papers by the likes of Bereiter (1963), Cattell (1963), Cattell (1966), Fiske and Rice (1955), Flugel (1928), Manning and DuBois (1962), Thouless (1936), Woodrow (1932) and many others intrigued me then and are still very much worth reading.

For me, one of the more stimulating pieces of work early on was the chapter by Bereiter (1963), titled "Some Persisting Dilemmas in the Measurement of Change". I wrestled with the issues raised by Bereiter, some of which I found to be quite abstract, such as the subjectivism versus physicalism dilemma.[2] I would think I understood the dilemmas and then, reading the chapter again to make sure, would become uneasy about one or another aspect. Still, I strug-

---

[1] I have a strong feeling of kinship with the University of Notre Dame Department of Psychology, having been a member of a reviewing committee several years ago that came to know the department rather well and made a number of recommendations designed to help strengthen an already fine program. One of those recommendations was to initiate a regular methodological dialogue such as that in which we are now participating. I am also proud to say that I had a hand in the graduate training of several of the current faculty members. In keeping with my intimate regard for the program and its faculty, I've purposefully injected a personal perspective into my comments. I hope they do not come across as overly egocentric.

[2] In 1964, Bereiter was slated to be the second reader on my master's thesis so I felt obliged to continue working on mastering his chapter. Bereiter left Illinois to take a position elsewhere, but I persisted.

gled with these and many other issues regarding the representation and measurement of psychological and behavioral change and carried these concerns with me when professional circumstances described elsewhere (Nesselroade, 2000) dictated that I become a life-span developmentalist. But that is another story. It didn't help my state of mind when, in 1970, Cronbach and Furby seemed to be saying not to bother any more with trying to measure psychological change at the individual level.

In the late 1970s, Paul Baltes and I made an attempt to organize some of the literature as well as our own thoughts about studying developmental changes with a discussion of longitudinal research methods. In preparing for this undertaking, to our surprise, we found such "comforting" thoughts as: "There is no hard and fast definition of what constitutes a longitudinal study. (Hindley, 1972, p. 23) and Zazzo's (1967) identification of *longitudinal* as a general term describing a variety of methods. To try to bring some closure to our own thinking regarding the term *longitudinal*, we concluded that "longitudinal methodology involves repeated, time-ordered observation of an individual or individuals with the goal of identifying processes and causes of intraindividual change and of interindividual patterns of intraindividual change [in behavioral development]" (Baltes & Nesselroade, 1979, p. 7). We observed that there is one sine qua non of longitudinal research, namely "the entity under investigation is observed repeatedly as it exists and evolves over time," and enunciated five reasons or rationales for why one would conduct longitudinal research. They are:

1. Direct identification of intraindividual change

2. Direct identification of interindividual differences in intraindividual change

3. Analysis of interrelationships in behavioral change

4. Analysis of causes (determinants) of intraindividual change, and

5. Analysis of causes (determinants) of interindividual differences in intraindividual change analysis.

I do believe that these rationale points were helpful in clarifying some of the purposes of developmental research and also in helping to demystify longitudinal research in general, although some of its mystique is clearly still alive today.

Along the way, one of the important views that students of change gradually came to accept, probably during the 1980s, is the perspective that, by and large, the effective study of change requires more than two occasions of measurement. Whether this realization helped to fuel the interest in growth curve modeling or vice versa, I'm not sure. In either case, because of this shift in perspective, we have been able to worry less about the use of simple measures of change, such as difference scores, and concentrate instead on the specification of more extensive change functions. Several of the chapters in this volume reflect this multi–occasion orientation.

It was about the time that Baltes and I were working on these ideas that I became better acquainted with the late Joachim F. (Jack) Wohlwill whom I had known since the late 1960s when he came to the first West Virginia Conference on Life–Span Development and delivered a paper titled, "Methodology and Research Strategy in the Study of Developmental Change." I was struck by Wohlwill's grasp of methodological issues pertinent to the study of developmental change as well as his knowledge of developmental theory.[3] In one of his last papers, a chapter published in 1991 in the *Annals of Theoretical Psychology*, Wohlwill once again turned to the relationship between theory and method in developmental research. He identified his preferred view of this relationship as the partial–isomorphism relationship between method and theory.

> This flexible, loose sort of linkage between theory and method will serve as a counterforce to sterile pursuit of methodology for its own sake, divorced from and uninformed by theory, such as would be encouraged if methodology were to be considered as completely independent of

---

[3]Ten years later, when Wohlwill and I were colleagues at Penn State, I relished our many lunch discussions concerning the study of change and development. These continued until his untimely death in 1987. Jack could and would "hold your feet to the fire" until he was satisfied that your case was stated unambiguously. Accepting your statement of the problem certainly did not mean that he would agree with your solution, as I learned over and over.

theory. At the same time the conception likewise avoids the excesses of theorizing without regard to methodological approach, or of subordinating method entirely to theory, which is apt to ensure the preservation of the theory in isolation from rival ones, and thus lead eventually to its dying on the vine. (Wohlwill, 1991, p. 91)

Wohlwill elegantly made the point that theory is not always in the driver's seat, nor, indeed, should it be, although many of us have been "hammered," over and over, with the idea that theory should drive method and not vice versa. Rather, Wohlwill was describing a productive tension between theory and method such that the one reinforced and pulled along the other. Indeed, theory may sometimes have to wait on method. But that does not mean that theory should contentedly rely on inadequate method. In a similar vein, the developer of method does not need to delay, until theory demands new products, promulgating something novel that may, in turn, elicit more advanced theoretical contributions.

In the second edition of the *Handbook of Multivariate Experimental Psychology* (Nesselroade, 1988), I had occasion to refer to Wohlwill's view of the theory-method interface and used the metaphor of a dance between two strong partners. I wrote:

First, substance, often in the form of elaborate but untested theory, takes a step and then methodological developments follow. Subsequently, methodology may glide out ahead, even far ahead of substantive gains. The partners in this seemingly cumbersome dance likely will never blend in a graceful pas de deux. Nor should we wish them to. Rather, a continuing imbalance seems to enable each in turn to elicit new stops from the other.[4] (p. 643)

Obviously, there are many instances in which theory has challenged, to good effect, the prevailing methodology. Looking back over

---

[4]I still remember a remark from my coeditor, Raymond B. Cattell, on reading this bit of prose, "Kind of abstract, isn't it?" This from the person who once described the hyperplane as "the footprint of a causal influence." I kept it in, anyway.

our history of the past 100 years, the development of factor analysis as a tool to help Spearman elaborate his concept of g, Thomson his "sampling bonds" theory, and subsequently, the development of multiple factor analysis by Thurstone to aid his theoretically guided search for multiple factors of human ability are cases in point.

Method Leading Theory

But this is a methodological conference, so I want to spend a little time on examining the other phase of this dance: how methodology has and must continue to challenge theories of adult development and aging. The chapter by Bergeman and Wallace thoughtfully addresses some of these key matters.

Modeling

One pertinent example of methodological concerns forcing theory to do better can be seen in the aftermath of the presentation of Schaie's general developmental model (see also Baltes, 1968) and parallel developments in the life-course research of some sociologists. Once researchers became convinced of the importance of identifying cohort and time of measurement effects, for example, it didn't take long for theoretical concerns to force researchers to begin to grapple with the "unpacking" of these generalized combinations of influences into their key, distinct components. The detailed identification by Baltes, Cornelius, and Nesselroade (1978), for example, of age-graded, history-graded, and nonnormative life events illustrates an advance in the theory of cohort and time of measurement effects that was elicited, in large part, by the methodological tension created by the appearance of the general developmental model.

Measurement

I want to say a word or two regarding measurement issues and describe a situation where I would like to see method exert more of an influence on theory development. It is in this context that I have come to reinterpret the contemporary phrase, "thinking outside the box." I will illustrate this in a moment but first, let me explain a bit more. The past two decades have witnessed an increased interest in modeling short-term, intraindividual variability in a variety of substantive domains, including temperament and human abilities. Coincidentally, developments in dynamic factor analysis (e.g., Browne & Nesselroade, 2005; J. J. McArdle, 1982; Molenaar, 1985; Nesselroade & Molenaar, 1999), as well as other kinds of dynamic modeling such as those presented in the chapters coauthored by Boker and by Wenger and Schuster, have blossomed. The appearance and preliminary application of these methods have given us some important new insights into the nature of behavior and behavior change and, I very much believe, have raised some promising possibilities about the way we conceptualize and measure variables.

Consider, for example, variables such as rhythmicity (a temperament dimension measured in young children) and rigidity (a personality characteristic studied at many age levels). Typically, these are measured by assigning a person a score indicating how much or how little of the attribute is manifested. For example, how much rhythmicity does a participant have? How high does someone score on rigidity? This kind of conceptualization is the traditional thinking within the "box," as represented in Fig. 1.1.

But, it is possible to think outside the "box" with such variables and many others, I'm convinced, and to conceptualize and measure them with actual intraindividual variability in the pertinent behavior rather than an estimate of a static amount. Consider the concept of socialization, for example. *Socialized* behavior is behavior that varies appropriately from situation to situation while still falling within acceptable limits; it is not behavior that is so highly constrained and repetitive as to be considered pathological. It is my expectation that work on intraindividual variability that has been largely methodologically oriented will challenge substantive researchers to consider these implications as they conceptualize their variables and build measurement devices for them.

There are many other aspects of measurement that space constraints preclude addressing here. The chapter by Schuster examines some additional critical aspects.

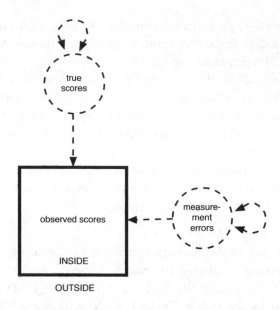

Figure 1.1: The "box."

Design

In a similar vein of methodological emphases running ahead of theoretical concerns, about 15 years ago I argued, on the strength of results from a series of intraindividual variability modeling studies, in favor of incorporating "bursts" of measurement into longitudinal designs. It took a while, but that methodologically leading step was followed by compelling theoretical rationale, and now, for example, the Victoria Longitudinal Study (Hultsch, Hertzog, Dixon, & Small, 1998) includes such a design feature.

Method and Theory in Aging Research

Despite a number of interesting and promising methodological developments of the past couple of decades, there are still many aspects of the study of aging for which theory has led the dance for a long time, perhaps long enough that it is time for a change. Developmental systems theorists (e.g., Ford, 1987; Ford & Lerner, 1992) have pushed some interesting substantive ideas well beyond the capabilities of the currently popular methods. Theorists in lifespan development and aging, such as Paul Baltes and Margret Baltes, Laura Carstensen, Gisela Labouvie–Vicf, and others, have advanced the development and presentation of theory to a considerable level, one involving complexities and abstractions such as multidimensionality, multidirectionality, and gains and losses and process notions of continuing adaptation such as selection, optimization, and compensation, socioemotional selectivity, and so forth. But the tools by which many of these conceptions are being empirically tested are the "work horses" of yesteryear, such as multiple regression, with some extensions.

For example, running through most of the theoretical arguments referred to earlier (and rightly so) is the notion of process, and that notion, I believe, challenges both the methodologist and the theorist more importantly now than at any point in our history. One of the arenas where method is already daring theory is growth curve modeling (J. J. McArdle & Nesselroade, 2003). Since the papers by Rao (1958) and by Tucker (1958) with key followups by J. McArdle and Epstein (1987); Meredith and Tisak (1984, 1990); Rogosa, Brandt, and Zimowski (1982), and others, the technology of fitting growth curves can be argued to have grown, to some extent, somewhat beyond the features of many of the data to which these models are fitted—the methods are more interesting than the data, in many cases. Theorists will do well to strengthen their conceptions and measures to take advantage of the benefits of these recently developed technologies. The chapter by Curran, Bauer, and Willoughby explores some key aspects and novel applications of growth curve modeling. But the theoretical arguments involving process concepts are crying out for other methodological approaches as well, including the linear oscillator discussed by Boker and latent change models by McArdle.

Projections

I want to look down the road a bit farther and prod you, the reader, perhaps even irritate you a little, regarding the current state of the method–theory interface. To do this, I am going to use theory to challenge measurement, design, and modeling methodology.

I call attention to a specter that I see slowly growing but not yet substantial; hulking but not yet sharply defined; advancing but not yet truly threatening. Yet, there are signs of it in the titles and content of many papers that are found in today's literature. I do not believe that this specter can be ignored.

I will cast this particular devil within the framework of the so–called idiographic versus nomothetic debate. The psychological literature contains an old distinction between idiographic and nomothetic concerns (e.g., Allport, 1937; Lamiell, 1981, 1988; Rosenzweig, 1958, 1986; Zevon & Tellegen, 1982) pertaining especially to the study of personality, but the concerns hold for any domain studied via differences among persons, I would argue. In developmental science, for example, the distinction between person–centered and variable–centered approaches to the study of behavior and its development (Bergman, Magnusson, & El-Kouri, 2003; Magnusson, 1998) is, in part, an acknowledgment of some of these same ideas. Valsiner's (1984) discussion of typological versus variational modes of thought also bears on the topic. Recent discussions by Lamiell (1998) and van Kampen (2000) illustrate those features of the debate of most centrality to the present discussion. Idiographic concerns center on the uniqueness of the individual, whereas nomothetic concerns emphasize the generality of lawfulness in behavior.

These two conceptual domains are often regarded as antithetical from the standpoint of building a science of behavior, but I subscribe to the spirit of rapprochement expressed by authors such as Lamiell (1981), who argued for integrating the two into an "idiothetic" approach, and Zevon and Tellegen (1982; see also Nesselroade & Ford, 1985), who proposed that idiographic information can and should be put to the service of developing nomothetic relationships (see also Molenaar, Huizenga, & Nesselroade, 2003). These and other writers have dared to raise questions regarding the validity of some of our most cherished group–analysis concepts, including means, variances, and covariances or correlations, All of us are familiar with examples in which the mean is not a very workable concept; where it applies to no one. For example, statistically speaking, the average number of bedrooms in single family dwellings implies a lot of unfinished houses, just as the average number of children living in these houses implies a lot of partial children. Far more serious, I contend, are the questions being raised regarding variances and covariances because those are the "stuff" that many of us study the most intensively. Correlations, and the statements of structure derived from them, are group, not individual representations. Just what is the role of the individual in these kinds of group modeling efforts? This is one of the key questions that is being asked.

Behavior patterns have both idiosyncratic and general features. To illustrate the basic idea more concretely, two speakers find themselves in front of large audiences, preparing to deliver addresses. One is painfully aware of the size of the audience, the fact that many of its members are well–dressed, professional–looking people, and that they seem to be a serious, humorless bunch. Waiting to be introduced, he feels his heart start to pound and his hands begin to tremble as his breathing becomes more and more shallow. The other speaker, somewhat by contrast, is also painfully aware of the size of his audience, notices that they appear to be "organized" into small groups of seemingly intimate acquaintances, and many of them have their eyes on the clock. His hands begin to sweat, his shirt collar feels very tight, and his heart begins to pound. In stimulus–response terms, both speakers are experiencing a stress response to a threatening situation. Clearly, some of what is happening is common to the two of them. But, there are also substantial idiosyncratic elements in both the perception of the stimulus situation and the pattern of response.

These idiosyncratic features of behavior are shaped by genetics and experience. There is much in common to the two speakers' experiences. Both perceive the situation as threatening, both have heightened sympathetic nervous system activity, and both are subjectively aware of their discomfort. They have inherited a number of physical and physiological attributes common to human beings that influence their perceptions of a situation and their reactions to it. But, their perceptions and reactions also have unique characteristics that introduce considerable idiosyncrasy into the mix. One sees the crowd as hostile; the other sees it as aloof. One breaks into a cold sweat; the other's shirt collar seems to be choking him. These perceptions and behavior patterns are, in part, functions of the unique genetic makeup and histories of conditioning and learning each has undergone over the course of his lifetime. Thus, the two speakers' perceptions and behaviors are similar in some ways and different in others.

Now, in this simple example, it is not amiss to aggregate information over the two speakers at the level of "experiencing a stress response to a threatening situation." However, there is much less justification for aggregation at the level of the speakers' self–reported perceptions of the stimulus situation and self–reported or objectively measured responses. For instance, "shallow breathing" holds for one, but not for the other. Aggregating over these kinds of "individual differences" might lead to relationships, but they will not be nearly as strong as is implied by the nomothetic components (e.g., anxiety response to a threatening situation).

Another example of the difficulties created by these kinds of individual differences comes from an earlier foray into *p–technique research*, this time with Linda Mitteness (Mitteness & Nesselroade, 1987). During debriefing, we found that two participants (a mother and daughter), whose daily emotion self–reports we were trying to relate, were responding quite differently to the stimulus, "Are you anxious?" One of the individuals was interpreting "anxious" to mean "anxious" and the other was interpreting "anxious," to mean "eager." Because of their unique phenotypic histories, these two individuals had different ideas about what the item signified and responded according to their respective views. In analyzing such data, we typically ignore the possibility that the content of the item might have been construed differently by different respondents and proceed to aggregate the information they have supplied across persons as though it were perfectly meaningful to do so.

Elsewhere, Molenaar et al. (2003) explored these issues in considerable detail within the framework of modeling single subject and group data. Another important key is the breaking down of data into groups and levels. Multilevel models, for example, involve the systematic recognition of differences among subgroups that would obscure relationships if ignored. The chapters by Curran et al. (ch. 4), by Johnson and Raudenbush (ch. 5), and by Neale et al. (ch. 9) examine various aspects of this matter. Furthermore, the growing interest in "mixture models" offers additional evidence that some researchers are becoming aware of and are trying to deal with these matters. I underscore the seriousness of the implications for our science.

There may be even "tougher" issues here than many of us would like to confront at this time. Avoiding the extreme question. "What if we are all different from each other?" we may still ask, "Just which individual differences can we aggregate over in order to develop meaningful, powerful lawful relationships among theoretically interesting variables?" "How can we identify, measure, and model them?" Clearly, these are important theoretical issues. They are there, beckoning to the methodologist to catch up, perhaps even to glide on by in some new and radical steps.

Metaphors, like analogies, break down at some point. Just who is leading who and when they are ahead in the method and theory dance is not always clear. I am convinced that the key is in the tension; the dynamic that inheres in theories that demand stronger ways to evaluate their empirical implications and methods that can elicit from the theorists more precise statements of compelling relationships to be evaluated. I am looking forward to what the future brings in this regard. Until these issues are clarified, I cannot be optimistic regarding the probable rate of progress in building compelling explanatory systems regarding adult development and aging or behavior in general, for that matter.

Concluding Remarks

In their sweeping overview chapter, Bergeman and Wallace (ch. 2) set the stage for a discussion of methodological issues that is appropriately grounded in the key theoretical issues of human development and change. They identify a number of developmental methodology issues and convey a sound impression of the importance of design, measurement, and analysis or modeling concerns. Despite the frank overall orientation of the volume toward methodological issues, Bergeman and Wallace's emphasis on the productive interplay between method and theory keeps the reader aware of the vital role that theory and theory development play in the generation of knowledge. No doubt methodologists need this kind of reminder on occasion—especially when several of them are brought together under one roof.

This first volume in what we hope will be a long and successful series is pointed toward the future; a future which I believe will witness the development and incorporation of powerful linear and nonlinear dynamical systems modeling tools that will first titillate only the younger theorists while offending the sensitivities of the older ones.

But the dancing will continue. As it does, these newer methodologies will eventually gain the momentum and purchase to wrench adult development and aging theory out of its comfortable reliance on the methodologies that have reigned over the past century and lure it into trying out some new steps.

References

Allport, G. W. (1937). *Personality: A psychological interpretation.* New York: Holt, Rinehart & Winston.

Baltes, P. B. (1968). Longitudinal and cross–sectional sequences in the study of age and generation effects. *Human Development, 11,* 145–171.

Baltes, P. B., Cornelius, S. W., & Nesselroade, J. R. (1978). Cohort effects in developmental psychology: Theoretical and methodological perspectives. In W. A. Collins (Ed.), *Minnesota symposium on child psychology* (Vol. 2, pp. 1–63). Hillsdale, NJ: Lawrence Erlbaum Associates.

Baltes, P. B., & Nesselroade, J. R. (1979). History and rationale of longitudinal research. In J. R. Nesselroade & P. B. Baltes (Eds.), *Longitudinal research in the study of behavior and development* (pp. 1–39). New York: Academic Press.

Bereiter, C. (1963). Some persisting dilemmas in the measurement of change. In C. W. Harris (Ed.), *Problems in measuring change.* Madison: University of Wisconsin Press.

Bergman, L. R., Magnusson, D., & El-Kouri, B. M. (2003). *Studying individual development in an interindividual context.* Mahwah, NJ: Lawrence Erlbaum Associates.

Browne, M. W., & Nesselroade, J. R. (2005). Representing psychological processes with dynamic factor models: Some promising uses and extensions of ARMA time series models. In A. Maydeu–Olivares & J. J. McArdle (Eds.), *Psychometrics: A festschrift to Roderick P. McDonald* (p. 415-452). Mahwah, NJ: Lawrence Erlbaum Associates.

Cattell, R. B. (1963). The interaction of hereditary and environmental influences. *The British Journal of Statistical Psychology, 16,* 191–210.

Cattell, R. B. (1966). Guest editorial: Multivariate behavioral research and the integrative challenge. *Multivariate Behavioral Research, 1,* 4–23.

Cronbach, L. J., & Furby, L. (1970). How should we measure "change"–or should we? *Psychological Bulletin, 74*(1), 68–80.

Fiske, D. W., & Rice, L. (1955). Intra–individual response variability. *Psychological Bulletin, 52,* 217–250.

Flugel, J. C. (1928). Practice, fatigue, and oscillation. *British Journal of Psychology, Monograph Supplement, 4,* 1–92.

Ford, D. H. (1987). *Humans as self-constructing living systems.* Hillsdale, NJ: Lawrence Erlbaum Associates.

Ford, D. H., & Lerner, R. M. (1992). *Developmental systems theory: An integrative approach.* Newbury Park, CA: Sage.

Hindley, C. B. (1972). The place of longitudinal methods in the study of development. In F. J. Monks, W. W. Hartup, & J. De Witt (Eds.), *Determinants of behavioral development* (pp. 22–51). New York: Academic Press.

Hultsch, D. F., Hertzog, C., Dixon, R. A., & Small, B. J. (1998). *Memory change in the aged.* Cambridge, UK: Cambridge University Press.

Lamiell, J. T. (1981). Toward an idiothetic psychology of personality. *American Psychologist, 36,* 276–289.

Lamiell, J. T. (1988, August). Once more into the breach: Why individual differences research cannot advance personality theory. (Paper presented at the annual meeting of the American Psychological Association, August, Atlanta, GA)

Lamiell, J. T. (1998). 'Nomothetic' and 'idiographic': Contrasting Windelband's understanding with contemporary usage. *Theory and psychology, 8*(1), 23–38.

Magnusson, D. (1998). The logic and implications of a person–oriented approach. In R. B. Cairns, L. R. Bergman, & J. Kagan (Eds.), *Methods and models for studying the individual* (pp. 33–64). Thousand Oaks, CA: Sage.

Manning, W. H., & DuBois, P. H. (1962). Correlational methods in research on human learning. *Perceptual and Motor Skills, 15,* 287–321.

McArdle, J., & Epstein, D. B. (1987). Latent growth curves within developmental structural equation models. *Child Development, 58*(1), 110–133.

McArdle, J. J. (1982). *Structural equation modeling of an individual system: Preliminary results from "A case study in episodic alcoholism".* (Unpublished manuscript, Department of Psychology, University of Denver)

McArdle, J. J., & Nesselroade, J. R. (2003). Growth curve analysis in developmental research. In J. Schinka & W. Velicer (Eds.), *Comprehensive handbook of psychology: Vol 2, Research methods in psychology.* New York: Pergamon Press.

Meredith, W., & Tisak, J. (1984). *"Tuckerizing" curves.* Paper presented at the annual meeting of the Psychometric Society, Santa Barbara, CA.

Meredith, W., & Tisak, J. (1990). Latent curve analysis. *Psychometrika, 55,* 107–122.

Mitteness, L. S., & Nesselroade, J. R. (1987). Attachment in adulthood: Longitudinal investigation of mother-daughter affective interdependencies by p-technique factor analysis. *The Southern Psychologist, 3,* 37–44.

Molenaar, P. C. M. (1985). A dynamic factor model for the analysis of multivariate time series. *Psychometrika, 50*(2), 181–202.

Molenaar, P. C. M., Huizenga, H. M., & Nesselroade, J. R. (2003). The relationship between the structure of interindividual and intraindividual variability: A theoretical and empirical vindication of developmental systems theory. In U. M. Staudinger & U. Lindenberger (Eds.), *Understanding human development: Dialogues with lifespan psychology* (pp. 339–360). Norwell, MA: Kluwer Academic.

Nesselroade, J. R. (1988). Sampling and generalizability: Adult development and aging research issues examined within the general methodological framework of selection. In K. W. Schaie, R. T. Campbell, W. Meredith, & S. C. Rawlings (Eds.), *Methodological issues in aging research* (pp. 13–42). New York: Springer.

Nesselroade, J. R. (2000). Getting here was half the fun. In J. E. Birren & J. J. F. Schroots (Eds.), *A history of geropsychology in autobiography* (pp. 211–224). Washington, DC: American Psychological Association.

Nesselroade, J. R., & Ford, D. H. (1985). P–technique comes of age: Multivariate, replicated, single–subject designs for research on older adults. *Research on Aging*, *7*, 46–80.

Nesselroade, J. R., & Molcnaar, P. C. M. (1999). Pooling lagged covariance structures based on short, multivariate time–series for dynamic factor analysis. In R. H. Hoyle (Ed.), *Statistical strategies for small sample research*. Thousand Oaks, CA: Sage.

Rao, C. R. (1958). Some statistical methods for the comparison of growth curves. *Biometrics*, *14*, 1–17.

Rogosa, D. R., Brandt, D., & Zimowski, M. (1982). A growth curve approach to the measurement of change. *Psychological Bulletin*, *92*, 726–748.

Rosenzweig, S. (1958). The place of the individual and of idiodynamics in psychology: A dialogue. *Journal of Individual Psychology*, *14*, 3–20.

Rosenzweig, S. (1986). Idiodynamics vis-à-vis psychology. *The American Psychologist*, *41*, 241–245.

Thouless, R. H. (1936). Test unrcliability and function fluctuation. *British Journal of Psychology*, *26*, 325–343.

Tucker, L. R. (1958). Determination of parameters of a functional relation by factor analysis. *Psychometrika*, *23*(1), 19–23.

Valsiner, J. (1984). Two alternative epistemological frameworks in psychology: The typological and variational modes of thinking. *The Journal of Mind and Behavior*, *5*(4), 449–470.

van Kampen, V. (2000). Idiographic complexity and the common personality dimensions of insensitivity, extraversion, neuroticism, and orderliness. *European Journal of Personality*, *14*, 217–243.

Wohlwill, J. F. (1991). Relations between method and theory in developmental research: A partial–isomorphism view. In P. van Geert & L. P. Mos (Eds.), *Annals of theoretical psychology* (Vol. 7, pp. 91–138). New York: Plenum Press.

Woodrow, H. (1932). Quotidian variability. *Psychological Review*, *39*, 245-256.

Zazzo, R. (1967). Diversité, realité, et mirages de la méthode longitudinale. *Enfance*, *20*, 131–136.

Zevon, M., & Tellegen, A. (1982). The structure of mood change: Idiographic/nomothetic analysis. *Journal of Personality and Social Pyschology*, *43*(1), 111–122.

2

The Theory-Methods Interface

Cindy S. Bergeman
University of Notre Dame

Kimberly A. Wallace
University of Montana

Questions in aging research are complex, intricate, and diverse. There is little doubt that the next generation in gerontology will demand more sophisticated research techniques to address this complexity and to accommodate the differential and multifaceted patterns of aging. Methodological designs and analytical techniques are needed to obviate threats to internal validity (i.e., distinguish age-related change from cohort and time of measurement effects); assess construct equivalence over time; detect increased heterogeneity with age; understand potential selection effects; and accommodate missing data due to systematic participant attrition, longer time intervals between occasions of measure, decreased health and functional status, and increased mortality. On a positive note, new analytical techniques in the areas of structural equation modeling, latent class analysis, hierarchical linear growth curve modeling, dynamical systems analysis, multivariate, multilevel Rasch models, survival analysis, and quantitative genetic methodologies provide researchers with tools to assess the dynamic nature of aging. A well-thought-out and executed program of study, integrating these new techniques, will contribute to theory development and advance powerful insights into the determinants of the aging process.

2.1   Introduction

One approach to studying the aging process is theoretically based in
a lifespan developmental perspective. From this perspective (e.g., see
Baltes, 1987), development is viewed as a dynamic and continuous
interplay between growth (gain) and decline (loss). As such, development is not seen as a period of growth until an individual reaches
young adulthood followed by a time of decline during the last three
quarters of the lifespan, nor is development viewed as a unidirec-
tional process of loss in adaptive capacity; rather, it is defined as any
change in the adaptive capacity of an organism, whether positive or
negative. This perspective also suggests that there is much intraindividual plasticity or within-person variability. That is, even in late
life, individuals have the potential for different forms of development
and can improve or modify their behavior. Knowing the range and
limits of intraindividual functioning is a cornerstone of the lifespan
perspective. This perspective, in turn, conveys the dynamic and developmental nature of aging with a primary focus on the process of
aging, not just outcomes at the end of life. Applying this framework to the study of developmental processes results in a complex
conceptualization of change.

    The purpose of the present chapter is not only to examine issues
related to the study of change, but also to do so within the context
of the continuous and synergetic interplay between developmental
theory and methodology. The discussion of these issues, in turn,
serves as an introduction to the collection of chapters in this book,
each of which explores a different, and oftentimes new, quantitative
application in developmental research.

2.2   Understanding Change

Developmental research in gerontology is concerned with identifying
sources of causation for individual constancy and change. Within the
field of gerontology, there has been an increasing awareness that there
may be many sources of causation for individual variability and that
multiple measures of each participant must be collected in order to
observe the developmental trajectory of an individual. The key question then is, "Which methodology is most appropriate for assessing

change?" In order to answer this, one must understand which type of change is being measured: interindividual differences, intraindividual change, or intraindividual variability. According to Baltes, Reese, and Nesselroade (1988), *interindividual differences* refer to differences between individuals on a given behavior or characteristic, whereas *intraindividual change* refers to within-person differences in the same behavior across time. *Intraindividual variability*, in turn, refers to relatively short-term changes that occur rapidly (Nesselroade, 1991a). Although this type of variability is typically viewed as random noise that is not part of the conceptualization of change, it may, in fact, be indicative of changes in attributes in the organism (Nesselroade, 1991b).

In addition to the different conceptualizations of change, an important piece of the research puzzle is to understand the relation between the theory of interest and the process of collecting data. Reese (1994) referred to this as the "data theory dialect." He defines *methods* as the ways of obtaining information or "data" (i.e., how we test the theoretical propositions); *theory* as the stipulated relationship among two or more constructs (i.e., our interpretation); and *knowledge* as our understanding of why a given theoretical proposition is true or false after it is put to a test. A "dialect" by definition is the contradiction between two conflicting forces viewed as the determining factor in their continued interaction. A "dialect" has also been defined as the Hegelian process of change whereby an ideational entity (a thesis) is transformed into its opposite (an antithesis) and preserved and fulfilled by it, the combination of the two being resolved in a higher form of truth (a synthesis; *Webster's II New Riverside University Dictionary*, 1984). As is discussed in more detail in Nesselroade (chap. 1, this volume), there is a continuous and dynamic interplay, or dance, that occurs between the opposing forces of theory and method, with knowledge as the synthesizing outcome. To understand this dance, researchers must consider three key areas: research design, measurement, and the selection of appropriate analytical techniques.

2.3   Research Design

Fundamental to the field of gerontology and our understanding of
change and individual development are research design issues. If
knowledge is considered to be the outcome of the dance between
the opposing forces of theory and method, then the quality of that
outcome is dependent, in part, on the quality of each component, as
well as the nature of the interplay between them. As such, research
design, or the structure of investigation, must be crafted with care.
One primary methodological consideration involves the type of data
that the researcher plans to collect: qualitative and/or quantitative.
Although the focus of this edited collection is on quantitative approaches in gerontology, it is important to explicate the notion that
both quantitative and qualitative data are essential for the continued
advancement of our understanding of adult development and aging
and to consider the potential contribution of qualitative methodologies.

Qualitative research encompasses a number of different approaches,
including ethnographies and participant observation, open–ended in-
terviewing and focus groups, oral histories and life stories, and content analysis (Hendricks, 1996; Maxwell, 1998; Strauss & Corbin,
1998). Across these approaches, the goal is to gather in-depth information and to understand the meaning of events and behavior as
they occur in context. This type of data collection lends itself well
to the field of gerontology and complex inquiries into continuity and
change. Additionally, qualitative research plays an important role
in the theory–method interface and may, in some cases, provide a
theoretical framework that would have been overlooked using more
traditional quantitative approaches. This, then, speaks to the importance of the synthesis between qualitative and quantitative methodologies and to the need for both to be applied in concert to further
scientific inquiry. Having acknowledged the dependence between the
two, the remaining discussion will focus more specifically on quantitative methodology. For a more in–depth examination of the contribution of qualitative research to gerontology, see Hendricks (1996)
and Gubrium and Sankar (1994).

In addition to determining which type of information a researcher
will collect (i.e., qualitative and/or quantitative), there are several

broad methodological concerns that investigators should consider. These methodological concerns cut across various types of designs and include sampling, external validity, and internal validity. *Sampling* refers to the selection of possible participants from the population of interest. Given the implication that sampling has for the validity of a study, defining the population and choosing and employing an appropriate sampling technique are critical (for further discussion, see Nesselroade, 1988). For instance, sampling decisions affect the degree to which results of the study attain broader generalizability. The possibility of a selection effect must be examined carefully and the consequences must be anticipated in shaping research paradigms.

Because much of what we know about the aging process is based on samples of convenience, it is fundamentally important to select a representative sample. Additionally, even if a study starts with a representative sample, various forms of attrition, nonresponse, and missing data can jeopardize generalizability (Jackson & Antonucci, 2001). For instance, because data may be missing for a variety of reasons, a researcher interested in the process of change must consider the issue of missingness. It is possible that data are missing completely at random, which is missingness due to variables that are irrelevant to the theoretical question. In contrast, data may also be missing at random, which is missingness due to variables that are measured and in the model, or not missing at random, which is missingness that is related to the levels of the outcome variable (e.g., Little & Rubin, 1987; Schafer & Graham, 2002). For a more in-depth review of approaches to missing data, such as maximum likelihood (ML) or Bayesian multiple imputation, as well as newer developments in the handling of missing data, see Schafer and Graham (2002). A related issue regarding missing data concerns survivorship and mortality. As a group is followed over time and participants drop out of a study, a researcher may effectively be studying survivors. If survivorship were a randomly distributed variable, this situation would not be a cause for concern. In many studies, particularly in gerontology, however, the result of this phenomenon is that samples get "healthier" over time. Mortality is not only a contaminant in gerontological research, but may be considered to be an outcome in its own right. This issue needs to be dealt with both conceptually and methodologically (see Lebowitz, 1989).

External validity refers to the issue of generality. More specifically, external validity is defined as the stability across other contexts of the causal relationship observed in a study (Cook & Campbell, 1979; Shadish, Cook, & Campbell, 2002). Although this type of generality is perhaps most often thought of in terms of the participants in a study, we must also consider other components of a study, including variables (measures), settings, occasions of measurement (times), and treatments. Across these dimensions, one must determine whether the sample component actually reflects the underlying domain of theoretical interest. Certain threats to external validity have been identified, including context–dependent mediation and interactions between the causal relationship of interest and units, treatment variations, outcomes, or settings (Cook & Campbell, 1979; Shadish et al., 2002).

Whereas these threats are clearly relevant in experimental aging research in which a variable or variables are manipulated and causal inferences are plausible, they are also of importance in the types of quasi-experimental designs typically used in developmental research to examine growth, change, and development (e.g., longitudinal and sequential designs). In particular, although researchers using developmental designs to study constancy and change may not manipulate a variable per se, the generality of findings across persons, settings, times, and measures are key to the broader application of one's scientific results. In fact, the issue of generality in terms of occasions of measurement (time) is a particularly important, albeit complex issue. For instance, Nesselroade and Boker (1994) have demonstrated that when occasions of measurement are defined too narrowly, conclusions about stability and change may be jeopardized, whereas Cole and Maxwell (2003) have discussed how the effect of timing of assessment on mediational research depends on the nature of the underlying causal relation. Finally, as mentioned previously, the issue of sampling is inextricably linked to external validity and generality in terms of participants. When our samples are nonrepresentative, we do not know whether the age trend or age differences observed in a particular study are representative of the larger population of interest.

Internal validity, on the other hand, refers to the validity of one's hypothesis about the relation between specific variables of interest.

Threats to internal validity, which have been discussed in detail elsewhere (e.g., Cook & Campbell, 1979; Shadish et al., 2002), exist when there is a potential rival or alternative explanation for the relation between the variables of interest, irrespective of the hypothesized substantive relation. Some examples that are salient to aging research include reactivity, practice effects, instrumentation, statistical regression, subject mortality bias, selection effects, and selection-maturation interaction (Campbell & Stanley, 1963; Schaie & Hofer, 2001). One threat of considerable consequence with regard to developmental research design is that of history. The threat of *history effects*, which may be evinced in terms of cohort or time of measurement effects, is perhaps best explained within the framework of the general developmental model (Schaie, 1965). According to this model, all developmental change (R) can be explained in terms of three constituent factors:

$$R = f(A, C, T)$$

in which, A is "age" or maturational changes, C refers to differences between cohorts in terms of experiences, and T reflects influences that occur between two points of measurement, referred to as "period" or "time of measurement" effects. More specifically, developmental change is a function of the main effects of age, cohort, and time of measurement, as well as the two- and three-way interactions between these terms, such that (Schaie, 1986):

$$X_{ijk} = a_i + c_j + t_k + ac_{ij} + at_{ik} + ct_{jk} + act_{ijk} + e_{ijk}$$

Traditional developmental designs, such as cross-sectional, longitudinal, and the less frequently described time–lag designs, are merely variations of this equation with one of the terms set to zero while the other two are confounded. In the case of *cross–sectional* designs, data are collected at one point in time from individuals from different age groups; period effects (t_k) are set to zero, and the change in observed response is a function of differences in age and cohort, which cannot be distinguished. *Longitudinal* designs use time series data from the same individuals at two or more points in time. Because all subjects are from the same birth cohort, no cohort differences are reflected in designs of this type (therefore, $c_j = 0$), and the confounded effects of age-related change and period effects explain changes in the observed response. Finally, *time–lag* designs use two or more samples of the same chronological age, assessed at different time points, which results in a comparison of the life–course patterns of successive cohorts. Thus, there is no variability due to age ($a_i = 0$), and change is a function of cohort and time of measurement effects, which are inextricably entwined. Although all three of these approaches are essential to testing theory in gerontology, they have widely differing implications. The failure to acknowledge this can result in misleading and erroneous interpretations, which are due to the confounding of variables in each of these designs as noted.

To put this in a historical context, as researchers began to assess the effects of methodology on the results of research in gerontology, they found that the age differences from cross–sectional studies could not be replicated in longitudinal studies, which led to the realization that what had been attributed to age–related maturation was most likely due to cohort (history) effects, and was an artifact of research design and not necessarily reflective of the aging process. To overcome these limitations, a variety of sequential designs were suggested to answer different types of developmental questions. Two examples are the cross-sectional sequence and the longitudinal sequence. The *cross–sectional sequence* consists of two or more cross-sectional studies, whereas the *longitudinal sequence* comprises a staggered sequence of longitudinal studies (Schaie, 1986; Schaie & Baltes, 1975). When cross-sectional and longitudinal sequential designs are combined in a systematic way, Schaie's Most Efficient Design results (Schaie, 1965, 1977, 1996). Using this design, age, cohort, and time of measurement effects can be disentangled using a systematic series of analyses (Schaie, 1965).

Clearly important information about individual development can be obtained using these more complex sequential designs. It is an interesting paradox, however, in that although it is the complexity of these designs that allow for the examination of more detailed developmental questions and potential history effects, it is also the complexity of these designs that make them difficult for researchers to apply in practice. As such, longitudinal designs, with their inherent limitations, are more often utilized and, in fact, have been referred to as "the lifeblood of developmental psychology" (McCall, 1977, p. 341). In particular, longitudinal data allow for the investigation of five broad developmental issues (Baltes & Nesselroade, 1979; Schaie & Hofer, 2001). The first issue is the direct identification of intraindividual change, which involves studying the behavior of interest across time to assess constancy or change in the relevant attribute. For instance, how does physical health change (or remain the same) with age? In this way, longitudinal studies also help to pinpoint the temporal order of events, conditions, and experiences (Alwin & Campbell, 2001). The second developmental issue is the assessment of interindividual differences in intraindividual change-assessing differences in the change trajectories. In other words, do people age differently? This approach also allows one to test ideas of increases in heterogeneity with age discussed in the literature (e.g., Dannefer & Sell, 1988). The third developmental issue that can be assessed with longitudinal data is the relationship among attributes undergoing intraindividual change; that is, are there changes in the ipsative relations among variables across maturation? Do attributes change in similar ways? The fourth developmental issue relates to the determinants of intraindividual change, that is, identifying the factors that predict within-person change. For example, to what extent does a person's sense of control (or social support) affect change in physical or mental health? The final developmental issue that can be addressed with longitudinal data focuses on interindividual differences in the determinants of intraindividual change. In other words, longitudinal data can be used to identify attributes (e.g., resilience mechanisms, vulnerability factors) that might explain why people age differently.

To exemplify these developmental issues (listed in Table 2.1 consider the Notre Dame Widowhood Study, which focused on emotion regulation after the loss of a spouse. The study was designed to examine all five developmental issues described by Baltes and Nesselroade (1979), by assessing interindividual differences in intraindividual change and variability and by analyzing the data from a variety of viewpoints.

Because the death of a spouse is consistently rated as the most stressful life event, researchers in the area of stress and illness have a strong interest in bereavement issues. Interestingly, there are large

Table 2.1: Five Developmental Issues That Can Be Examined With Longitudinal Data.

1) Direct identification of intraindividual change
2) Assessment of interindividual differences in intraindividual change
3) Relationships among attributes undergoing intraindividual change
4) Determinants of intraindividual change
5) Interindividual differences in the determinants of intraindividual change

Note: From Baltes & Nesselroade, 1979; Schaie & Hofer, 2001.

individual differences in how older people adapt to loss. What are the turning points that change an individual's trajectory and which qualities result in more optimal outcomes? The Notre Dame Widowhood Study (Bergeman, Bisconti, & Boker, 1999; Bisconti, 2001) is exploratory in nature, assessing both the process of initial emotion regulation and the long-term adjustment to conjugal loss. The study has three primary objectives: to examine the initial process of emotional regulation after conjugal loss, to look at the long-term trajectory of adjustment, and to identify resilience resources that may contribute importantly to more optimal bereavement outcomes.

Participants comprise a target group and a control group of recently bereaved widows. These individuals were first contacted approximately 2 weeks after the death of the spouse. Subjects in both groups participated in pre– and postinterviews, and were asked to complete self-report questionnaires at the pre- and postinterviews, as well as at 8, 12, 16, 20, and 24 months postloss. This resulted in seven occasions of measurement across the 2–year period. In addition to the interview and questionnaire data, the participants in the target group were asked to answer a series of questions on a daily basis regarding their emotions/affect during a 3–month period. To assess whether the experience of reporting one's feelings on a daily basis enhanced health and well-being outcomes, the control group did not participate in the daily assessments of emotions/affect.

A dynamical systems approach can be used to identify the intraindividual variability in emotional response following the loss of a spouse. In particular, to understand emotion regulation after a significant life event, a methodology that allows for the possibility of oscillation across time is needed. One such approach is dynamical systems, which allows for a unique investigative opportunity in the study of bereavement in later life. A basic assumption of dynamical systems is that all systems change and evolve in time. The knowledge of a system's current state contributes to the prediction of the future state of the system (Nowak & Lowenstein, 1994). According to Smith and Thelen (1993), there is a geometric way of understanding a dynamical system. The set of numbers $x_1(t), x_2(t), ..., x_n(t)$ may be considered coordinates of a point in an n dimensional space, called a *phase space*. The actual state of the system, described by the dynamical variables, is represented as a point in this space. This motion draws a curve, or a sequence of points, in the phase space that is often referred to as a *trajectory*. In other words, a trajectory is a set of points "visited" by the system during its time evolution (Nowak & Lowenstein, 1994). Analyses of this type can depict an individual's course of adjustment (the first developmental issue described by Baltes & Nesselroade, 1979) and can be used to compare the trajectories of different widows (the second broad developmental issue described earlier).

Dynamical systems are made up of dynamical variables, which are numbers that change in time and that characterize the relevant properties of the state of the system. Nowak and Lowenstein (1994) make the distinction between *order parameters*, which are macroscopic global parameters internal to the system, and *control parameters*, which represent conditions or influences external to the system itself but that determine to a great extent the character of the dynamics observed. A dynamical systems approach allows the parameters of the system to be estimated. For example, in the Notre Dame Widowhood Study, order parameters include the variability in emotion, the frequency of mood shifts, and the rate at which the mood shifts diminish. Using this framework, it was hypothesized that in normal older adults, the day–to–day change in a person's mood has a point attractor and an equilibrium point that is between emotionally stable and unstable. A stressful life event, like the death of a spouse, perturbs the emotional regulation of the individual away from equilibrium, which contributes to emotional shifts that vacillate between negative and positive affect, thus resulting in emotional lability. The dynamical systems analysis tracks this trajectory. Described in more detail later, control parameters are exemplified (in the Notre Dame Widowhood study) by individual differences in aspects of the social support system that contribute to differences in the trajectory of grief resolution. For a more in–depth discussion of the preliminary findings on intraindividual variability, see Boker and Bisconti (chap. 7, this volume) and Bisconti, Bergeman, and Boker (2004).

In addition to the use of a dynamical systems approach to identify intraindividual variability, information regarding emotion regulation is enhanced by concomitant information on long–term adjustment. Consequently, an analytical technique like hierarchical linear modeling (HLM) can be used to assess growth trajectories over the 2–year period following conjugal loss and intraindividual change in variables such as depression, life satisfaction, self–reported health and grief resolution. The third developmental issue can be represented by assessing the relationship among the attributes undergoing intraindividual change. Questions such as "What is the relationship between physical health and psychological well–being across the adjustment process?" or "How do the different emotions typically experienced by widows (e.g., anxiety, depression, happiness, loss of control) interrelate as a widow adapts to conjugal loss?" can be asked and empirically tested.

Clearly, consideration of both intraindividual variability and intraindividual change is important for advancing our understanding of sources of causation. Researchers must not stop there, however. Also important is the identification of the dispositional and environmental factors that influence these growth trajectories. In looking at both intraindividual change and variability, the assessment of protective mechanisms (e.g., social support, sense of control) that promote more optimal outcomes (e.g., grief resolution, dampened emotional lability) can be included in second–level models (as control parameters) and interindividual differences in intraindividual change and variability can be examined. Because stress and coping is an unfolding, dynamic process by which personal, social, and external resources serve to moderate all aspects of both the stressful event and a person's methods of coping with it, it is fundamental to assess both the determinants of these processes (fourth developmental issue) and the interindividual differences in the determinants of these processes (fifth developmental issue). That is, it is important to understand which protective factors ameliorate the debilitating effects of the event itself, and thus lead to more successful adaptation, and how individual differences in these attributes lead to differences in grief resolution over time. Generally, the emotions following the death of one's spouse can best be illustrated as a "roller coaster," with many ups and downs. Of particular interest are the mechanisms by which individuals reorganize their emotional system, resolve their grief, and eventually adapt to conjugal loss.

In sum, the Notre Dame Widowhood Study was designed to answer a variety of questions by assessing interindividual differences in intraindividual change and variability (for more details see Bisconti, 2001; Bisconti et al., 2004).

Although the previously mentioned example is specific to the domain of loss and bereavement, an important, underlying issue cuts across substantive areas to focus on the relationship between theory and methodology. That is, the ability to identify the change components of interest and to match the theoretical question with appropriate analytical techniques is fundamental to the purpose of this book and a key challenge to gerontologists today. As such, it is important to remember the interface between theory and method described previously. Clearly, research design serves as a core component of this dynamic partnership, and consideration must be given to issues of sampling, validity, and structure. Problems that arise due to selection or validity threats can undermine one's ability to advance scientific knowledge. Similarly, if our methods of data collection are not designed to assess change, we will not be able to understand it; nor will we be able to advance developmental theory. One area in which research design has been applied to advance our understanding of change is developmental behavioral genetics. Because this is a topic that is examined in more detail in the chapter by Neale, Boker, Bergeman, and Maes (chap. 9, this volume), only a brief overview is provided here.

Behavioral geneticists assess the etiology of individual differences in behavior and attribute these differences to genetic and environmental components of variance. Thus, quantitative behavioral genetic methodologies serve as a tool for estimating the degree to which complex traits or characteristics are influenced by genetic and environmental factors. Identical and fraternal twins, family members, and adopted siblings serve as pairs of individuals who differ in genetic relatedness. In addition, these family members may have been reared together or apart (i.e., adopted apart), providing groups of individuals who differ in environmental similarity as well. Such methods allow for the exploration of questions such as "Why do people age differently?" and "To what extent are characteristics associated with the aging process influenced by genetic predispositions, environmental factors, or both?" Using older samples, researchers have assessed attributes such as physical health, life satisfaction, personality, cognitive functioning, and psychopathology from a behavioral genetic perspective. For a review of the research in this area, see Bergeman (1997), Bergeman and Plomin (1996), or McClearn and Vogler (2001).

One issue that can be addressed with a longitudinal behavioral genetic design is the etiology of continuity and change in genetic and environmental influences in an attribute or attributes over time. To say that genetic influences can contribute to the stability of a behavior is not surprising, but to say that genetic influences contribute to change may be more counterintuitive. Because we are born with a full complement of genes, it is often assumed that genetic influences are "locked in" at the moment of conception with a continuous influence across the lifespan. Research in developmental behavioral genetics indicates that genes turn on and off during development. New or "innovative" genetic effects may come in to play at selected developmental stages or at any point across the lifespan. For a more in–depth discussion of how models of development and various hypotheses about growth may be examined using behavioral genetic data, see the chapter by Neale et al. (chap. 9, this volume) and Neale and Cardon (1992).

In sum, research design issues are fundamental to understanding the interplay between theory and methodology. As mentioned previously, the quality of such a dynamic, and thus the resultant knowledge as outcome, depends in part on the quality of the design that comprises the methodology. Sampling and the potential for selection effects, as well as the various threats to internal and external validity are cause for concern and must be considered in our studies of age–related change. Of course, research design is not the only issue relevant to the theory–method interface; the issue of measurement must be examined as well.

2.4   Measurement

Measurement is the second key component to understanding the complex partnership between theory and method. Without valid and reliable measurement, the application of one's method in terms of the assessment of the constructs of interest is problematic, and thus the ability to test, advance, and refine theory is jeopardized. One of the main measurement concerns in research designed to assess constancy and change over time is that of equivalence. The issue here deals with whether the quantitative comparisons that are being made have the same meaning over time and/or across individuals (Cavanaugh & Whitbourne, 1999; Labouvie, 1980). That is, with the goal of attributing observed change to the underlying process of interest, researchers need to determine whether the assumption of construct or factorial invariance is tenable. As discussed by Rudinger and Rietz (2001), this type of invariance concerns both measurement equivalence (i.e., the relative magnitude of factor loadings remaining the same over time) and structural equivalence (i.e., the degree of relations between factors remaining consistent over time). With regard to a related concern, researchers interested in stability and change must be aware of how possible alterations in the wording and context of questions, mode of administration (i.e., mail, face–to–face, telephone), process of editing and coding, data management techniques, and analysis and interpretation can impact constancy or change in the measure over time (Jackson & Antonucci, 2001). In other words, changes in any one or several of these areas may serve as a rival or alternative explanation for an observed change in the construct of interest.

Another issue that must be considered is error of measurement. Because measurement error can affect all types of survey data (e.g., opinions, information of a factual nature, reports of subjective states), its impact on the quality of the data obtained, and ultimately the ability to advance theory, may be quite pervasive. Alwin (1999) describes six components of the response process in survey analyses that affect the reliability of survey assessment. The first component is *content validity*; that is, how well does the measure assess the phenomenon of interest? The second is *comprehension*; how well does the respondent understand the information that is being requested? The third, *accessibility*, focuses on whether the respondents have access to the information of interest. Do they have an opinion? Fourth, *retrieval*, is concerned with whether the respondent can develop a response on the basis of the internal cognitive or affective cues related to his/her attitude or level of agreement, and the fifth, *communication*, reflects whether the participant translates that response into the categories provided by the survey question. Finally, the sixth component is *motivation*; how willing is the respondent to provide an accurate response? Clearly, these concerns are not just a problem in samples of older adults, but there may be characteristics of the aging process that increase the salience of these issues. That is, there may be cognitive decrements, motivation or confidence differences, or physical changes associated with aging that impair reliable reporting of information in survey research (e.g., Alwin, 1999; Alwin & Campbell, 2001).

Interestingly, Alwin (1999) suggested that the variability across age in measurement reliability might be due, in part, to cohort effects. That is, it is possible that the differences in measurement reliability observed in different age groups are reflective of effects associated with historical time of birth. The ability to distinguish age–related changes associated with errors of measurement from cohort differences depends on identifying theoretically relevant, cohort–related factors that are also associated with errors of measurement. Possible examples include level of schooling or exposure to standardized testing and survey completion. Results from a study by Alwin (1999) indicate that there is a difference in the reliability of self–report data based on level of schooling, with college graduates reporting information in surveys at a level of reliability that is roughly 1% higher than high school graduates. To examine the hypothesis that cohort differences in education could play a role in patterns of reliability by age, Alwin assessed the reliability by age for both *factual data*, defined as objective information concerning the participant or members of his/her household, and *nonfactual measures*, which included *beliefs* (i.e., subjective assessments of states and/or outcomes), *attitudes* (i.e., affective responses), and *self–descriptions* (i.e., subjective evaluations of the state of the participant). For factual measures, there were virtually no detectable differences in reliability by age. Among nonfactual measures, particularly attitudes and beliefs, there was a clear pattern in the unadjusted reliabilities with those individuals in the oldest age groups producing more measurement errors. When the age–education and education–reliability relationships were taken into account, however, a generally positive relationship between age and reliability of measurement emerged, implicating cohort differences, rather than age differences, in errors of measurement.

Overall, measurement concerns are inextricably linked to the ability to conduct sound research. Consideration of the equivalence in constructs and measures over time, as well as the role of measurement error, is essential to one's ability to rule out alternative explanations for observed change. These issues occur in conjunction with those discussed previously in terms of research design. That is, weaknesses in either measurement and/or research design can interrupt the dynamic interplay between method and theory. The picture is not complete, however, without considering the impact of data analytic technique, a topic that is discussed in more detail in the next section and throughout the remainder of this edited collection.

2.5   Data Analysis

Although a clearly delineated theoretical question may be examined using strong research design and measurement, one's ability to advance scientific knowledge still depends, in part, on the match between the substantive question of interest and the appropriate statistical technique. As such, data analytic techniques can inform the relation between the opposing forces of theory and method by providing a link between the two. In many ways, advancements in data analytic techniques have served to strengthen the methodological quality of the research in gerontology. For instance, structural equation modeling (SEM) allows researchers to examine constancy and change on the underlying, or latent, level. In addition, SEM and latent variable analyses provide other important advantages over more traditional analytic techniques. More specifically, much research in gerontology is limited by the use of a single measure per trait and as a result, problems with error of measurement cannot be adequately addressed. In addition, when only one measure per construct is used, the results are limited to the measure (e.g., the Geriatric Depression Scale) and not the construct (e.g., depression). The inclusion of measurement error in the specified model is particularly important given the potential problems that such error can cause. For instance, error of measurement can bias structural parameter estimates. In addition, error is often a problem in longitudinal designs because of the potential confound between it and true individual change, which may then bias the estimates of relationships over time (Alwin, 1988). Random error that is due to the unreliability of a measure may attenuate bivariate relationships between interpersonal variables, and in behavioral genetic model–fitting analyses, errors of measurement contribute to nonshared environment (because error contributes to differences between family members); if this error is accounted for using SEM, then more reliable parameter estimates can be obtained.

Structural modeling techniques have also been successfully applied when testing for factor invariance of a measurement across groups, across time, or across individuals, which allows the researcher to argue the case that the instrument used is measuring the same latent phenomenon. Building a strong and invariant measurement model is especially important when making comparisons across age groups. For a more in–depth discussion of longitudinal SEM, see McArdle and Hamagami (chap. 3, this volume), in which several model–based dynamics are examined. Although not limited to these, there are other areas in which advancements in data analytic strategies have informed developmental theory and methodology. For instance, Boker and Bisconti (chap. 7, this volume) apply linear differential equations models of short– and long–term dynamics to longitudinal data in gerontology. Curran, Bauer, and Willoughby (chap. 4, this volume) demonstrate how techniques for testing and probing higher–order interactions can be used in hierarchical linear models. In addition, Johnson and Raudenbush (chap. 5) examine the application of a multivariate, multilevel Rasch model, whereas Schuster (chap. 6) overviews latent class analysis approaches to the determination of the reliability of nominal classifications. Finally, Wenger, Schuster, Petersen and Petersen (chap. 8) investigate the application of proportional hazards models and frailty models to response time data to explicate the viability of the technique.

Overall, there is a thread that runs through each of these analytic techniques and methodological approaches: There is an intimate connection between appropriate statistical analysis and sound experimental design. Of course, the characteristics of the theory and methodology are expected to influence the choice of appropriate data analytic techniques to answer the chosen theoretic question. At the same time, prior knowledge of constraints imposed by particular data analytic techniques can help the thoughtful researcher design experiments that answer the chosen theoretic question with sufficient power, but also with efficient use of resources. Methodological innovations have markedly increased our ability to assess development and change.

2.6 Summary

In order to enhance our understanding of individuals' developmental trajectories in a particular substantive area of interest, it is necessary that gerontologists match the appropriate methodology with their conceptualization(s) of change (i.e., interindividual differences, intraindividual change, intraindividual variability). In order to achieve such a match, we as scientists must understand the dialect between data and theory and between theory and methodology. As discussed in the present chapter, the three key components of this dialect, or interface, include research design (e.g., sampling, validity), measurement (e.g., equivalence, error), and analysis (e.g., the fit between the analytic technique and substantive question). In the field of gerontology thus far, the consideration of these components in empirical work has yielded important fruits, that is, in terms of the gains that have been made in establishing useful representations of change and process. Despite such progress, however, additional efforts are needed.

Questions concerning age–related change and development cannot be answered in a simple and straightforward manner. Interestingly, the field of gerontology and adult development and aging, which was once thought to represent relative stability, now appears to manifest complex patterns of change (McArdle & Nesselroade, 1994). As such, the complexity of development in later life has become increasingly apparent with advancements in methodology and analysis. Further refinements are needed in terms of both developmental theory and methods in order to fully capture the dynamic nature of change in later life. This book, which is a compilation of chapters that describe a number of advances in quantitative methodology in aging research,

serves as a step in this direction. The common thread that binds
these chapters together is the underlying importance in each chapter
of the symbiotic relationship, discussed here as the interplay, between
theory and method. Just as innovations in methodology may allow
gerontologists to examine theoretical models at a new conceptual level
or that were not previously specifiable (Schaie, 1992), innovations
in theory may force researchers to question and refine the existing
methodology. The continuation of the dance between theoretical refinement and methodological technique is essential to the evolution
of scientific knowledge in gerontology. Consider the challenge issued
by Nesselroade and Schmidt–McCollam (2000):

> Developmental science can ill afford to continue with "busi-
> ness as usual" when so many signs point toward both
> the need for advanced conceptions and the possibilities
> of their being within the methodological reach of those
> who dare to lean over the edge and stretch a bit. Build-
> ing more sensitive measurement devices, designing more
> changed–oriented studies, and employing more dynamical
> models is possible — and promises to be worth the invest-
> ment. If developmentalists do take on this challenge, the
> next millennium will be one of dramatic breakthroughs in
> our understanding of behavioural development. We hope
> the challenge will be accepted eagerly. (p. 299)

References

Alwin, D. F. (1988). Structural equation modeling in research on
human development and aging. In K. W. Schaie, R. T. Campbell, W. Meredith, & S. Rawlings (Eds.), *Methodological issues
in aging research* (pp. 71–170). New York: Springer.

Alwin, D. F. (1999). Aging and errors of measurement: Implications
for the study of life-span development. In N. Schwarz, D. C.
Park, B. Knauper, & S. Sudman (Eds.), *Cognition, aging and
self-reports* (pp. 365–385). Philadelphia: Psychology Press.

Alwin, D. F., & Campbell, R. T. (2001). Quantitative approaches:
Longitudinal methods in the study of human development and
aging. In R. H. Binstock & L. K. George (Eds.), *Handbook of*

aging and the social sciences (5th ed., pp. 22–43). San Diego, CA: Academic Press.

Baltes, P. B. (1987). Theoretical propositions of life-span developmental psychology: On the dynamics between growth and decline. *Developmental Psychology, 23*, 611–626.

Baltes, P. B., & Nesselroade, J. R. (1979). History and rationale of longitudinal research. In J. Nesselroade & P. B. Baltes (Eds.), *Longitudinal research in the study of behavior and development* (pp. 1–39). New York: Academic Press.

Baltes, P. B., Reese, H. W., & Nesselroade, J. R. (1988). *Introduction to research methods: Life-span developmental psychology.* Hillsdale, NJ: Lawrence Erlbaum & Associates.

Bergeman, C. S. (1997). *Aging: Genetic and environmental influences.* Thousand Oaks, CA: Sage.

Bergeman, C. S., Bisconti, T. L., & Boker, S. (1999). *Emotion regulation in recently bereaved widows: A dynamical systems approach.* National Institute of Aging-1 RO3 AG18570-01.

Bergeman, C. S., & Plomin, R. (1996). Behavioral genetics. In *Encyclopedia of gerontology* (Vol. 1, pp. 163–172). Orlando, FL: Academic Press.

Bisconti, T. L. (2001). *Widowhood in later life: A dynamical systems approach to emotion regulation.* Unpublished doctoral dissertation, University of Notre Dame, Notre Dame, IN.

Bisconti, T. L., Bergeman, C. S., & Boker, S. (2004). Emotion regulation in recently bereaved widows: A dynamical systems approach. *Journal of Gerontology: Psychological Sciences, 59*, 158-167.

Campbell, D. T., & Stanley, J. C. (1963). *Experimental and quasi-experimental designs for research.* Chicago: Rand McNally.

Cavanaugh, J. C., & Whitbourne, S. K. (1999). Research methods. In J. C. Cavanaugh & S. K. Whitbourne (Eds.), *Gerontology: An interdisciplinary perspective* (pp. 33–64). New York: Oxford University Press.

Cole, D. A., & Maxwell, S. E. (2003). Testing mediational models with longitudinal data: Myths and tips in the use of structural equation modeling. *Journal of Abnormal Psychology, 112*, 558–577.

Cook, T. D., & Campbell, D. T. (1979). *Quasi-experimentation:*

Design and analysis issues for field settings. Boston: Houghton Mifflin.

Dannefer, D., & Sell, R. R. (1988). Age structure, the life course and "aged heterogeneity": Prospects for research and theory. *Comprehensive Gerontology–B*, *2*, 1–10.

Gubrium, J. F., & Sankar, A. (1994). *Qualitative methods in aging research*. Thousand Oaks, CA: Sage.

Hendricks, J. (1996). Qualitative research: Contributions and advances. In R. H. Binstock & L. K. George (Eds.), *Handbook of aging and the social sciences* (4th ed., pp. 52–72). San Diego: Academic Press.

Jackson, J. S., & Antonucci, T. C. (2001). Survey methodology in life-span human development research. In S. H. Cohen & H. W. Reese (Eds.), *Life-span developmental psychology: Methodological contributions* (pp. 65–94). Mahwah, NJ: Lawrence Erlbaum & Associates.

Labouvie, E. W. (1980). Identity versus equivalence of psychological measures and constructs. In L. W. Poon (Ed.), *Aging in the 1980's: Psychological issues* (pp. 493–502). Washington, DC: American Psychological Association.

Lebowitz, B. D. (1989). Scientific change and longitudinal research: Subjects, methods and environments. In M. P. Lawton & A. R. Herzog (Eds.), *Special research methods for gerontology* (pp. 309–317). Amityville, NY: Baywood.

Little, R. J. A., & Rubin, D. B. (1987). *Statistical analysis with missing data*. New York: Wiley.

Maxwell, J. A. (1998). Designing a qualitative study. In L. Bickman & D. R. Rog (Eds.), *Handbook of applied social research methods* (pp. 69–100). Thousand Oaks, CA: Sage.

McArdle, J. J., & Nesselroade, J. R. (1994). Using multivariate data to structure developmental change. In S. H. Cohen & H. W. Reese (Eds.), *Life-span developmental psychology: Methodological contributions* (pp. 223–267). Hillsdale, NJ: Lawrence Erlbaum & Associates.

McCall, R. B. (1977). Challenges to a science of developmental psychology. *Child Development*, *48*, 333–344.

McClearn, G. E., & Vogler, G. P. (2001). The genetics of behavioral aging. In J. E. Birren & K. W. Schaie (Eds.), *Handbook of the psychology of aging* (5th ed., pp. 109–131). San Diego, CA: Academic Press.

Neale, M. C., & Cardon, L. R. (1992). *Methodology for genetic studies of twins and families.* Dordrecht, Netherlands: Kluwer.

Nesselroade, J. R. (1988). Sampling and generalizability: Adult development and aging research issues examined within the general methodological framework of selection. In K. W. Schaie, R. T. Campbell, W. Meredith, & S. Rawlings (Eds.), *Methodological issues in aging research* (pp. 13–42). New York: Springer.

Nesselroade, J. R. (1991a). Individual differences in intraindividual change. In L. M. Collins & J. L. Horn (Eds.), *Best methods for the analysis of change: Recent advances, unanswered questions, future directions* (pp. 92–105). Washington, DC: American Psychological Association.

Nesselroade, J. R. (1991b). The warp and the woof of the developmental fabric. In R. Donws, L. Liben, & D. S. Palermo (Eds.), *Visions of development, the environment, and aesthetics: The legacy of Joachim F. Wohlwill* (pp. 213–240). Hillsdale, NJ: Lawrence Erlbaum & Associates.

Nesselroade, J. R., & Boker, S. M. (1994). Assessing constancy and change. In T. F. Heatherton & J. L. Weinberger (Eds.), *Can personality change?* (pp. 121–147). Washington DC: American Psychological Association.

Nesselroade, J. R., & Schmidt–McCollam, K. (2000). Putting the process in developmental processes. *International Journal of Behavioral Development, 24,* 295–300.

Nowak, A., & Lowenstein, M. (1994). Dynamical systems: A tool for social psychology? In R. R. Vallacher & A. Nowak (Eds.), *Dynamical systems in social psychology* (pp. 17–53). San Diego, CA: Academic Press.

Reese, H. W. (1994). The data/theory dialectic: The nature of scientific progress. In S. H. Cohen & H. W. Reese (Eds.), *Life-span developmental psychology: Methodological contributions* (pp. 1–27). Hillsdale, NJ: Lawrence Erlbaum & Associates.

Rudinger, G., & Rietz, C. (2001). Structural equation modeling in longitudinal research on aging. In J. E. Birren & K. W. Schaie (Eds.), *Handbook of the psychology of aging* (5th ed., pp. 29–

52). San Diego, CA: Academic Press.

Schafer, J. L., & Graham, J. W. (2002). Missing data: Our view of the state of the art. *Psychological Methods, 7*, 147–177.

Schaie, K. W. (1965). A general model for the study of developmental problems. *Psychological Bulletin, 64*, 92–107.

Schaie, K. W. (1977). Quasi-experimental designs in the psychology of aging. In J. E. Birren & K. W. Schaie (Eds.), *Handbook of the psychology of aging* (pp. 39–58). New York: Van Nostrand Reinhold.

Schaie, K. W. (1986). Beyond calendar definitions of age, time, and cohort: The general developmental model revisited. *Developmental Review, 6*, 252–277.

Schaie, K. W. (1992). The impact of methodological changes in gerontology. *International Journal of Aging and Human Development, 35*, 19–29.

Schaie, K. W. (1996). *Intellectual development in adulthood: The Seattle Longitudinal Study.* Cambridge, UK: Cambridge University Press.

Schaie, K. W., & Baltes, P. B. (1975). On sequential strategies in developmental research: Description or explanation? *Human Development, 18*, 384–390.

Schaie, K. W., & Hofer, S. M. (2001). Longitudinal studies in aging research. In J. E. Birren & K. W. Schaie (Eds.), *Handbook of the psychology of aging* (5th ed., pp. 53–77). San Diego, CA: Academic Press.

Shadish, W. R., Cook, T. D., & Campbell, D. T. (2002). *Experimental and quasi-experimental designs for generalized causal inference.* Boston: Houghton Mifflin.

Smith, L. B., & Thelen, E. (1993). Can dynamic systems theory be usefully applied in areas other than motor development? In L. B. Smith & E. Thelen (Eds.), *A dynamic systems approach to development* (pp. 151–170). Cambridge, MA: MIT Press.

Strauss, A., & Corbin, S. (1998). *Basics of qualitative research: Techniques and procedures for developing grounded theory* (2nd ed.). Thousand Oaks, CA: Sage.

Webster's II New Riverside University Dictionary. (1984). New York: Houghton Mifflin.

3

Longitudinal Tests of Dynamic Hypotheses on Intellectual Abilities Measured Over Sixty Years

John J. McArdle and Fumiaki Hamagami
University of Virginia

In this research, we describe a longitudinal analysis of a dynamic hypothesis about the relationships among intellectual abilities. The *Bradway–McArdle Longitudinal study* includes 111 individuals who were repeatedly measured on up to six occasion between the ages of 4 and 64. In this research we first use contemporary measurement models to create comparable composite scores for both Verbal (g_c) and Non-Verbal $(g_f$ or $g_v)$ intelligence measures from the early Stanford–Binet tests (at ages of 4, 14, 30, and 42), as well as the WAIS tests (at average ages 30, 42, 56, and 64). To evaluate the validity of R. B. Cattell's dynamic growth hypothesis we use recent techniques of nonlinear structural analysis with incomplete data.

The statistical models presented are based on a *structural equation model* (SEM) form of Coleman's (1968) differential equations model of bivariate change (also see Arminger, 1987). Latent variables models allow us to represent levels and slopes in a bivariate dynamic model across different variables at different ages. These dynamic SEM form the basis of a dynamic interpretation of the developmental influences of g_f on g_c, and vice versa. This chapter emphasizes both methodological and substantive aspects of testing dynamic hypotheses and discusses implications for further experimental and developmental research.

3.0.1   The Investment Theory of Abilities

The psychometric concept of a single general factor of intelligence, originally labeled "g," has been promoted by psychologists from the turn of the century (by Spearman, 1904) to today (e.g., Jensen & Faulstich, 1988). Several alternative models of an increasing number of broad intellectual factors have been proposed, most notably by Burt (1912), Cattell (1941) and Thurstone (1947). Cattell (1941, 1971) proposed an alternative model based on developmental considerations and postulated the existence of at least two general cognitive ability factors: (1) *fluid intelligence* (g_f), indicated by reasoning abilities which are relatively independent of cultural influences, and (2) *crystallized intelligence* (g_c), indicated by knowledge abilities which are largely determined by acculturation. The developmental aspect of g_f - g_c theory was clearly postulated by Cattell (1971):

> "The investment theory supposes that in the development of the individual there is initially (perhaps after two or three years of maturational shaping from birth) a single, general, relational — perceiving ability connected with the total associational, neuron development of the cortex. This general power is applicable to any sensory or motor area and any process of selective retrieval from storage. Because it is not tied to any specific habits or sensory, motor, or memory area, we have called it *fluid* ability, g_f. [...] This investment of fluid ability in the experimentally–gained crystallized skills may, as far as we yet know, result in their having a life and durability of their own, in independence of the fluid ability which begot them. The term *crystallized* is meant to imply this freezing in a specific shape of what was once fluid ability. [...] For we have asserted that, like fluid ability, it is a broad, *general* factor [...] this theory, which recognizes the fact of a g_c and g_f duality, the *investment* theory. It says that g_c arises and has its particular form as a result of investing a general capacity, $g_{f(h)}$, in suitable learning experience." (p. 127).

In more formal terms Cattell (1971, p.127) hypothesized,

$$g_{c(a)} \;=\; \int_0^a (g_{f(h)} \times S_e)dt$$

or (3.1)

$$g_{c(a)} \;=\; \int_0^a (g_{f(h)} + S_e)dt,$$

where $g_{c(a)}$ is the level of crystallized ability at age a, $g_{f(h)}$ is the historical fluid ability level acting at age a, S_e is the form of the educational influence at age a, and the integral equation is used to represent *a process that accumulates over time*. The fact that the educational influence (S_e) might act in either a *multiplicative or additive* fashion did not seem to be a major concern of Cattell at the time.

These structural concepts were expanded and put to an empirical test in the seminal research of John L. Horn (1965; see also J. L. Horn & Cattell, 1966, 1967, 1982). These results suggested that, given a wide spread of developmental influences, the multiple factor $g_f - g_c$ model was a more effective organization of individual differences in abilities data. These results have been influential in casting doubt on the usefulness of a "g" theory, especially in test development and clinical practice. However, most of the information analyzed in previous work was collected from cross–sections of persons at different ages, and longitudinal analyses of $g_f - g_c$ abilities are rare. It follows that the developmental processes hypotheses represented by $g_f - g_c$ theory have not yet been given a rigorous test. It also follows that, even if longitudinal data are available, a statistical test(s) of proposition(s) raised by Equation 3.1 is not clear.

3.0.2 Contemporary Structural Equation Models

A great deal of prior work on *structural equation models* (SEM) has been devoted to problems of longitudinal analyses (J. Horn & McArdle, 1980; K. G. Jöreskog & Sörbom, 1979, 1993; R. P. McDonald, 1985; R. McDonald, 1999). This includes the seminal work by Jöreskog & Sörbom (K. G. Jöreskog, 1970, 1974, 1977; K. G. Jöreskog

& Sörbom, 1979; Sörbom, 1975, 1976) on formalizing and testing auto–regressive simplex models using latent variables. This SEM approach also provided a practical way to deal with the complex issue of measurement error in panel data (e.g., J. McArdle & Woodcock, 1997; Sörbom, 1975). Longitudinal SEMs were expanded in an important way with the addition of common factor models (e.g., K. G. Jöreskog, 1977). Research on covariance–based longitudinal SEMs was extended using concepts derived from auto–regressive models identifiable with longer time series. In important practical work, Molenaar (1985) presented multivariate LISREL models of individual time–series, and Arminger (1987) developed a way to use standard LISREL results (estimates and standard errors) from panel data using Coleman's (1964, 1968) differential equations (dY/dt) models. In related theoretical work, Maccallum and Ashby (1986) called for an integration of systems models and covariance–based LISREL model, and Gollob and Reichardt (1987) clarified inferences about the specific time–lags in longitudinal data using LISREL.

In a recent and important innovation, Meredith and Tisak (1990) showed how the "Tuckerized curve" models (named in recognition of Tucker's contributions) could be represented and fitted using structural equation modeling based on restricted common factors. These growth modeling results were important because they made it possible to represent a wide range of alternative growth models. This work also led to interest in methodological and substantive studies of growth processes using structural equation modeling techniques (J. J. McArdle, 1986; J. McArdle & Anderson, 1990; J. McArdle & Epstein, 1987; J. McArdle & Hamagami, 1991, 1992; J. McArdle & Woodcock, 1997). These latent growth models have since been expanded upon and used by many others (Browne & Arminger, 1995; Duncan & Duncan, 1995; J. McArdle & Bell, 2000; J. McArdle & Woodcock, 1997; Metha & West, 2000; B. Muthen & Curran, 1997; Willett & Sayer, 1994). The contemporary basis of latent growth curve analyses can also be found in the recent developments of *multilevel models* (A. S. Bryk & Raudenbush, 1987; A. Bryk & Raudenbush, 1992; Cnaan, Laird, & Slasor, 1997; Goldstein, 1995; Heck & Thomas, 1999; Hox, 2002; Kreft & De Leeuw, 1998; Snijders & Bosker, 1999) or *mixed–effects models* (Littell, Miliken, Stoup, & Wolfinger, 1996; McCulloch & Searle, 2000; Pinherio & Bates, 2000; Singer, 1998; Skrondal &

Rabe-Hesketh, 2004; Verbeke & Molenberghs, 2000). Perhaps most importantly, the work by Browne and Toit (1991) showed how the nonlinear dynamic models could be part of this same framework (see Cudeck & du Toit, 2001, 2003; Lindstrom & Bates, 1990; J. McArdle & Hamagami, 1996; J. McArdle, Hamagami, Meredith, & Bradway, 2001; Pinherio & Bates, 2000). For these reasons, the term "latent growth models" seems appropriate for any technique that describes the underlying growth in terms of latent changes using the classical assumptions (e.g., independence of residual errors).

The model–based fitting of structural assumptions about the group and individual differences holds the key to later substantive interpretations. From such formal assumptions, we can write the set of expectations for the means, variances, and covariances for all observed scores and use these expectations to identify, estimate, and examine the goodness–of–fit of latent variable models representing change over time. Most of the models discussed here are based on fitting observed raw–score longitudinal growth data to a theoretical model using likelihood–based techniques (as in Little & Rubin, 1987; J. McArdle & Bell, 2000). These theoretical restrictions may not hold exactly in the examination of real data, and this leads to the general issues of model testing and goodness–of–fit. Recent research has also produced a variety of new statistical and computational procedures for the analysis of latent growth curves, and their unique features are somewhat difficult to isolate. This means that the likelihood–based approach to the estimation and fitting of growth curve analyses can be accomplished using several widely available computer packages (e.g., SAS, Littell et al., 1996; Singer, 1998; Verbeke & Molenberghs, 2000; S–Plus, Pinherio & Bates, 2000; MIXREG, Hedecker & Gibbons, 1996, 1996). A few available computer programs, for instance Mx (Neale, M., Xie, & H., 2003), AMOS (Arbuckle & Wotke, 1999), Mplus (L. Muthen & Muthen, 1998), can be used to estimate the parameters of all analyses described herein.

In the chapter, we discuss the use of contemporary growth curve analyses of contemporary longitudinal data. To examine the basic questions of this research, we study the longitudinal growth data in Figure 3.1: These are age plots of data from a recent study of intellectual abilities (see next section). These are described in the methods section.. The models and results sections are organized into five sections based on specific kinds of problems in data analysis: (1) measurement models, (2) latent growth curves, (3) aspects of dynamic growth models, (4) multiple variables in dynamic analyses, and (5) multiple groups in dynamic growth curve models. We conclude with a discussion of future issues raised by the current growth models. In all sections we present a basic structural equation model to illustrate different kinds of mathematical and statistical issues for the analyses of these data.

The growth plots illustrate further complexity that needs to be dealt with in longitudinal growth curve analyses. Thus, most of these are SEMs designed to deal with the practical issues involving (a) alternative models of change, (b) unequal intervals, (c) unequal numbers of persons in different groups, (d) non–random attrition, (e) altering the measures over time, and (f) dealing with multiple and changing outcomes. We do not provide a detailed historical perspective on growth models (but see J. McArdle & Nesselroade, 2003) but we use these models to meet the essential goals of most longitudinal data analyses (e.g., Baltes & Nesselroade, 1979; Campbell, 1988; J. McArdle & Bell, 2000).

3.1   Methods

The Bradway–McArdle longitudinal data come from a classic study of 111 individuals who were repeatedly measured over time at four occasions (see Bradway & Thompson, 1962; Kangas & Bradway, 1971). In 1984 and 1992 when subjects were at average ages 56 and 64, the current authors, working with Bradway, measured as many of these same subjects as we could locate (about 50% participation). Some details on the longitudinal data follow.

3.1.1   Longitudinal Participants

The persons in this study were first measured in 1931 when they were aged 2 to 7 as part of the larger standardization sample of the Stanford–Binet test ($N = 212$). They were measured again about ten years later by Katherine P. Bradway as part of her doctoral dissertation in 1944 ($N = 138$). Many of these same persons were measured twice more by Bradway as adults at average ages of 30 and 42 using the Wechsler Adult Intelligence Scales ($N = 111$; For further details, see Bradway & Thompson, 1962; Kangas & Bradway, 1971). About half ($N = 55$) of the adolescents tested in 1944 were measured again in 1984 at ages 55 to 57 and in 1993–1997 at ages ranging from 64 to 72 (J. McArdle et al., 2001).

As with any data oriented study, the information in this data set has some clear limitations (e.g., Pinneau, 1961). Among these, the participants are all from one birth cohort (~1928) in the same geographical area (San Francisco), one ethnicity (Caucasian), and come from volunteer families with above–average socioeconomic status, and most score above–average on most cognitive tasks. Whereas the longitudinal age–span and the number of measures taken are large, the number of occasions of measurement was limited by practical concerns (e.g., cooperation, fatigue, and practice effects). The benefits and limitations of these classic longitudinal data make it possible to examine both the benefits and limitations of the new models for the growth and change discussed in this chapter.

3.1.2   Variables Measured

A great deal of variables has been measured on these participants but only two variables will be considered in detail here, and these data are described in the plots of Figure 3.1. The first plot (Fig. 3.1a) gives individual growth curve data for verbal ability (Rasch–scaled) at each age–at–testing for 29 individuals who were measured at each time–of–testing and for the 82 persons who were measured at some, but not all ages of testing. The second plot of Figure 3.1b is a similar plot for data from Non–Verbal measurements. Although not depicted here, multiple variables from the SB and the WAIS have been repeatedly measured, including separate measures of "Verbal" (or "Knowledge") scores, and of "Non-Verbal" (or "Reasoning") scores (for details, see J. McArdle & Nesselroade, 2003). Measurement problems arise in the fitting of any statistical model with longitudinal data, and these issues begin with scaling and metrics.

Our common problem in longitudinal data comes from the fact that the SB was the measure administered at early ages (4, 14, 30) and the Wechsler Adult Intelligence WAIS was used at the later ages (30, 42, 56, 64). While these are both measures of intellectual abili-

Figure 3.1: Longitudinal growth curves for Verbal and Non–Verbal abilities (Rasch–scaled and age–interpolated)

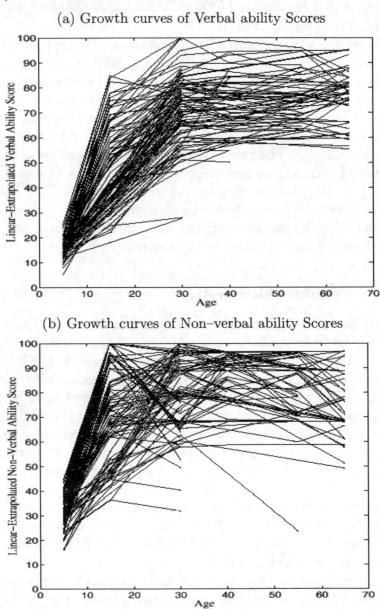

(a) Growth curves of Verbal ability Scores

(b) Growth curves of Non–verbal ability Scores

Table 3.1: Descriptive statistics for variables used in dynamic models

(a) Summary statistics for Verbal scores

Variable	N	Mean	Std Dev	Minimum	Maximum
V05	111	15.44	3.46	5.04	25.24
V15	111	47.19	15.35	18.17	84.72
V30	109	71.31	13.05	27.78	100.00
V40	49	73.23	11.24	50.11	98.81
V55	53	75.07	9.54	59.38	95.88
V65	49	76.39	10.39	55.36	95.28

(b) Descriptive Statistics for Non–Verbal scores

Variable	N	Mean	Std Dev	Minimum	Maximum
N05	111	32.13	5.73	15.94	44.60
N15	111	72.70	19.10	36.35	100.00
N30	110	80.42	14.23	31.90	100.00
N40	49	88.18	9.76	58.61	96.49
N55	52	82.43	14.30	23.50	96.49
N65	46	78.14	14.09	49.17	96.88

(c) Pair-wise correlations for Verbal scores

	V05	V15	V30	V45	V55	V65
V05	1.000					
V15	0.363	1.000				
V30	0.476	0.693	1.000			
V40	0.446	0.609	0.850	1.000		
V55	0.418	0.651	0.887	0.930	1.000	
V65	-0.007	0.529	0.735	0.767	0.767	1.000

V=Verbal, N=Nonverbal, 05, 15, 30, 45, 55, and 65 Reflect Age
Note: Original scores were Rasch-scaled over the SB and WAIS and then altered by linear age extrapolation within occasion; see text for details.

Table 3.1: (continued)

(d) Pair-wise correlations for Non–Verbal scores

	N05	N15	N30	N45	N55	N65
N05	1.000					
N15	0.466	1.000				
N30	0.155	0.228	1.000			
N40	0.010	0.251	0.748	1.000		
N55	0.032	0.336	0.622	0.760	1.000	
N65	0.170	0.386	0.533	0.779	0.743	1.000

(e) Pair-wise correlations for Verbal and Non–Verbal scores

	V05	V15	V30	V45	V55	V65
N05	0.426	0.173	0.315	0.232	0.266	0.017
N15	0.261	0.180	0.370	0.273	0.195	0.248
N30	0.261	0.217	0.292	0.376	0.158	0.197
N40	0.012	-0.076	0.112	0.118	-0.010	0.087
N55	0.072	0.110	0.045	-0.055	0.126	-0.084
N65	-0.017	0.102	0.302	0.221	0.170	0.239

V=Verbal, N=Nonverbal, 05, 15, 30, 45, 55, and 65 Reflect Age
Note: Original scores were Rasch-scaled over the SB and WAIS and then altered
by linear age extrapolation within occasion; see text for details.

ties, they are not scored in the same way, and they may measure different intellectual abilities at the same or different ages. These data were examined using set of structural equation models with common factors for composite scores from the SB and WAIS. That is, the original scores have been transformed using models to be described few but, as we illustrate, the comparability of scales from one age to another is not assured and can be a fairly complex problem.

3.1.3   Summary Data Description

Table 3.1 is a listing of numerical information from this study that is used in subsequent examples. The overall subject participation shows a nearly continual loss of participants over the sixty years. The means and standard deviations for two composite variables (see Table 3.1, a and b) show early increases followed by less change in the later years. The correlations of these measures over six occasions are listed in Table 3.1 (c, d, and e) and here we find a complex pattern of results: some correlations suggesting high stability of individual differences (e.g., $r > .9$) and others suggesting low long–term stability ($r < .1$). The summary information presented in Tables 3.1 is limited to those 29 participants with complete data at all 6 time points of measurement, but information on $N = 111$ available through adulthood will be used in the growth curve examples to follow.

3.2 Models

Multivariate growth curve data are characterized as having multiple observations based on *longitudinal* or *repeated measures*. This means the scores to be modeled are assumed to (a) be measured on the same persons, (b) be measured under the same conditions, (c) represent the same constructs, and (d) be scored in the same units at each occasion. To evaluate these assumptions, previous researchers have considered the application of standard multivariate models to growth data (e.g., Harris, 1963; J. Horn, 1972). In this section, we focus on the SEMs used to deal with the measurement, growth, and dynamic relationships among the variables.

3.2.1 SEM for Measurement Calibration

One way to use these measurement concepts is to use a so–called "measurement model" embedded in longitudinal structural models (as in J. McArdle, 1988; J. McArdle & Woodcock, 1997). Assume we observe scores on two scales at multiple occasions ($t = 1$ to T) on a constant set of persons ($n = 1$ to N). To deal with the measurement issues in this analysis,

$$SB[t]_n = \nu_s + \lambda_s y[t]_n + e_{sb}[t]_n,$$
$$\text{and} \tag{3.2}$$
$$WS[t]_n = \nu_w + \lambda_w y[t]_n + e_{ws}[t]_n,$$

where the observed variables for the Stanford–Binet ($SB[t]$) and the WAIS ($WS[t]$) are each related to a common factor ($f[t]$) with time–invariant factor loadings (λ_j), unique components (u_j), and scaling intercepts (v_j). Although we are only considering two variables, the assumption of a single common factor model represents a restrictive and testable hypothesis about the proportionality of the responses within an occasion. It is not commonly recognized that these kinds of models can be fitted even if both variables are not measured at the same occasion (see J. McArdle, 1994; J. McArdle & Woodcock, 1997).

To clarify measurement models we the *path diagram* displayed as Figure 3.2 (for details on these diagrams, see J. J. McArdle & Boker, 1990). In this representation, the observed variables are drawn as squares, the unobserved variables are drawn as circles, and the implied unit constant (i.e., scores of one before the intercept parameter in Eq. 3.2) is included as a triangle. Model parameters representing "fixed" or "group" coefficients are drawn as one-headed arrows while "random" or "individual" features are drawn as two-headed arrows. The observed variables ($SB[t]$ and $WS[t]$) are seen here in the pattern of measured (squares) and unmeasured (circles) variables depending on the occasion (e.g., the $SB[4]$ is measured but the $WS[4]$ is not). However, for each occasion, we postulate a single latent common factor ($y[t]$) with two loadings (λ_s and λ_w) and two error variances (ψ_s^2 and ψ_w^2) which are allowed to be different with an occasion but are fixed to be the same across all occasions. In order to estimate unique parameters, we add a typical restriction on one of the factor loadings (e.g., $\lambda_w = 1$).

The expectations from this kind of a model can be seen as *proportional growth curves*, even if the model includes additional variables or factors. To the degree multiple measurements are made, this common factor hypothesis about the change pattern is a strongly rejectable model (e.g., J. McArdle & Woodcock, 1997). To further reduce the complexity of this model we also postulate two second–order common factors (f_1 and f_2). These factors are not formally necessary, but they have means and covariances with unrestricted loadings, and this help limit the means and covariances implied for the latent variables $y[t]$ at all six occasions.

In a related but simpler analysis, Bayley (1956) showed how the deviations of scores from different scales measured on persons at the same occasion could be used to create comparable longitudinal scores (i.e., 16 D scores for the Berkeley Growth Study children). This classical calibration may be further improved by estimating latent traits with equal intervals in the form of *item response theory* (IRT) latent trait models (Embretson, 1996; Fischer & Molenaar, 1995).

Although IRT models are often considered in a separate context, the single parameter "Rasch" IRT models can be easily and directly related to these kinds of SEM (R. McDonald, 1999), and this IRT approach will be used here as well.

Figure 3.2: A structural equation model for scaling a comparable ability on the Stanford–Binet (SB[t]) and the WAIS (WS[t]) over the six–occasions of longitudinal data (Note: For further restrictions two common factors are included at the second level)

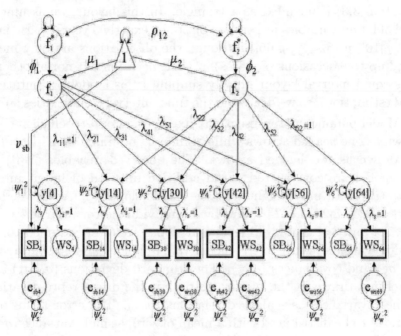

3.2.2   SEM based on Latent Growth Curves

Assuming we observe variable Y at multiple occasions on the same persons, we can write

$$Y[t]_n = y_{0,n} + A[t]y_{s,n} + e[t]_n \tag{3.3}$$

where the y_0 are scores representing an individual's initial level (e.g., intercept), the y_s are scores representing the individual *linear change over time* (e.g., slopes), the set of $A[t]$ are termed "basis" weights which define the timing or "shape" of the change over time for the group (e.g., age at testing), and (d) the $e[t]$ are error scores at each measurement.

This latent growth model (Equation 3.3) can be seen as a common factor model, and this is clear in the path diagram of Figure 3.3a. In this diagram, the observed variables are drawn as squares, the unobserved or unmeasured variables are drawn as circles, and the implied unit constant (i.e., scores of one before the intercept parameter in Equation 3.3) is included as a triangle. In this layout, we assume a level of latent variables $y[t]$ spread out to be exactly 5 years apart (i.e., $y[5]$, $y[10]$, $y[15]$, ..., $y[65]$) although the observations are only measured up to 6 occasions (squares) at some occasion but not at others. This equal interval layout greatly simplifies this model presentation (and estimation), so we deal with the time–interval complexities later.

Model parameters representing "fixed" or "group" coefficients are drawn as one headed arrows while "random" or "individual" features are drawn as two–headed arrows. The observed variables ($Y[t]$) in this model are constructed as an additive function of latent intercepts (y_0) with unit weights, by the latent slopes (y_s) with weights ($A[t] = [a[1], a[2], ..., a[T]]$), and by an individual error term ($e[t]$). In Eqs. 3.4 and 3.5, the initial level and slopes are often assumed to be random variables with "fixed" means (μ_0, μ_s) but "random" variances (σ_0^2, σ_s^2) and covariances ($\sigma_{0,s}$). The standard deviations (σ_0, σ_s) are sometimes drawn in the picture to permit the direct representation of the covariances as scaled correlations ($\rho_{0,s}$). The error terms are assumed to be distributed with a mean of zero, a single variance (σ_e^2), and no correlation with any of the other latent scores. Further statistical tests may assume these errors follow a normal distribution as well.

In this latent growth model, change from any one time to another ($\Delta y_n / \Delta_t$) is a function of the slope score (y_s) and the change in the factor loadings ($\Delta A[t]$). It follows that a class of alternative models can be based on the form of the $A[t]$ basis coefficients. These coefficients determine the metric or scaling and interpretation of these scores, so alterations of $A[t]$ can lead to many different models. If, for example, we require all $A[t] = 0$, this parameter constraint would effectively eliminate all slope parameters and create a "baseline" or "no–growth" alternative. Another alternative is to fix $A[t] = t$ to represent a "straight line" or "linear" growth curve or other interpretations of the shape of the changes (e.g., $A[t] = [1, 2, 2, 1]$). We can allow the curve basis to take on a number of restrictive nonlinear forms to reflect specific nonlinear hypothesis (J. McArdle & Hamagami, 1996; J. McArdle & Nesselroade, 2003). We can also allow the curve basis to take on a shape based on the empirical data (Meredith & Tisak, 1990). In this approach, we fit a factor model based on two common factor scores, an intercept (y_0) with unit loadings, a linear slope (y_s), and independent unique factor scores ($e[t]$), but the factor loadings ($A[t]$) are now estimated from the data as any factor loadings and we obtain what should be an *optimal shape* for the group curve. Additional models can be considered by adding more factors or adding structure to the specific factors (e.g., Cnaan et al., 1997; Littell et al., 1996).

3.2.3 Structural Equation Models Based on Latent Difference Scores

In recent research, we have considered some ways to improve the clarity of the basic dynamic change interpretations, but we use conventional analytic techniques. This has led us to recast the previous growth models using *latent difference scores* (see J. McArdle, 2001). In this approach we first assume we have a pair of observed scores $Y[t]$ and $Y[t - 1]$ measured over a defined interval of time ($\Delta t = 1$), and we write

$$
\begin{aligned}
Y[t]_n &= y[t]_n + e[t]_n, \\
Y[t - 1]_n &= y[t - 1]_n + e[t - 1]_n \\
&\text{and} \\
y[t]_n &= y[t - 1]_n + \Delta y[t]_n \\
&\text{so} \\
\Delta y[t]_n &= (y[t]_n - y[t - 1]_n),
\end{aligned}
\tag{3.4}
$$

with latent scores $y[t]$ and $y[t-1]$, and errors of measurement $e[t]$ and $e[t-1]$, and where the new latent variable $\Delta y[t]$ is directly interpreted as a *latent difference score*. This simple algebraic device allows us to

Figure 3.3: Alternative path diagrams of univariate latent growth models

(a) A standard path diagram of a univariate latent growth model

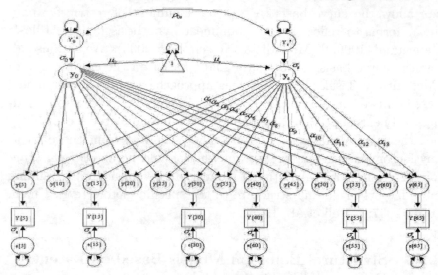

(b) An alternative path diagram of latent growth based on latent difference score model with constant change (a)

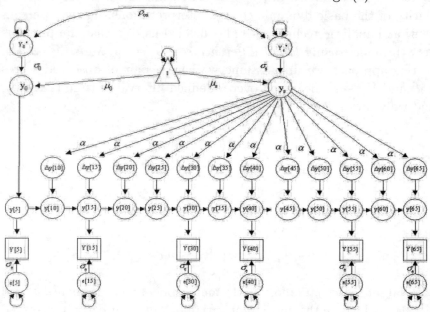

generally define the trajectory equation as

$$Y[t]_n = y_{o,n} + \left(\sum_{i=1}^{t} \Delta y[i]_n\right) + e[t]_n, \qquad (3.5)$$

where the summation $(\sum_{i=1,t})$ or accumulation of the latent changes $(\Delta y[t])$ up to time t is included. In this latent difference score approach, we do not directly define the $A[t]$ coefficients, but instead we directly define *changes as an accumulation of the first differences among latent variables.*

Following this logic, the traditional linear change score model can be drawn in terms of first differences as Figure 3.3b. Here we use: (a) *unit–valued regression weights* among variables by fixed non–zero constraints (as in J. McArdle & Nesselroade, 1994), (b) a *constant timelag* by using additional latent variables as placeholders (as in J. Horn & McArdle, 1980), (c) each *latent change score as the focal outcome variable,* and (d) a repetition (by equality constraints) of the α structural coefficients. Following the standard linear growth models, we include the unobserved initial level mean and variance (i.e., μ_0 and σ_0^2), while the error of measurement has mean zero, constant variance $(\sigma_e^2 > 0)$, and is uncorrelated with every other component. As in the linear change model, this constant change component (y_s) has a non–zero mean (i.e., μ_s, the average of the latent change scores), a non–zero variance (i.e., σ_s^2, the variability of the latent change scores), and a non–zero correlation with the latent initial levels (i.e., ρ_{0s}).

This latent difference score $(\Delta y[t]_n)$ of Eqs. 3.4 and 3.5 is not the same as an observed difference score $(\Delta Y[t]_n)$ because the latent score is considered separate from the removal of the model based error component. While this difference $\Delta y[t]_n$ is a theoretical score, it has immediate practical value because now we can write a structural model for *any latent change concept* without immediate concern about the resulting trajectory (as in J. McArdle, 2001; J. McArdle et al., 2001; J. McArdle & Nesselroade, 1994). For example, a composite change expression model is written as

$$\Delta y[t]_n = \alpha y_{s,n} + \beta y[t-1]_n. \qquad (3.6)$$

where the y_s is a latent slope score which is constant over time, and the α and β are coefficients describing the change. This combines an additive change model such as Figure 3.3b with a multiplicative change model drawn as Figure 3.4a. We refer to this combination in Figure 3.4b as a *dual change score* (DCS) model because it permits both a systematic constant change (α) and a systematic proportional change (β) over time, and no stochastic residual is added (i.e., $z[t]$; see J. McArdle, 2001). This is an interesting linear difference score model because the expectations lead to a mixed–effects model trajectory with a distinct nonlinear form from a simple accumulation of first differences (Eq. 3.6), and it can be fitted using standard SEM software (e.g., LISREL, Mx, etc.).

3.2.4 Structural Equation Models for Dynamic Interrelationships Among Growth Curves

The collection of multiple variables at each occasion of measurement leads naturally to questions about relationships among growth processes and multivariate growth models. Some recent SEMs described in the statistical literature have emphasized the examination of *parallel growth curves*, including the correlation of various components (J. McArdle, 1988, 1991; Willett & Sayer, 1994). The models fitted here can be represented in latent growth notation for two variables by

$$Y[t]_n = y_{0,n} + A_y[t]y_{s,n} + e_y[t]_n$$
$$\text{and} \tag{3.7}$$
$$X[t]_n = x_{0,n} + A_x[t]x_{s,n} + e_x[t]_n,$$

where $Y[t]$ and $X[t]$ are two different variables observed over time, and there are two basis functions ($A_y[t]$ and $A_x[t]$), with covariances (e.g., $E\{y_s, x_s\} = \sigma_{ys,xs}$) allowed among the common latent variables. The hypothesis here relies on the equality of the basis coefficients (e.g., $A_y[t] = A_x[t]$) to examine the overall shape of the two curves and about any non–zero covariance of initial levels (i.e., $|\sigma_{y0,x0}| > 0$) and *covariance of slopes* (i.e., $|\sigma_{ys,xs}| > 0$).

Another popular alternative is to assume a variable $X[t]$ is measured at multiple occasions and that we want to examine its influence in the context of a growth model for $Y[t]$. One popular model used in multilevel and mixed effects modeling is based on the analysis of

Figure 3.4: Alternative forms of latent difference score models

(a) A path diagram of a univariate proportional change score model (β)

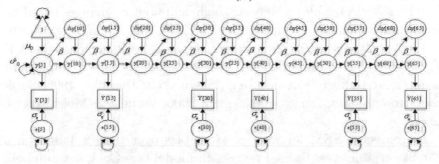

(b) A path diagram of a univariate dual change score model

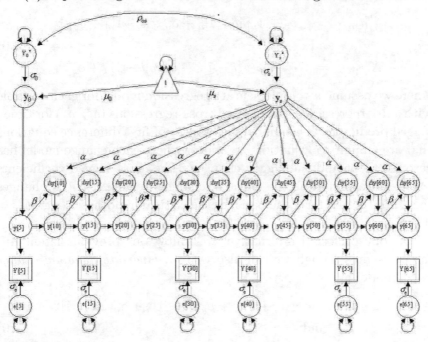

covariance (Eq. 3.3) with $X[t]$ as a "time–varying" predictor. We can write

$$Y[t]_n = y_{0:xn} + A[t]y_{s:x,n} + \delta X[t]_n + e[t]_n \qquad (3.8)$$

where the δ are fixed (group) coefficients with the same effect on $Y[t]$ scores at all occasions. In this case, the growth parameters ($\mu_{0:x}, \mu_{s:x}, \sigma_{s:x}$, etc.) are conditional on the expected values of the external $X[t]$ variable. The basis coefficients reflect changes based on a constant slope ($y_{s:x}$) independent of $X[t]$, and the new coefficient (δ) represents the effect of changes in X (i.e., $\Delta X[t]$) on changes in Y (i.e., $\Delta y[t]$). This time–varying covariate model is easy to implement using mixed–effects software (e.g., Sliwinski & Buschke, 1999; Sullivan, Rosenbloom, Lim, & Pfefferman, 2000; Verbeke & Molenberghs, 2000).

A classical SEM for multiple variables over time is based on a latent variable cross–lagged regression model (see Cook & Campbell, 1979; Rogosa, 1978). This model can be written for latent scores as

$$Y[t]_n \quad = \quad \nu_y + \phi_y y[t-1]_n + \delta_{yx} x[t-1]_n + e_y[t]_n$$
$$\text{and} \qquad\qquad\qquad\qquad\qquad\qquad\qquad (3.9)$$
$$X[t]_n \quad = \quad \nu_x + \phi_x x[t-1]_n + \delta_{xy} y[t-1]_n + e_x[t]_n,$$

where we assume a complementary regression model for each variable with auto–regressions (ϕ_y, ϕ_x) and cross-regressions (δ_{yx}, δ_x) for time–lagged predictors. This model yields a set of first difference equations that are similar to Equation 3.8 above, where each change model has zero intercept and the lagged changes. The cross–lagged coefficients (δ) are interpreted as the effect of changes (e.g., $\Delta x[t]$) on changes (e.g., $\Delta y[t]$), and form the basis for the critical hypotheses (e.g., $\delta_{yx} > 0$ but $\delta_{xy} = 0$).

As our preferred alternative, we follow our previous latent difference scores model; we can also write a *bivariate dynamic change score* model as

$$\Delta y[t]_n \quad = \quad \alpha_y + y_{s,n} + \beta_y y[t-1]_n + \gamma_{yx} x[t-1]_n$$
$$\text{and} \qquad\qquad\qquad\qquad\qquad\qquad\qquad (3.10)$$
$$\Delta x[t]_n \quad = \quad \alpha_x + x_{s,n} + \beta_x x[t-1]_n + \gamma_{xy} y[t-1]_n.$$

In the first part of each change score, we assume a dual change score model represented by parameters α and β. This model also permits a *coupling* parameter (γ_{yx}), representing the time–dependent effect of latent $x[t]$ on $y[t]$, and another coupling parameter (γ_{xy}), representing the time–dependent effect of latent $y[t]$ on $x[t]$. This is not the same as the correlated growth (Equation 3.7), time–varying covariate (Equation 3.8), or cross–lagged models (Equation 3.9). The latent changes in this system of equations have an intercept (α) and the coupling parameters (γ) are direct effects from prior time–varying levels $(x[t-1]$ and $y[t-1])$. Results from these alternative models can be quite different (see J. McArdle et al., 2001).

This bivariate dynamic model is described in the path diagram of Fig. 3.5. The key features of this model include the use of fixed unit values (to define $\Delta y[t]$ and $\Delta x[t]$) and equality constraints (for the $\alpha, \beta,$ and γ parameters). These latent difference score models can lead to more complex nonlinear trajectory equations (e.g., nonhomogeneous equations) but these can be described simply by writing the respective bases $(A_j[t])$ as the linear accumulation of first differences (Eq. 3.6) for each variable:

$$Y[t]_n \quad = \quad y_{0,n} + (\sum_{i=1}^{t} \Delta y[i]_n) + e_y[t]_n$$

$$\text{and} \tag{3.11}$$

$$X[t]_n \quad = \quad x_{0,n} + (\sum_{i=1}^{t} \Delta x[i]_n) + e_x[t]_n.$$

This makes it practical to analyze a variety of dynamic models using standard SEM.

3.2.5   Structural Equation Models with Multiple Groups

In contemporary SEM, we can consider analyses which include more detailed information about group differences. In contemporary SEM, we can consider group differences in (a) the fixed components, (b) the random components, (c) different patterns of observed data, and (d) latent groups of persons for all of the above.

Assume a variable termed Z indicates some measurable characteristic of the person (e.g., sex, educational level, etc.) that is constant

Figure 3.5: A path diagram representing a bivariate dual change score model fitted to incomplete and unequal interval data from the Bradway–McArdle Longitudinal study (from McArdle, 2001; McArdle & Hamagami, 2001).

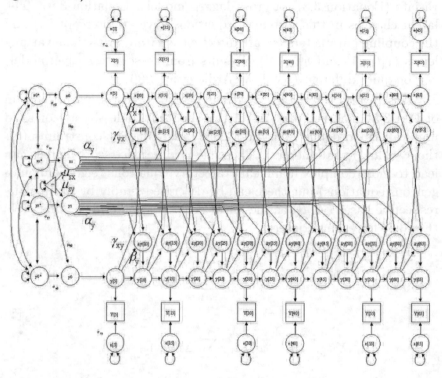

over occasions. We can write

$$Y[t]_n = y_{0:x,n} + (\sum_{i=1}^{t} \Delta y[i]_n) + \omega Z_n + e[t]_n, \qquad (3.12)$$

where the w are fixed (group) coefficients with the same–sized effect on the measured $Y[t]$ scores at all occasions and the X is an independent observed (or assigned) predictor variable. This use of "adjusted" growth parameters is popularly represented in the techniques of the analysis of covariance, and the reduction of error from one model to the next is considered as a way to index the impact (see Snijders & Bosker, 1999).

An alternative way to add another variable to a growth model is to write expressions where the Z variable has a direct effect on the individual differences scores of the growth factors. This can be stated as

$$Y[t]_n = y_{0,n} + (\sum_{i=1}^{t} \Delta y[i]_n) + e[t]_n$$

with

$$y_{0n} = \nu_{00} + \nu_{0z} Z_n + e_{0n}, \qquad (3.13)$$

and

$$y_{sn} = \nu_{s0} + \nu_{sz} X_n + e_{sn},$$

where the regression of the latent variables (y_0, y_s) on Z includes intercepts (ν_{00}, ν_{s0}) and slopes (ν_{0z}, ν_{sz}). In this simple latent growth model, as in more complex models to follow, we can always add other predictors Z for the intercepts and the slopes because these models are simply latent growth models with "extension variables" (e.g., J. McArdle & Epstein, 1987). Such models have been termed "random–coefficients" or "multilevel models," or "slopes as outcomes," or "mixed–effects" models (Littell et al., 1996; A. S. Bryk & Raudenbush, 1987; A. Bryk & Raudenbush, 1992). Variations on these models can be compared for goodness–of–fit indices, and we can examine changes in the model variance explained at both the first and the second level (see Snijders & Bosker, 1999).

A third and less restrictive treatment of the group problem model uses concepts derived from multiple–group factor analysis (e.g., J. Horn & McArdle, 1992; K. Jöreskog & Sörbom, 1999; J. McArdle & Cattell, 1994). In these kinds of models, each group, $g = 1$ to G, is assumed to follow some kind of latent growth accumulation, such as

$$Y[t]_n^{(g)} = y_{0,n}^{(g)} + (\sum_{i=1}^{t} \Delta y[i]_n^{(g)}) + e[t]_n^{(g)}, \qquad (3.14)$$

with the changes $\Delta y[i]_n^{(g)}$ are defined by substantive application. The persons in the groups are assumed to be independent, so this kind of grouping can only be done for observed categorical variables (i.e., sex). The multiple group growth model permits the examination of the presumed invariance of the latent basis functions and the rejection of these constraints (based on χ^2/df) implies that some independent groups have a different basic shape of the growth curve. Additional tests of the equality of the means and variances of the latent levels and slopes may be informative as well.

Multiple group models can be a useful way to express problems of incomplete data. Longitudinal data collections often include different numbers of data points for different people and different variables, and one good ways to deal with these kinds of statistical problems is to include multiple group models permit different numbers of data points on each person (e.g., Little & Rubin, 1987; J. McArdle, 1994). In order to uniquely identify and estimate the model parameters from this collection of data, all parameters are *forced to be invariant over all groups* (for further details, see J. McArdle & Anderson, 1990; J. McArdle & Hamagami, 1992). The key assumption in our use of these *MLE*-based techniques is that the incomplete data are *missing at random* (*MAR*, Little & Rubin, 1987). This assumption does not require the data to be *missing completely at random* (*MCAR*), but *MAR* does assume there is some observed information that allows us to account for and remove the bias in the model estimates created by the lack of complete data (e.g., Hedecker & Gibbons, 1997; J. McArdle, 1994; J. McArdle & Bell, 2000; J. McArdle & Hamagami, 1992; Miyazaki & Raudenbush, 2000). In many cases, this *MAR* assumption is a convenient starting point and allows us to use all the available information in one analysis.

Another final problem is the discrimination of (a) models of multiple curves for a single group of subjects from (b) models of multiple groups of subjects with different curves. These practical problems set the stage for models that test hypotheses about *growth curves between latent groups*. The recent series of models termed *growth mixture models* have been developed for this purpose (Nagin, 1999; Hagenaar & McCutcheon, 2002). We can write this model as a weighted sum of accumulations

$$Y[t]_n = \sum_{c=1}^{C}(P\{c_n\}.\{y_{0,n}^{(c)} + (\sum_{i=1}^{t}\Delta y[i]_n^{(c)}) + e[t]_n^{(c)}\}),$$

with   (3.15)

$$\sum_{c=1}^{C}(P\{c_n\}) = 1,$$

where $P\{c_n\}$ is the constrained to sum to unity so it acts as a "probability of class membership" for the person in $c = 1$ to C classes. In these kinds of analyses, the distribution of the latent parameters is assumed to come from a "mixture" of two or more overlapping distributions. Using growth–mixture models we can estimate the most likely threshold parameter for each latent distribution (τ_p, for the pth parameter) while simultaneously estimating the separate model parameters for the resulting latent groups. A variety of new program scripts (e.g., Nagin, 1999) and computer programs (e.g., Mplus, by L. Muthen & Muthen, 1998) permit these analyses.

3.3 Results

3.3.1 Results from Fitting Measurement Models

The initial SEM of Fig. 3.2 was fitted using all the available information from the SB and WAIS. The parameters of this model were largely identified from the information at the age 30 and age 42 occasions where both measurements were made, but we assumed invariance across all measures at other occasions. In model fitting, the factor loading of the first variable was fixed ($\lambda_y = 1$) to identify the factor scores, and the other loading ($\lambda_x = .84$) was estimated and required to be invariant over all times of measurement. The results quickly showed that a single common factor at the first level ($y[t]$) did not produce a good fit ($\chi^2 = 473, df = 34$) even though most of the parameter estimates seem reasonable ($\sigma_s = 1.39; \sigma_{ew} = .06; \sigma_{ws} = 5.3$). In subsequent analyses, the items in each scale (SB & WAIS) were separated on a theoretical basis: some were considered as "Verbal" items and these were separated from the items that were considered as "Non-Verbal" items in each scale ("Memory" and "Number" items were deleted; see Hamagami, 1998). The single factor model was refitted to each new scale, and each of these models fits much better than before ($\chi^2 = 63, df = 32$). This result suggests that at least two separate constructs were needed to reflect the time–sequence information in the inter-battery data. We could now use this kind of a model as a first level for all subsequent SEM analyses.

As a simpler alternative, we tried to create factor scores $y[t]$ from a joint IRT calibration of the items of the SB and the WAIS. Here we only used the Verbal and Non-Verbal items of the SB and WAIS at ages 30 and 42. An IRT analysis using the MSTEPS program suggested 95% of the items could be used to form a consistent scale, and the relationships among the scores are presented in Figs. 3.6a and 3.7a. The second set of plots (Figs. 3.6b and 3.7b) show the new scoring system as "translation table" for each construct from the SB and WAIS measures by using IRT calibration based on the data from the age 30 testing. These analyses resulted in new and hopefully "age-comparable" scales for the Verbal and Non-Verbal items from all occasions.

It is possible to write SEM to deal with the exact ages of the persons at each time of measurement. This may be needed because the ages within each occasion vary by about 5 years (i.e., 2 to 7), and because the interval of time between testings was not forced to be of equal duration. However, to make our computer programming task more practical (e.g., Mx), we made a small linear extrapolation of the scores. The original data were (a) linearly extrapolated within occasion to the average age, and then (b) linearly extrapolated across occasions into 5–year age segments (i.e., 5 to 10, 10 to 15, etc.). These adjustments yield scores that a person would have at ages 5, 15, 30, 45, 55, and 65, and these are the data listed in Table 3.1. Whenever possible (i.e., in mixed models to follow), these age–adjusted scores were compared to the original scores.

3.3.2 Results from Fitting Latent Growth Models

The complete and incomplete data from the six–occasion Bradway–McArdle longitudinal study (Fig. 3.1) have been fitted and reported in J. McArdle and Hamagami (1996) and J. McArdle et al. (2001). On a computational note, the standard HLM, MLn, VARCL, MX, and SAS PROC MIXED programs produced similar results for all models with a fixed basis. The models with estimated factor loadings $(A[t])$ were fitted using the general Mx unbalanced raw data option (e.g., the variable length approach) and with SAS PROC NLMIXED, the results are similar. The basic models were nearly identical before and after this age–adjusted approximation.

Our initial results are presented in detail in Table 3.2. The first model (labeled $V0$ or $N0$) was a no–growth model estimated with

Figure 3.6: Results from IRT scaling of the Verbal abilities from the Stanford–Binet and the WAIS (Data from 1957 and 1969 testing)

(a) An expected total test score as a function of ability measures for Vocabulary

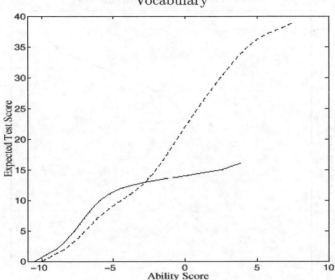

(b) A comparison of ability measures between Stanford–Binet items and WAIS items for Vocabulary

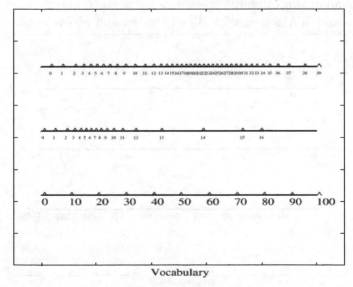

Vocabulary

Figure 3.7: Results from an IRT scaling of the Non–Verbal abilities from
the Stanford–Binet and the WAIS (Data from 1957 and 1969 testing)

(a) An expected total test score as a function of ability measures for
Block Design and equivalents

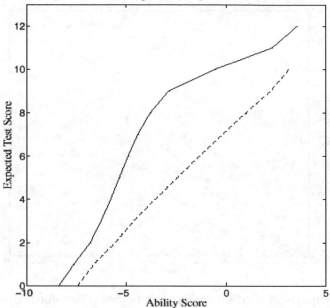

(b) A comparison of ability measures between Stanford-Binet items
and WAIS items for Block Design and equivalents

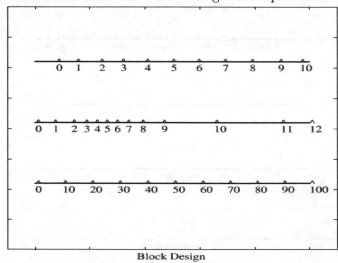

only three parameters to obtained baseline fits $(-2logL = 4515, 4423)$. The parameters estimated include initial level means $(\mu_0 = 54.0, 68.2)$, small initial level standard deviations $(\sigma_0 = 0.001, 0.001)$, and large error deviations $(\sigma_e = 26.2, 24.5)$. The second model fitted was a linear growth model $(V1$ or $N1)$ with a fixed basis and six free parameters. This basis was first formed by using the mean age of the persons at the time of measurement $A[t] = [5, 15, 30, 45, 55, 65]$, then placed in the centered and rescaled form of $A[t] = (Age[t] - 5)/60 = [0, 0.16, 0.42, 0.58, 0.83, 1.00]$; In this metric the weights are proportional to the range of data between the initial age of 5 and the oldest age of 56. Estimates obtained yielded fits $(-2logL = 4069, 4215)$, which represented a clear improvement over the baselines $(\chi^2 = 456, 208$ on $df = 3)$, and the error variances were reduced substantially (to $\sigma_e\{1\} = 15.8, 19.4)$. The mean and variance of the intercept and slope parameters yielded a function which increases over all ages.

This latent basis model $(V2$ or $N2)$ was fitted next. For the purposes of estimation, the $A[1] = 0$ (at Age=5) and $A[6] = 1$ (at Age=65) were fixed (as proportions) but the four other coefficients were estimated from the data. This resulted in likelihoods $(L = 3450, 3759)$ that is substantially better than both the baseline models $(\chi^2 = 1065, 669$ on $df = 7)$ and the linear models $(\chi^2 = 619, 422$ on $df = 4)$, and the error variance has been substantially reduced (to $\sigma_e\{2\} - 6.7, 10.3)$. For the Verbal scores, the basis coefficients were $A[t] = [0, 0.55, 0.95, 0.96, 0.97, 1]$, with slope means $\mu_l = 58.8$ and $\sigma_s = 9.1$. This leads to a group trajectory which rises linearly between ages 4 and 30 and then shows no decline by age 65. For the Non–Verbal scores, the basis coefficients were $A[t] = [0, 0.93, 1.09, 1.20, 1.10, 1]$, with slope means $\mu_l = 44.0$ and $\sigma_s = 7.9$. This leads to a group trajectory which rises rapidly between ages 4 and 14, peaks at age 42, and starts a small but clear downward decline at ages 55 to 65. These group curves are plotted as a dashed line in Fig. 3.8. and are very similar to the general features of the raw data in Fig. 3.1. The individual differences in this model are not seen in the means but in the large variances for the level (σ_0) and the slope (σ_s) parameters. The latent level and slope scores required a bounded correlation $(\rho_{ls} =< .99)$.

The improved fit of this latent basis compared to the linear basis model suggests the need for some form of a nonlinear curve. To

Table 3.2: Univariate modeling results for Verbal (V) and Nonverbal (N) scores for alternative growth curve models

(a): Univariate modeling results for Verbal scores

Model Parameters	V0: No change (NCS)	V1: Linear Change (LCS)	V2: Latent Growth (LGM)	V3: Partial Adjustment (PAM)	V4: Mono-molecular change (SPAM)
Fixed Effects					
Initial Mean μ_0	54.0	30.3	15.2	74.9	74.7
Slope Mean μ_s	=0	61.8	58.8	-.508	.48
Growth Rate π				4.77	4.82
Loading $\alpha_{[5]}$	=0	=0	=0	=118	=-124
Loading $\alpha_{[15]}$	=0	=.1667	.55	=53.1	=-55.5
Loading $\alpha_{[30]}$	=0	=.4167	.95	=7.9	=-8.1
Loading $\alpha_{[40]}$	=0	=.5833	.96	=7.3	=-7.5
Loading $\alpha_{[55]}$	=0	=.8333	.97	=2.2	=-2.2
Loading $\alpha_{[65]}$	=0	=1	=1	=1.0	=-1.0
Random Effects					
Error Dev. σ_e	26.2	15.8	6.70	6.85	7.04
Initial Dev. σ_0	.001	3.22	3.13	10.89	12.07
Slope Dev. σ_s	=0	4.78	9.08	0.07	.07
Rate Dev. σ_π	–	–	–	–	.01
Correlation ρ_{0s}	=0	<.99	<.99	.90	<.99
Goodness-of-Fit					
Likelihood - 2ll	4515	4069	3450	3472	3455
Parameters	3	6	10	7	8

Table 3.2: (continued)

(b) Univariate modeling results for Non-verbal scores

Model Parameters	N0: No change (NCS)	N1: Linear Change (LCS)	N2: Latent Growth (LGM)	N3: Partial Adjustment (PAM)	N4: Mono-molecular change (SPAM)
			Fixed Effects		
Initial Mean μ_0	68.2	51.3	32.0	81.5	81.4
Slope Mean μ_s	=0	44.6	44.0	-.006	.005
Growth Rate π				9.055	9.16
Loading $\alpha_{[05]}$	=0	=0	=0	=8562	=-9511
Loading $\alpha_{[15]}$	=0	=.167	.93	=1893	=-2066
Loading $\alpha_{[30]}$	=0	=.417	1.09	=50.6	=-52.9
Loading $\alpha_{[40]}$	=0	=.583	1.20	=43.5	=-45.5
Loading $\alpha_{[55]}$	=0	=.833	1.10	=4.5	=-4.6
Loading $\alpha_{[65]}$	=0	=1	=1	=1.0	=-1.0
			Random Effects		
Error Dev. σ_e	24.5	19.4	10.3	10.8	10.7
Initial Dev. σ_0	.001	1.13	2.45	10.6	11.4
Slope Dev. σ_s	=0	5.84	7.90	0.01	.01
Rate Dev. σ_π	—	—	—	—	—
Correlation ρ_{0s}	=0	<.99	<.99	.90	<.99
			Goodness-of-Fit		
Likelihood - 2ll	4423	4215	3759	3793	3785
Parameters	3	6	10	7	8

explore the addition of fixed higher order growth components, the quadratic polynomial model was fitted to these data using the same procedures, but this led to convergence problems, and the goodness–of–fit was only slightly improved. An alternative nonlinear model was used ($V3$ or $N3$) based on the representation of "change as a partial adjustment" (PAM) and fitted with an exponential basis, $A[t] = [exp(-t - 1)\pi]$, with growth rate parameter π. This model required 4 free parameters with individual differences in the initial level variance (an asymptote) and in the latent slope (the distance from asymptote) parameters. This model requires all loadings to have an exponential function formed from a growth rate parameter (estimated at $\pi = 4.8, 9.1$). This model fit was much different from the latent basis model ($\chi^2 = 22, 34$ on $df = 3$), and the error variance is similar ($\sigma_e\{3\} = 6.9, 10.8$). A second model of this type was fit allowing individual coefficients in the rate parameter (π_n): Model 4 is labeled as a stochastic partial adjustments model (SPAM). The resulting fitted curves show only a small change in the average rate; the random variance of these rates is very small ($\sigma_\pi < .01$), and the fit is not much better than the simpler partial adjustment model ($\chi^2 = 13, 8; df = 4$).

The expected trajectories of this nonlinear model are drawn as solid lines in Fig. 3.8. In contrast to the previous latent basis model, this is an exponential shape that rises rapidly and then stays fairly constant at the asymptote (or equilibrium point) from age 42 to age 65. Also, unlike the latent basis model, this negative exponential model makes explicit predictions at all ages. The comparison of the latent basis ($M2$) and the partial adjustment models ($M3$ or $M4$) suggests that the decline in Non–Verbal intellectual abilities by age 65 is relatively small. The expectations from these two models yield only minor departures of the exploratory latent basis model ($M2$) from the partial adjustment model ($M3$). The further comparison of the stochastic adjustment ($M4$) and the partial adjustment model ($M3$) suggests that the same shape of change in Non–Verbal intellectual abilities can be applied to all persons.

Figure 3.8: Visual displays of two latent growth model expectations fitted to the Bradway–McArdle data

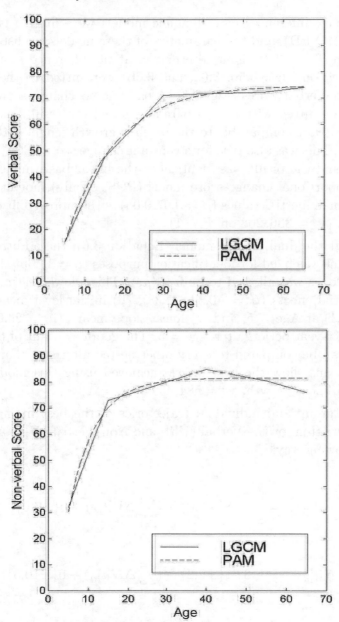

3.3.3   Results from Fitting Latent Difference Score Models

The latent difference score dynamic models were fitted (using Mx and NLMIXED), and the parameters of these models are listed some detail in Table 3.3. Four alternative latent difference score models (based on Figs. 3.5b, 3.6a, and 3.6b) were fitted to the Verbal and Non–Verbal scores (Fig. 3.1). A baseline no–change score model (NCS) was fitted with only 3 parameters and the results using this approach were comparable to the baseline growth model ($M0$ of Table 3.2). This was also true for a constant change score (CCS; α only) model, and the result was identical to the linear basis model ($M1$). The proportional change score model (PCS; β only), not fit earlier, yields small inertial values ($\beta = 0.07, 0.05$) with improved fit over the baseline ($\chi^2 = 336, 208$ on $df = 1$).

To fit the dual change model (Equation 3.6), the additive slope coefficient was fixed for identification purposes ($\alpha = 1$) but the mean of the slopes was allowed to be free (μ_s). This allowed estimation of (a) inertial effects ($\beta = -0.34, -1.38$), (b) initial level means ($\mu = 14.8, 32.1$) at Age $= 5$, and (c) linear slope means ($\mu_s = 26.0, 110.1$) for each 5-year period after Age $= 5$. The goodness-of-fit of the DCS model can be compared to every other nested alternative, and these comparisons show the best fit was achieved using this model (e.g., versus a linear growth, $\chi^2 = 584, 439$ on $df = 1$).

The group and individual trajectories of the best fitting model can be written for the Verbal ($V[t]$) and Non–Verbal ($N[t]$) scores in the following way:

$$V[t]_n \quad = \quad 14.8\{\pm3.0\} + (\sum_{i=1}^{t} \Delta V[t]_n) + 0\{\pm7.0\},$$

$$\text{and} \tag{3.16}$$

$$N[t]_n \quad = \quad 32.1\{\pm2.2\} + (\sum_{i=1}^{t} \Delta N[t]_n) + 0\{\pm10.5\}.$$

More fundamentally, the respective latent change scores were modeled as

Table 3.3: Univariate modeling results for (a) Verbal and (b) Non–verbal scores

(a) Univariate modeling results for Verbal scores

Model Parameters	V0: No change (NCS)	V1: Constant Change (CCS)	V5: Proportional Change (PCS)	V6: Dual Change (DCS)
Fixed Effects				
Initial Mean μ_0	54.0	30.3	37.1	14.8
Slope Mean μ_s	$=0$	5.14	$=0$	26.04
Loading α	$=0$	$=1$	$=0$	$=1$
Proportion β	$=0$	$=0$	0.076	-.343
Random Effects				
Error Dev. σ_e	26.2	15.8	18.3	7.04
Initial Dev. σ_0	.001	3.23	3.78	2.97
Slope Dev. σ_s	$=0$	0.40	$=0$	4.23
Correlation ρ_{0s}	$=0$	$< .99$	$=0$	$< .99$
Goodness-of-Fit				
Likelihood - 2ll	4515	4069	4179	3485
Parameters	3	6	4	7

(b) Univariate modeling results for Non-verbal scores

Model Parameters	N0: No change (NCS)	N1: Constant Change (CCS)	N5: Proportional Change (PCS)	N6: Dual Change (DCS)
Fixed Effects				
Initial Mean μ_0	68.2	51.3	55.0	32.1
Slope Mean μ_s	$=0$	3.71	$=0$	110.8
Loading α	$=0$	$=1$	$=0$	$=1$
Proportion β	$=0$	$=0$	.045	-1.38
Random Effects				
Error Dev. σ_e	24.5	19.4	20.4	10.5
Initial Dev. σ_0	.001	1.12	2.02	2.22
Slope Dev. σ_s	$=0$	.487	$=0$	15.38
Correlation ρ_{0s}	$=0$	$< .99$	$=0$	$< .99$
Goodness-of-Fit				
Likelihood - 2ll	4423	4215	4251	3776
Parameters	3	6	4	7

$$\Delta V[t]_n = 26.0\{\pm 4.2\} + V_{s,n} + -0.34V[t-1]_n,$$
$$\text{and} \tag{3.17}$$
$$\Delta N[t]_n = 32.1\{\pm 2.2\} + N_{s,n} + -1.38N[t-1]_n.$$

From these estimates we calculate the expected group trajectories and the five–year latent change accumulation as the combination of Eqs. 3.6 and 3.7, and we find the expected trajectory over time for these variables represented in this way is very close to the previous nonlinear solid line in Fig. 3.8.

3.3.4 Results from Fitting Multiple Variable Dynamic Models

Several alternative Verbal versus Non–Verbal bivariate coupling models based on Fig. 3.5 were fitted to the data. A first model included all the bivariate change parameters described above (Equations 3.10 and 3.11). This includes six dynamic coefficients (two each for α, β, γ), four latent means (μ), six latent deviations (σ), and six latent correlations (ρ). This model was fitted to 111 individuals with at least one point of data and 498 individual data observations, and yield one overall fit ($-2logL = 7118$) which was different from a random baseline ($\chi^2 = 379$ on $df = 16$). The group and individual trajectories of the best fitting model can be written for the Verbal ($V[t]$) and Non-Verbal ($N[t]$) scores in the following way:

$$V[t]_n = 15.4\{\pm 1.4\} + (\sum_{i=1}^{t} \Delta V[t]_n) + 0\{\pm 4.7\},$$
$$\text{and}$$
$$N[t]_n = 33.4\{\pm 7.9\} + (\sum_{i=1}^{t} \Delta N[t]_n) + 0\{\pm 11.5\}, \tag{3.18}$$
$$\text{with}$$
$$\sigma_{y0,x0} = .78, \sigma_{y0,xs} =< 99, \sigma_{ys,x0} = .09, \sigma_{ys,xs} = -.06.$$

More fundamentally, the respective latent change scores were modeled as

$$\Delta V[t]_n = -10.1\{\pm 11.2\}V_{s,n} + -1.00V[t-1]_n + 1.02N[t-1]_n,$$
$$\text{and}$$
$$\Delta N[t]_n = 34.6\{\pm 4.3\}N_{s,n} + -0.28N[t-1]_n + -0.17V[t-1]_n.$$

The parameters can be used to form the expected values described in Fig. 3.9. These parameters are specific to the time interval chosen (i.e., $\Delta t = 5$). Any calculation of the other information (e.g., explained latent variance) requires a specific interval of age. However, these seemingly small differences can accumulate over longer periods of time so the larger $N[t]$ is expected to account for an increasing variance in $\Delta V[t]$ over age.

Table 3.4: Results of two baseline Verbal–Nonverbal Bivariate Dynamic Models

Model Parameters	M1: Bivariate Dual Change		M2: Bivariate Proportion Change	
	Verbal	Non-verbal	Verbal	Non-verbal
(a) Fixed Effects				
Initial Mean μ_0	15.4	33.4	14.5	35.2
Slope Mean μ_s	-10.1	34.5	—	—
Loading α	=1	=1	=0	=0
Proportion β	-1.00	-0.28	-1.24	1.09
Coupling from Verbal γ_{nv}	—	-0.17	—	-1.08
Coupling from Non-Verbal γ_{vn}	1.02	—	0.94	—
(b) Random Effects				
Error Deviation σ_e	4.74	11.5	7.86	13.4
Initial Deviation σ_0	1.38	7.85	2.59	5.18
Slope Deviation σ_s	11.2	4.20	—	—
Correlation ρ_{0s}	< 0.99	0.40	—	—
Correlation ρ_{y0x0}	0.78		—	
Correlation ρ_{ysxs}	-0.06		—	
Correlation ρ_{y0xs}	< 0.99		—	
Correlation ρ_{ysx0}	0.09		—	
(c) Goodness-of-Fit				
-2logL	7118		7413	
Parameters	20		10	

The fitting of a further sequence of alternative models is needed to interpret the replicability of the *coupling* across the $V[t]$ and $N[t]$ variables. Table 3.5 gives details of several popular goodness–of–fit for two additional models fit to examine whether one or more of the coupling parameters (γ) were different from zero. In the first alternative model, the parameter representing the effect of $N[t]$ on $\delta V[t]$ was fixed to zero ($\gamma_x = 0$), and this led to a notable loss of fit ($\chi^2 = 123$ on $df = 1$). The second alternative assumed no effect from $V[t]$ on $\Delta N[t]$ ($\gamma_y = 0$) and this is a much smaller loss of fit ($\chi^2 = 27$ on $df = 1$). Table 3.6 gives summary results of additional models fit to check on this hypothesis in other ways. Model M5 assumed no coupling ($\gamma_x = 0$ and $\gamma_y = 0$), and this resulted in a clear loss of fit ($\chi^2 = 126$ on $df = 2$). Model M6 assumed equal coupling ($\gamma_x = \gamma_y$) and yielded another loss of fit ($\chi^2 = 143$ on $df = 1$), but this is confounded with likely scaling differences (i.e., even IRT scales are not invariant to affine transformation). Model M7 assumed pure equality of each parameter ($\alpha_x = \alpha_y$ and $\gamma_x = \gamma_y$) and this resulted in another loss of fit ($\chi^2 = 187$ on $df = 2$). Model M8 used a nonlinear constraint to test the equality of the net output of the resulting system ($\alpha_x \gamma_x = \alpha_y \gamma_y$); This resulted in smaller but still clear loss of fit ($\chi^2 = 80$ on $df = 2$). These comparisons suggest that models M1 and M4 are the most reasonable representations of these longitudinal data.

The estimated model parameters are highly dependent on the scalings used, but the trajectory expectations allows us to interpret the results in a relatively "scale–free" form, are these are displayed in Fig. 3.9 (model M1). Figures 3.9a and 3.9b are trajectory plots of the estimated factor scores for each person from the parameters of this model. Figure 3.9c is a state–space plot of the same estimated factor scores; here we plot the $v[t]$ and $n[t]$ pair for each person collapsed over time. Figure 3.9d gives a summary of this state–space plot as a *vector field plot* (for details, see Boker & McArdle, 1995; J. McArdle et al., 2001). Any pair of coordinates is a starting point (y_0, x_0) and the directional arrow is a display of the expected pair of 5-year changes (Δ_y, Δ_x) from this point. The last two figures show an interesting dynamic property: *the change expectations of a dynamic model depend on the starting point.* From this perspective, we can also interpret the positive level–level correlation ($\rho_{y0,x0} = 0.78$), which describes the placement of the individuals in the vector field, and the small slope–slope correlation ($\rho_{ys,xs} = -0.06$), which describes the location of the subsequent change scores for individuals in the vector field. The resulting "flow" shows a dynamic process where scores on

Table 3.5: Results of two additional Verbal–Nonverbal Bivariate Dynamics Models

Model Parameters	M3: No Coupling from Non-Verbal		M4: No Coupling from Verbal	
	Verbal	Non-verbal	Verbal	Non-verbal
(a) Fixed Effects				
Initial Mean μ_0	14.8	32.1	15.5	31.8
Slope Mean μ_s	26.1	42.4	0.01	46.7
Loading α	=1	=1	=1	=1
Proportion β	-0.34	-0.40	-0.77	-0.58
Coupling from Verbal γ_{nv}	—	-0.17	—	-1.08
Coupling from Non-Verbal γ_{vn}	-0.15	—	=0	—
(b) Random Effects				
Error Deviation σ_e	7.04	10.5	5.85	10.8
Initial Deviation σ_0	2.87	2.84	1.64	4.92
Slope Deviation σ_s	4.29	5.52	8.82	6.34
Correlation ρ_{0s}	< 0.99	0.40	< 0.99	0.52
Correlation ρ_{y0x0}	< 0.99		< 0.99	
Correlation ρ_{ysxs}	0.63		0.39	
Correlation ρ_{y0xs}	0.44		< 0.99	
Correlation ρ_{ysx0}	0.85		-0.39	
(c) Goodness-of-Fit				
-2ll	7241		7145	
Parameters	19		19	

Table 3.6: Summary of goodness-of-fit model comparison among alternatives to baseline model for the Verbal and Non-Verbal bivariate dynamic models

Model Fit	Likelihood 2logL	Parameters	$\Delta\chi^2$	Δdf	RMSEA	Prob	BIC	TLI
M0: Null Model $(\sigma_v, \sigma_n, \mu_v and \mu_n)$	1939	4	-	-	-	-	8958	-
M1: Full Coupling Model	118	20	-	-	-	-	7212	.841
M2: No Slopes, $\gamma_{vn} = 0$	413	10	305	10	.518 (.459 - .578)	0	7460	.668
M3: No $N->V$ Coupling, $\gamma_{vn} = 0$	241	19	123	1	1.048 (.866-1.240)	0	7330	.830
M4: No $V->N$ Coupling, $\gamma_{nv} = 0$	145	19	27	1	.486 (.309-.682)	0	7234	.890
M5: No Coupling at all, $\gamma_{vn} = \gamma_{nv} = 0$	244	18	126	2	.751 (.621-.886)	0	7329	.820
M6: Equal Coupling, $\gamma_{vn} = \gamma_{nv}$	261	19	143	1	1.136 (.953-1.327)	0	7350	.829
M7: Equal System, $\gamma_{vn} = \gamma_{nv}, \alpha_{vn} = \alpha_{nv}$	305	18	187	2	.917 (.787-1.052)	0	7390	.818
M8: Equal Net, $\alpha_{vn}\gamma_{vn} = \alpha_{nv}\gamma_{nv}$	198	18	80	2	.595 (.467-.732)	0	7283	.821

Note:

Goodness of fit comparison is performed the null model (M0) against the alternative dynamics model (M1 through M8); TLI is Tucker-Lewis (1973) goodness-of-fit index calculated as $TLI = \frac{\frac{F0}{df0} - \frac{Fa}{dfa}}{\frac{F0}{df0}}$, in which F0 denotes a 2llf for the Null model with df0 degrees of freedom and Fa denotes a 2llf for the alternative model with dfa degrees of freedom; BIC is a Bayesian Information Criterion computed as BIC=−2llf + log(N)*P in which 2llf is a 2 log likelihood function value, N denotes a sample size, and P denotes the number of parameters in the alternative model;

$RMSEA = \sqrt{\frac{fa}{dfa}}$, in which fa denotes a minimum likelihood function value for the alternative model with dfa degrees of freedom.

Non–Verbal abilities have a tendency to impact score changes on the Verbal scores (as in Eq. 3.1), but there is no notable reverse effect.

3.3.5   Results from Fitting Group Growth Models

We have studied a variety of mixed–effect or multilevel models of the Bradway data. To allow some flexibility, we used the same latent basis curve and dual change score models but added a few additional variables as predictors. These variables included various aspects of demographic (e.g., gender, educational attainment by age 56, etc.), self–reported health behaviors (e.g., smoking, drinking, physical exercise, etc.), health problems (e.g., general health, illness, medical procedures, etc.), and personality measures (e.g., 16 PF factors). As one example, in a mixed–effects model (Equation 3.6), we added gender as an effect–coded variable (i.e., Females = - 0.5 and Males = + 0.5). The results obtained for Non-Verbal scales included the latent basis $A[t] = [= 0, 0.93, 1.01, 1.06, = 1, .97]$ as before. Now, in the same model, we found the Males start at slightly lower initial levels ($\nu_{0x} = -0.06$) but had larger positive changes over time ($\nu_{sx} = 0.30$). The addition of gender does not produce large changes in fit ($\chi^2 = 10$ on $df = 4$), so all gender mean differences may be accounted for using the latent variables, but gender does not account for much of the variance of the latent scores (0.03, 0.05). To account for more of this variance we used basic principles of multiple regression: in a third model, we added educational attainment; in a fourth model, we added both gender and education; and in a fifth model, we added an interaction of sex and education.

Group differences in the Bradway–McArdle data were also studied using multiple group growth curves. In a general model, the latent means, deviations, and basis shape of the changes were considered different for the males and the females. The key results for males and females show some lack of invariance for the initial basis hypothesis ($A[t]^{(m)} = A[t]^{(f)}, \chi^2 = 40$ on $df = 5$). The separate group results show the females have a higher basis function, and this implies more growth over time (e.g., J. McArdle & Epstein, 1987). This result includes both mean and covariance differences, and it may be worth pursuing.

Figure 3.9: The expected trajectories from the bivariate dual change score model (see Figure 3.5 and Table 3.5, M1)

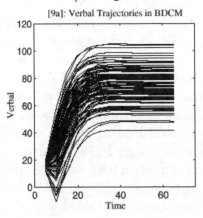

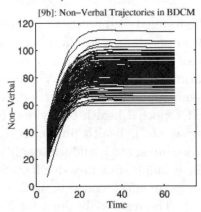

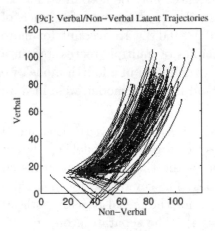

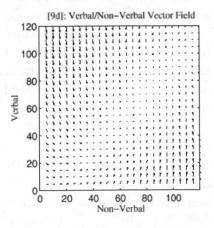

Multiple group growth models have been used in all prior analyses described in this chapter to fit the complete and incomplete subsets of the Bradway–McArdle data (Fig. 3.1). We compared the numerical results for the complete data versus the complete and incomplete data together, and the parameters remain the same. As a statistical test for parameter invariance over these groups, we calculated from the difference in the model likelihoods, and these differences were trivial ($\chi^2 < 20$ on $df = 20$). This suggests that selective dropout or subject attrition can be considered random with respect to the Non-Verbal abilities. This last result allows us to combine the complete and incomplete data sets in the hopes for a more accurate, powerful, and unbiased analysis.

In our final set of multiple group models, we used the latent mixture approach to estimate latent groupings Verbal and Non–Verbal scores. In a first latent mixture model, we allowed the additional possibility of two latent classes ($C = 2$) with different parameters for the latent means and variance but assuming the same growth basis. The two–class growth model assumed the same free basis coefficients as above, smaller latent variances, an estimated class threshold ($z = 2.48$) separating Class 1 with 92% of the people with high latent means ($\mu_0 = 25, \mu_s = 58$), from Class 2 with 8% of the people with lower latent means ($\mu_0 = 16, \mu_s = 53$). This two class model yielded a likelihood which (assuming these two models are nested) represents a notable change in fit ($\chi^2 = 30$ on $df = 3$). This result suggests that a small group of the Bradway persons may have started at a lower average score with a smaller change. A sequence of parameters were compared under the assumption of two classes. The two-class growth model yielded an estimated class threshold ($z = -0.72$) separating two classes with 33% and 67% of the people. This complete two-class growth-mixture model yielded only a small improvement in fit ($L = -1628, \chi^2 = 34$, on $df = 12$) so we conclude that only one class of persons is needed to account for the basic growth curves underlying these data. This result was found using several alternatives.

Additional models were fit to examine a common growth factor model proportionality hypothesis. In this case, the factor model has two indicators at each time, $V[t]$ and $N[t]$, and it was combined with the previous dual change model. The basic model required only 9 parameters in common factor loadings ($\lambda_y = 1, \lambda_x = .35$) and common factor dynamic parameters ($\alpha_z = 1$, $\beta_z = .14$, $\mu_{sz} = -0.13$, with no γ) and achieved convergence. However, the fit of this common factor DCS was much worse than the bivariate DCS model ($\chi^2 = 1262$ on $df = 11$), and this is additional evidence that separate process models are needed for Verbal and Non-Verbal growth processes.

Differences between various Bradway demographic groups were examined using multiple group bivariate dynamic growth models. First we examined results when the data for Males and Females were considered separately, and the results are presented in Table 3.7. Here we found that an overall test of invariance across groups now yielded only a small difference ($\chi^2_{(m+f)} = 41$ on $df = 20$). To be specific, the sum of the likelihoods for the Male and Female groups is $-2logL = 3821 + 3256 = 7077$ on $df = 40$, and the baseline M1 yielded $-2logL = 7118$ on $df = 20$, so the difference is $\Delta\chi^2 = 41$ on $\Delta df = 20$. In a more specific hypothesis tests, we also found no difference in the coupling hypothesis across gender groups ($\chi^2_{(m)} = 10$ on $df = 2$). This is not simply a result of low N leading to low power; the parameters in Table 3.7 are much the same across these separate groups.

The same kinds of dynamic comparisons were calculated for participants with some college experience (ce) versus those with no college education (nc). Here we found that an overall test of invariance across groups yields another small difference ($\chi^2_{ce+nc} = 32$ on $df = 20$). However, when we pursue this result in more detail we do find a slightly larger difference in the coupling hypothesis across these groups: the Non–Verbal to Verbal coupling effect is enhanced in the group with some college education ($\gamma = -0.28$, $\chi^2_{ce} = 25$ on $df = 1$) even though both groups started at similar initial levels.

The final group model was designed to answer several questions about non–random attrition. This was addressed by comparing results for subjects with complete six–occasion longitudinal data ($n = 29$) from those with some incomplete data ($n = 82$). The differences in fit due to the assumption of invariance of the dynamic process over data groups is relatively small, but nontrivial ($\chi^2_{(c+i)} = 54$ on $df = 20$). This means that the results were interpreted differently by using all available data rather than just the persons with all data at all time points. This leaves us with a complex issue that requires further investigation.

Table 3.7: Summary of results from separate bivariate dynamic models (model M1) fitted to the Female and Male groups

Model Parameters	Female (N=59) Bivariate Dual Change		Male (N=52) Bivariate Dual Change	
	Verbal	Non-verbal	Verbal	Non-verbal
(a) Fixed Effects				
Initial Mean μ_0	16.1	34.3	14.5	32.3
Slope Mean μ_s	-24.7	41.9	-2.6	25.7
Loading α	=1	=1	=1	=1
Proportion β	-1.00	-0.43	-1.00	-.05
Coupling from Verbal γ_{nv}	—	-0.12	—	-.33
Coupling from Non-Verbal γ_{vn}	1.28	—	0.86	—
(b) Random Effects				
Error Deviation σ_e	5.00	11.9	4.40	13.4
Initial Deviation σ_0	1.12	7.70	1.22	7.70
Slope Deviation σ_s	11.2	4.65	9.57	4.14
Correlation ρ_{0o}	< 0.99	.28	-.30	.33
Correlation ρ_{y0x0}		< 0.99		0.58
Correlation ρ_{ysxs}		-0.44		0.56
Correlation ρ_{y0xs}		< 0.99		< 0.99
Correlation ρ_{ysx0}		0.13		-0.18
(c) Goodness-of-Fit				
-2ll		3821		3256
Parameters		20		20

Note:
The sum of the likelihoods for the Male and Female groups is -2logL = 3821 + 3256 = 7077 on df=40. The baseline M1 yielded -2logL = 7118 on df=20, so difference is $\Delta\chi^2 = 41$ on Δ df=20.

3.4   Discussion

The overall longitudinal modeling results suggest a dynamic system which is fairly close to Cattell's investment–theory hypothesis of Equation 3.1: *The Non–Verbal ability is a positive leading indicator of changes on Verbal ability, but the negative effect of Verbal ability on the Non–Verbal changes is not as strong.* The substantive conclusions that can be drawn from these analyses are limited by the methodology used, so we focus on these limitations now.

The measurement assumptions we made may be evaluated whenever we fit the longitudinal measurement hypothesis — i.e., is $\lambda[t] = \lambda[t + 1]$? It may be useful to examine the assumption of "metric factorial invariance" over occasions without the necessity of a simple structure basis to the measurement model (J. Horn & McArdle, 1992; J. McArdle & Cattell, 1994; J. McArdle & Nesselroade, 1994). When this kind of restrictive model of "changes in the factor scores" among multiple variables provides a reasonable fit to the data, we then have evidence for the "dynamic construct validity" of the common factor (as in J. McArdle & Prescott, 1992). Unfortunately, when the data are less than complete we can lose some or all of the statistical power of such tests. In these data, the SB and the WAIS were only measured together at age 30 and 42, and these may limit the clarity of any incomplete data SEM (Fig. 3.2) or the Rasch–based IRT analysis. The basic requirements of meaningful and age–equivalent measurement models are a key problem in the behavioral sciences, and future research is needed to address these fundamental concerns (see Burr & Nesselroade, 1990; Fischer & Molenaar, 1995).

The latent difference score approach used here is not identical to the differential equations considered earlier (e.g., Arminger, 1987; Coleman, 1968) nor is it the same as the differential equation models proposed by others, including the new models of Boker (2001). But it does offer a practical approximation with dynamic interpretations for traditional linear growth models. That is, a key advantage of this approach is that this dynamic model can fitted using standard structural modeling software. The structural path diagram in Figs. 3.3 – 3.5 illustrate how fundamental change score concepts can be directly represented using standard longitudinal structural SEMs. As in other latent growth models, the numerical values of the parameters (α, β and γ) can now be combined to form many different kinds of individual and group trajectories over age or time, including the addition of covariates. All these features are apparent without directly specifying an integral equation for the trajectory over time.

Nevertheless, the dynamic curve models fitted here, either in latent curve form or latent change form, are limited in several ways. For example, a reasonable alternative model using "segments" fitted to the Bradway–McArdle data has been published by Cudeck and du Toit (2001). Using data from persons that had data on at least one of the last three occasions ($N = 74$), these authors fit a nonlinear mixed model concluded, "Although the trend is decreasing overall, a few individuals actually exhibit increases, while for others the response is essentially constant into old age . . . ." (Cudeck & du Toit, 2001, p.13). The addition of individual differences in "transition points" may be needed to better understand these growth curves.

On a formal basis, this bivariate dynamic approach permits hypotheses to be formed about (a) parallel growth, (b) covariance among latent components, (c) proportional growth, and (d) dynamic coupling over time. That is, in addition to the previous restrictions on the dynamic parameters ($\alpha = 0$, $\alpha = 1$ and/or $\beta = 0$), we can focus on evaluating models where one or more of the coupling parameters is restricted (i.e., $\gamma_{yx} = 0$ and/or $\gamma_{xy} = 0$). If only one of these coupling parameters is large and reliable, we may say we have estimated a coupled dynamic system with "leading indicators" in the presence of growth. To the degree these parameters are zero, we can say we have estimated an "uncoupled system." Additional descriptions of the relevant dynamic aspects of these model coefficients, including the stability or instability of long–run behaviors, can be evaluated from additional calculations (e.g., eigenvalues and equilibrium formulas; Arminger, 1987; Tuma & Hannan, 1984).

This means that the bivariate dynamic models fitted here, while directly related to Cattell's original arguments, were only one set of a much larger family of such models. Also, while this SEM was a direct test with these two variables, we recognize that many other variables might play an important role here. In other work, we have examined four variables in a dynamic system over the adult part of the life span and concluded that the network of cognitive dynamic relationships is far more complex than the one portrayed herein (J.

McArdle et al., 2001). Perhaps the only way to fully examine these relationships is to examine other longitudinal experiments.

> "The identification of relationships that remain invariant among variables under different conditions and transformations is a major goal of empirical research [...] For the purpose of assessing changes, invariant loading patterns in factor-analytic models and, more generally, invariant measurement models in structural–causal analysis with latent variables provide stable reference frames against which changes can be measured and interpreted [...] Demonstration of factor invariance is one particular realization of a major goal of science — namely the identification of invariant relationships. The invariant relationships involved are those between factors (unobserved or latent variables) and observed variables or, in higher order analyses, other factors. At the first order of analysis for example, factor invariance signals a kind of constancy of a measurement system and thus the reasonableness of comparing phenomena in quantitative rather than in qualitative terms ... " (from John R. Nesselroade, 1983, p. 59, 62-63).

The same can be said about the recent uses of the growth–mixture models. These analyses provide a test of the invariance of growth model parameters without knowing exactly the group membership of each individual. By combining some aspects of the previous sections, we can consider a *group difference dynamic change score* model in different ways. In one model, we add the group contrasts as a covariate in the difference model. In another model, we add a multilevel prediction structure of the dynamic slopes. In general, we can always consider that a model where multiple groups are independent or probabilistic, and where the group dynamics are different. Our future task is clear: it is to find the invariant dynamical systems that help us understand our own group dynamics.

References

Arbuckle, J., & Wotke, W. (1999). *Amos.* Smallwaters. Chicago. (Users Guide)

Arminger, G. (1987). Linear stochastic differential equation models for panel data with unobserved variables. In N. Tuma (Ed.), *Sociological methodology* (pp. 187–212). San Francisco: Jossey Bass.

Baltes, P., & Nesselroade, J. (1979). Longitudinal research in the study of behavior and development. In J. Nesselroade & P. Baltes (Eds.), *History and rationale of longitudinal research.* New York: Academic Press.

Bayley, N. (1956). Individual patterns of development. *Child Development, 27*(1), 45–74.

Boker, S. (2001). Differential models and differential structural equation modeling of intraindividual variability. In L. Collins & A. Sayer (Eds.), *New methods for the analysis of change* (pp. 5–27). Washington, D.C.: American Psychological Association.

Boker, S., & McArdle, J. (1995). A statistical vector field analysis of longitudinal aging data. *Experimental Aging Research, 21,* 77–93.

Bradway, K., & Thompson, C. (1962). Intelligence at adulthood: A 25 year follow-up. *Journal of Educational Psychology, 53*(1), 1–14.

Browne, M., & Arminger, G. (1995). Specification and estimation of mean– and covariance–structure models. In G. Arminger, C. C. Clogg, & M. E. Sobel (Eds.), *Handbook of statistical modeling for the social and behavioral sciences* (pp. 311–359). New York: Plenum Press.

Browne, M., & Toit, S. H. du. (1991). Best methods for the analysis of change. In L. Collins & J. L. Horn (Eds.), *Models for learning data* (pp. 47–68). Washington, D.C.: APA Press.

Bryk, A., & Raudenbush, S. (1992). *Hierarchical linear models: Applications and data analysis methods.* Newbury Park: CA: SAGE.

Bryk, A. S., & Raudenbush, S. W. (1987). Application of hierarchical linear models to assessing change. *Psychological Bulletin, 101*(1), 147–158.

Burr, J., & Nesselroade, J. (1990). New statistical methods in developmental research. In A. von Eye (Ed.), *Change measurement* (pp. 3–34). New York: Academic Press.

Burt, C. (1912). The inheritance of mental characteristics. *Eugenics Review, 4*, 168–200.

Campbell, R. T. (1988). Methodological issues in aging research. In K. W. Schaie, R. T. Campbell, W. Meredith, & S. C. Rawlings (Eds.), *Integrating conceptualization, design, and analysis in panel studies of the life course* (pp. 43–69). New York: Springer Publishing Company, Inc.

Cattell, R. B. (1941). Some theoretical issues in adult intelligence testing. *Psychological Bulletin, 38*, 592.

Cattell, R. B. (1971). *Abilities: Their structure, growth and action.* Boston: Houghton-Mifflin.

Cnaan, A., Laird, N., & Slasor, P. (1997). Using the general linear mixed model to analyse unbalanced repeated measures and longitudinal data. *Statistics in Medicine, 16*, 2349–2380.

Coleman, J. (1964). *Introduction to mathematical sociology.* New York: Free Press.

Coleman, J. (1968). Methodology in social research. In H. M. Blalock & A. B. Blalock (Eds.), *The mathematical study of change* (pp. 428–475). New York: McGraw-Hill.

Cook, T., & Campbell, D. (1979). *Quasi-experimentation design and analysis issues for field settings.* Skokie, IL: Rand-McNally.

Cudeck, R., & du Toit, S. H. (2001). Mixed-effects models in the study of individual differences with repeated measures data. *Multivariate Behavioral Research, 31*, 371–403.

Cudeck, R., & du Toit, S. H. (2003). Nonlinear multilevel models for repeated measures data. In N. Duan & S. P. Reise (Eds.), *Multilevel modeling: Methodological advances, issues, and applications. multivariate applications* (pp. 1–24). Mahwah, NJ: Lawrence Erlbaum Associates.

Duncan, S. C., & Duncan, T. E. (1995). Modeling the processes of development via latent variable growth curve methodology. *Structural equation modeling, 2*, 187–213.

Embretson, S. E. (1996). The new rules of measurement. *Psychological Assessment, 4*, 341–349.

Fischer, G. H., & Molenaar, I. (1995). *Rasch models – foundations, recent developments, and applications.* New York: Springer.

Goldstein, H. (1995). *Multilevel statistical models.* London: Edward Arnold.

Gollob, H. F., & Reichardt, C. S. (1987). Taking account of time lags in causal models. *Child Development, 58*, 80–92.

Hagenaar, J. A., & McCutcheon, A. L. (2002). *Applied latent class analysis.* London: Cambridge University Press.

Hamagami, F. (1998). A developmental-based item factor analysis. In J. McArdle & R. Woodcock (Eds.), *Human abilities in theory and practice* (pp. 231–246). Mahwah, NJ: Erlbaum.

Harris, C. (Ed.). (1963). *Problems in measuring change.* Madison, WI: University of Wisconsin Press.

Heck, R. H., & Thomas, S. L. (1999). *An introduction to multilevel modeling techniques.* Mahwah, NJ: Lawrence Erlbaum Associates.

Hedecker, D., & Gibbons, R. (1996). Mixreg: A computer program for mixed-effects regression analysis with autocorrelated errors. *Computer Methods and Programs in Biomedicine, 49*, 229–252.

Hedecker, D., & Gibbons, R. (1997). Application of random-effects pattern-mixture models for missing data in longitudinal studies. *Psychological Methods, 2*, 64–78.

Horn, J. (1972). The state, trait, and change dimensions of intelligence. *British Journal of Educational Psychology, 2*, 159–185.

Horn, J., & McArdle, J. (1980). Perspectives on mathematical and statistical model building (masmob) in research on aging. In *Aging in the 1980's: Psychological issues* (pp. 503–541). Washington, D. C.: American Psychological Association.

Horn, J., & McArdle, J. (1992). A practical guide to measurement invariance in research on aging. *Experimental Aging Research, 18*(3), 117-144.

Horn, J. L. (1965). *Fluid and crystallized intelligence: A factor analytic and developmental study of the structure among primary mental abilities.* Unpublished doctoral dissertation, University of Illinois, Champaign, IL. (Unpublished doctoral dissertation)

Horn, J. L., & Cattell, R. B. (1966). Refinement and test of the theory of fluid and crystallized intelligence. *Journal of Educational Psychology, 57*, 253–270.

Horn, J. L., & Cattell, R. B. (1967). Age differences in fluid and crystallized intelligence. *Acta Psychologica, 26*, 107–129.

Horn, J. L., & Cattell, R. B. (1982). Whimsy and misunderstandings of Gf-Gc theory: A comment on Gilford. *Psychological Bulletin, 91*, 623–633.

Hox, J. J. (2002). *Multilevel analyses: Techniques and applications.* Mahwah, NJ: Lawrence Erlbaum Associates.

Jensen, A. R., & Faulstich, M. E. (1988). Difference between prisoners and the general population in psychometric g. *Personality & Individual Differences, 9*, 925–928.

Jöreskog, K., & Sörbom, D. (1999). *LISREL 8.30: LISREL 8: Structural equation modeling with the SIMPLIS command language.* Scientific Software International. Hillsdale, NJ.

Jöreskog, K. G. (1970). Estimation and testing of simplex models. *British Journal of Mathematical & Statistical Psychology, 23*, 121–145.

Jöreskog, K. G. (1974). Analyzing psychological data by structural analysis of covariance matrics. In R. C. Atkinson (Ed.), *Contemporary developments in mathematical psychology* (pp. 1–56). San Francisco: Freeman.

Jöreskog, K. G. (1977). Structural equation models in the social sciences: Specification, estimation, and testing. In I. P. Krishnaiah (Ed.), *Applications of statistics* (pp. 265–287). Amsterdam: North-Holland Publishing Company.

Jöreskog, K. G., & Sörbom, D. (1979). *Advances in factor analysis and structural equation models.* Cambridge, MA: Abt Books.

Jöreskog, K. G., & Sörbom, D. (1993). *LISREL 8: Structural equation modeling with the SIMPLIS command language.* Hillsdale, NJ: Lawrence Erlbaum Associates.

Kangas, J., & Bradway, K. P. (1971). Intelligence at middle age: A thirty-eight year follow-up. *Developmental Psychology, 5*(2), 333–337.

Kreft, I. G., & De Leeuw, J. (1998). *Introducing multilevel modeling.* Thousand Oaks, CA: SAGE.

Lindstrom, J., M, & Bates, D. M. (1990). Nonlinear mixed–effects models for repeated measures data. *Biometrics, 46*, 673–687.

Littell, R., Miliken, G., Stoup, W., & Wolfinger, R. (1996). *Sas system for mixed models.* Cary, N.C.: SAS institute.

Little, R., & Rubin, D. (1987). *Statistical analysis with missing data.*

New York: Wiley.

Maccallum, R., & Ashby, F. G. (1986). Relationships between linear systems theory and covariance structure modeling. *Journal of Mathematical Psychology*, *30*, 1–27.

McArdle, J. (1988). Dynamic but structural equation modeling of repeated measures data. In J. Nesselroade & R. Cattell (Eds.), *The handbook of multivariate experimental psychology* (Vol. 2, pp. 561–614). New York: Plenum Press.

McArdle, J. (1991). Structural models of developmental theory in psychology. In P. Van Geert & L. Mos (Eds.), *Annals of theoretical psychology* (Vol. VII, pp. 139–160.). New York: Plenum Publishers.

McArdle, J. (1994). Structural factor analysis experiments with incomplete data. *Multivariate Behavioral Research*, *29*(4), 409–454.

McArdle, J. (2001). A latent difference score approach to longitudinal dynamic structural analyses. In R. Cudeck, S. du Toit, & D. Sörbom (Eds.), *Structural equation modeling: Present and future* (pp. 342–380). Lincolnwood, IL: Scientific Software International.

McArdle, J., & Anderson, E. (1990). Latent variable growth models for research on aging. In J. Birren & K. Schaie (Eds.), *The handbook of the psychology of aging* (pp. 21 43). New York: Plenum Press.

McArdle, J., & Bell, R. (2000). Recent trends in modeling longitudinal data by latent growth curve methods. In T. Little, K. Schnabel, & J. Baumert (Eds.), *Modeling longitudinal and multiple-group data: practical issues, applied approaches, and scientific examples* (pp. 69–108). Mahwah, NJ: Erlbaum.

McArdle, J., & Cattell, R. (1994). Structural equation models of factorial invariance in parallel proportional profiles and oblique confactor problems. *Multivariate Behavioral Research*, *29*(1), 63–113.

McArdle, J., & Epstein, D. (1987). Latent growth curves within developmental structural equation models. *Child Development*, *58*(1), 110–133.

McArdle, J., & Hamagami, E. (1991). Modeling incomplete longitudinal and cross-sectional data using latent growth structural models. In L. M. Collins & J. L. Horn (Eds.), *Best methods for the analysis of change: Recent advances, unanswered questions, future directions.* (pp. 276–304). Washington, DC: American Psychological Association.

McArdle, J., & Hamagami, E. (1992). Modeling incomplete longitudinal and cross-sectional data using latent growth structural models. *Experimental Aging Research, 18*(3), 145–156.

McArdle, J., & Hamagami, F. (1996). Multilevel models from a multiple group structural equation perspective. In G. Marcoulides & R. Schumacker (Eds.), *Advanced structural equation modeling techniques* (pp. 89–124). Hillsdale, N.J.: Erlbaum.

McArdle, J., Hamagami, F., Meredith, W., & Bradway, K. (2001). Modeling the dynamic hypotheses of gf-gc theory using longitudinal life-span data. *Learning and Individual Differences, 12,* 53–79.

McArdle, J., & Nesselroade, J. (1994). Structuring data to study development and change. In S. Cohen & H. Reese (Eds.), *Life-span developmental psychology: Methodological innovations* (pp. 223–267). Hillsdale, N.J.: Erlbaum.

McArdle, J., & Nesselroade, J. (2003). Growth curve analyses in contemporary psychological research. In J. Schinka & W. Velicer (Eds.), *Comprehensive handbook of psychology, volume two: Research methods in psychology* (pp. 447–480). New York: Pergamon Press.

McArdle, J., & Prescott, C. (1992). Age-based construct validation using structural equation models. *Experimental Aging Research, 18*(3), 87–115.

McArdle, J., & Woodcock, J. (1997). Expanding test-rest designs to include developmental time-lag components. *Psychological Methods, 2*(4), 403–435.

McArdle, J. J. (1986). Latent growth within behavior genetic models. *Behavior Genetics, 16,* 163–200.

McArdle, J. J., & Boker, S. M. (1990). *RAMpath: A computer program for automatic path diagrams.* Hillsdale, NJ: Lawrence Erlbaum Associates.

McCulloch, C. E., & Searle, S. R. (2000). *Generalized, linear, and mixed models.* New York: Wiley.

McDonald, R. (1999). *Test theory: A unified treatment.* Mahwah,

NJ: Erlbaum.

McDonald, R. P. (1985). *Factor analysis and related methods.* Mahwah, NJ: Lawrence Erlbaum Associates.

Meredith, W., & Tisak, J. (1990). Latent curve analysis. *Psychometrika, 55,* 107–122.

Metha, P., & West, S. (2000). Putting the individual back into individual growth curves. *Psychological Methods, 5*(1), 23 43.

Miyazaki, Y., & Raudenbush, S. (2000). Tests for linkage of multiple cohorts in an accelerated longitudinal design. *Psychological Methods, 5*(1), 24 63.

Molenaar, P. C. (1985). A dynamic factor model for the analysis of multivariate time series. *Psychometrika, 50,* 181–202.

Muthen, B., & Curran, P. (1997). General longitudinal modeling of individual differences in experimental designs: A latent variable framework for analysis and power estimation. *Psychological Methods, 2,* 371–402.

Muthen, L., & Muthen, B. (1998). *Mplus, the comprehensive modeling program for applied researchers users guide.* Muthen and Muthen. Los Angeles, CA.

Nagin, D. (1999). Analyzing developmental trajectories: Semi–parametric group–based approach. *Psychological Methods, 4,* 139–177.

Neale, M., M., B. S., Xie, G., & H., M. H. (2003). *Mx: Statistical modeling* (6th ed.). VCU Box 900126, Richmond, VA 23298: Department of Psychiatry.

Nesselroade, J. R. (1983). Temporal selection and factor invariance in the study of development and change. *Life-Span Development and Behavior, 5,* 59–87.

Pinherio, J. C., & Bates, D. M. (2000). *Mixed effects models in S and S–Plus.* New York: Springer–Verlag.

Pinneau, S. R. (1961). *Changes in intelligence quotient: Infancy to maturity.* Oxford, England: Houghton Mifflin.

Rogosa, D. (1978). Causal models in longitudinal research: Rationale, formulation, and interpretation. In J. Nesselroade & P. Baltes (Eds.), *Longitudinal research in the study of behavior and development.* New York: Academic Press.

Singer, J. (1998). Using SAS PROC MIXED to fit multilevel models, hierarchical models, and individual growth models. *Journal of*

Educational and Behavioral Statistics, 24(4), 323–355.

Skrondal, A., & Rabe-Hesketh, S. (2004). *Generalized latent variable modeling: Multilevel, longitudinal, and structural equation models.* New York: Chapman & Hall/CRC.

Sliwinski, M., & Buschke, H. (1999). Cross-sectional and longitudinal relationships among age, cognition, and processing speed. *Psychology and Aging, 14*(1), 18–33.

Snijders, T., & Bosker, R. (1999). *Multilevel analysis: An introduction to basic and advanced multilevel modeling.* Thousand Oaks, CA: SAGE.

Sörbom, D. (1975). Detection of correlated errors in longitudinal data. *British Journal of Mathematical & Statistical Psychology, 28*, 138–151.

Sörbom, D. (1976). A statistical model for the measurement of change in true scores. In D. N. M. de Gruijter & J. L. T. van der Kamp (Eds.), *Advances inpsychological and educational measurement* (pp. 159–169). New York: Wiley.

Spearman, C. (1904). 'General intelligence,' objectively determined and measured. *American Journal of Psychology, 15*(2), 201–293.

Sullivan, E., Rosenbloom, M., Lim, K., & Pfefferman, A. (2000). Longitudinal changes in cognition, gait, balance in abstinent and relapsed alcoholic men: Relationships to changes in brain structure. *Neuropsychology, 14*(2), 178–188.

Thurstone, L. L. (1947). *Multiple factor analysis.* Chicago: University of Chicago Press.

Tuma, N., & Hannan, M. (1984). *Social dynamics.* New York: Academic Press.

Verbeke, G., & Molenberghs, G. (2000). *Linear mixed models for longitudinal data.* New York: Springer.

Willett, J., & Sayer, A. (1994). Using covariance structure analysis to detect correlates and predictors of individual change over time. *Psychological Bulletin, 116*, 363–381.

4

Testing and Probing Interactions in Hierarchical Linear Growth Models

Patrick J. Curran, Daniel J. Bauer, and Michael T. Willoughby
University of North Carolina

Random effects growth models provide a powerful and flexible statistical tool to behavioral researchers for the study of individual differences in stability and change over time. Within the hierarchical linear modeling (HLM) framework, the functional form of the relationship between the repeated measures and time is specified in the level 1 model. Individual variability in initial levels and in rates of change may then be modeled as a function of one or more predictor variables specified in the level 2 model. In growth models, the inclusion of a main–effect predictor at level 2 represents an implicit "cross–level" interaction with the level 1 predictor, time. While this relation is clearly recognized within the HLM literature, cross–level interactions are not often more closely investigated using classical techniques such as testing of simple slopes and computing regions of significance. Here we demonstrate that methods for testing and probing interactions in the standard regression model can be generalized to a broad class of hierarchical linear models. Within the growth model, these techniques provide essential information for interpreting specifically how the relationships of predictors to the repeated measures change over time. This approach extends naturally to the examination of multiplicative interactions between level 2 variables, which then constitute three–way cross–level interactions with time. We present analytical developments and illustrate the use of these methods using an empirical example drawn from the Longitudinal Study of Optimal Aging.

4.1   Introduction

The basic premise behind growth modeling is that a set of repeated measures observed on a given individual can be used to estimate an unobserved trajectory that is believed to have given rise to the set of repeated measures. Once estimated, these trajectories then become the primary focus of analysis. Although easy to describe, growth models can be remarkably vexing to compute. Early examples of modeling individual trajectories include Gompertz (1825); Palmer, Kawakami, and Reed (1937); and Wishart (1938). Although both ingenious and well ahead of their time, these early attempts were limited by significant statistical and computational problems. Important recent developments in statistical theory and high–speed computing have allowed us to overcome many of these earlier limitations. Thanks to the work of Bryk and Raudenbush (1987); Goldstein (1986); McArdle (1988, 1989, 1991); Meredith and Tisak (1984, 1990), D. R. Rogosa and Willett (1985), and many others, there are now several statistical approaches that can be used to estimate a broad class of random effects trajectory models.

Within the social sciences, the two primary approaches to modeling longitudinal trajectories are based on the structural equation modeling (SEM) and the hierarchical linear modeling (HLM) framework. The SEM approach defines the repeated measures to be multiple indicators of one or more latent factors that are believed to represent the unobserved underlying random trajectories (e.g., Meredith & Tisak, 1984, 1990). In contrast, the HLM approach considers the repeated measures to be nonindependent observations nested within each individual and thus treats this as a hierarchically nested data problem (e.g., Bryk & Raudenbush, 1987). It has been shown that under some conditions, the SEM and HLM approaches to modeling trajectories are analytically equivalent, whereas in others they are not (MacCallum, Kim, Malarkey, & Kielcolt–Glaser, 1997; S. Raudenbush, 2001; Willett & Sayer, 1994).

Our topic of interest here is the testing and probing of higher–order interactions in the analysis of individual trajectories from the HLM perspective. It has long been known that a HLM with a single level 1 predictor and a single level 2 predictor results in a "cross–level" interaction in the reduced form model (e.g., Equation 2.21,

S. W. Raudenbush & Bryk, 2002). Such cross–level interactions are quite common in many HLM applications, especially models of individual trajectories. Despite the fact that cross–level interactions arise from the hierarchical nature of the model, this interaction is of the very same multiplicative form as occurs in the usual ordinary least squares (OLS) regression model (e.g., Aiken & West, 1991). In OLS regression, it has become standard to test and probe such higher–order interactions; however, there is limited evidence of widespread use of these same methods within HLM in general, and in the HLM approach to trajectory modeling in particular.

We are aware of a small number of examples in which probing of cross–level interactions has been used to aid in the interpretation of results from an HLM analysis (e.g., Bryk & Raudenbush, 1987, p. 154; Singer, 1998, p. 345; Willett, Singer, & Martin, 1998, p. 423). However, even in these important examples of probing cross–level interactions, the simple slopes of the probed relations were used more descriptively and were not formally tested as is typically done in OLS regression models. We believe that routinely incorporating such probing techniques in HLM would allow researchers to more fully capitalize on the information available from the models and would strengthen inferential tests of theoretically derived hypotheses.

It is not clear why these techniques are not more widely used in HLM applications. One reason may be that, to our knowledge, it has not yet been clearly demonstrated that methods developed in OLS regression can be generalized to the HLM setting. Our first motivating goal is thus to demonstrate that the methods used for testing and probing interactions in standard OLS regression can indeed be generalized directly to HLM as well. Further, although the methods we describe here apply to a broad class of HLMs, our second goal is to focus explicitly on the analysis of individual trajectories. We argue that the testing and probing of interactions is not only of great use when interpreting complex model results, but such techniques should almost always be used when considering the effects of predictors of individual change over time. Finally, we will augment our analytical developments with the presentation of a fully worked empirical example in hopes that applied researchers might consider using these techniques in practice.

Although we focus here exclusively on the HLM approach to modeling individual trajectories, all of our developments and conclusions generalize directly to the SEM approach as well. We detail these extensions to SEM in Curran, Bauer, and Willoughby (2004). Because of the analytical overlap in the SEM and HLM approaches, there is logically much corresponding overlap between the work we discuss here and that which we presented in Curran et al. (2004). The core differences between the 2004 paper and this chapter is that here we focus exclusively on the HLM approach to modeling trajectories and, in the spirit of the topic of this book, we present a detailed worked example drawn from the empirical study of aging. Please see Curran et al. (2004) for a presentation of these ideas as manifested within the SEM approach, and for the detailed explication of an alternative empirical example.

We begin with a brief introduction to the empirical data set we will use to demonstrate our various modeling strategies. We then introduce the unconditional trajectory model followed by a conditional trajectory model with a single dichotomous predictor and a single continuous predictor. We show how these conditional models contain implicit cross–level interactions with time, and we propose methods for testing and probing these interactions as might be done in the OLS regression model. We then extend this conditional HLM to include higher–order interactions within level 2 and similarly demonstrate how to test and probe the cross–level interactions of the level 2 interaction terms with time. We conclude with a discussion of potential limitations and directions for future research.

4.1.1　Motivating Empirical Example

To demonstrate our proposed methods, we fit a series of models to data drawn from the Longitudinal Study of Optimal Aging (LSOA; see Bisconti & Bergeman, 1999, and Wallace & Bergeman, 1997, for further details). Briefly, the LSOA was designed to follow the health outcomes of older adults and consists of two subsamples of participants. At the first wave of assessment, the first subsample consisted of 250 participants over 65 years of age. Three follow–up assessments were conducted, spaced approximately 3 years apart. The second subsample consisted of 301 participants over age 55 who were followed for

a total of three waves of data collection, again spaced approximately
3 years apart. The maximum age at assessment between the two
subsamples was 96 years of age. The high level of variability in age
of assessment suggested that HLM would be an optimal data analysis approach. Our analyses include respondents who had complete
data at their first wave of assessment, with possible missing data at
later time periods ($N = 439$). Up to four repeated measures were
obtained on a physical health scale scored as the sum of five items
which ranged from 0 to 14 with higher values indicating worse health.
Here we consider two predictors: the sex of the participant (where 0
denotes female and 1 denotes male) and perception of social support
received from relatives scored as the sum of eight items which ranged
from 8 to 34 with higher scores indicating greater support from relatives. Social support was grand mean centered for all analyses. The
substantive questions of interest center on the trajectories of change
over time in reported physical health problems and whether individual trajectories systematically vary as a function of (a) subject sex,
(b) perceived social support from relatives, and (c) the interaction
between sex and perceived social support.

4.1.2 The Unconditional Random Trajectory Model

The random effects trajectory model can be thought of as a two–level
model: The first level estimates a model within individual across time
(i.e., intraindividual change), and the second level estimates a model
across individuals (i.e., interindividual differences in intraindividual
change). The population level 1 (or within person) equation for the
standard linear growth model is

$$y_{it} = \alpha_i + \beta_i a_{it} + \varepsilon_{it}, \qquad (4.1)$$

where y_{it} is the dependent measure assessed on individual $i = 1, 2, ...N$
at timepoint $t = 1, 2, ...T$, a_{it} is the measure of time that is allowed
to vary over individual i and is typically coded $a_{it} = 0, 1, ..., T_i - 1$,
and ε_{it} is the random residual error for individual i at timepoint t.[1,2]

---

[1]Although our notation differs substantially from the standard HLM notation
used by S. W. Raudenbush and Bryk (2002), we retain our current notational
scheme to correspond to similar models used in the SEM trajectory model.

[2]There are many different strategies available to code the passage of time, but
we do not explore these in detail here. Throughout this discussion, we utilize a

Given this formulation, α_i and β_i represent the individual specific intercept and slope of the trajectory of y_t over time for person i. These individually varying intercepts and slopes are then treated as random variables and can be expressed as a population level 2 model such that

$$\alpha_i = \mu_\alpha + \zeta_{\alpha_i} \qquad\qquad (4.2)$$
$$\beta_i = \mu_\beta + \zeta_{\beta_i}.$$

The level 1 and level 2 distinction is for heuristic value only, and the level 2 equations can be substituted into level 1 to result in the "reduced form" equation

$$y_{it} = [\mu_\alpha + \mu_\beta a_{it}] + [\zeta_{\alpha_i} + a_{it}\zeta_{\beta_i} + \varepsilon_{it}]. \qquad (4.3)$$

From this, the population mean of y at time t can be expressed as

$$\mu_{y_t} = \mu_\alpha + \mu_\beta a_t. \qquad\qquad (4.4)$$

The expected values (or fixed effects) of the intercept and slope are $E(\alpha_i) = \mu_\alpha$ and $E(\beta_i) = \mu_\beta$, respectively, and these values represent the mean intercept and mean slope of the trajectory pooling over all individuals in the sample. The variances (or random effects) of the intercept and slope are $VAR(\alpha_i) = \psi_\alpha$ and $VAR(\beta_i) = \psi_\beta$, respectively, with covariance $COV(\alpha_i\beta_i) = \psi_{\alpha\beta}$, and these values represent the degree of individual variability around the mean intercept and slope values. Finally, the variance of the level 1 residual is $VAR(\varepsilon_{it}) = \sigma^2$, highlighting the standard (but not required) assumption of homoscedasticity of residuals over individual and time. This value represents the degree of error that exists in the estimation of the trajectory parameters. The analytical goal of the model is to estimate these parameters from our observed data.

To demonstrate the model in Equations 4.1 and 4.2, we fit an unconditional HLM to the four repeated measures of health perceptions from the LSOA. Time (i.e., a_{it}) was measured in years and centered

---

time coding scheme that begins with zero and allows for the intercept factor to be interpreted as the beginning of the trajectory. See Biesanz, Deeb–Sossa, Aubrecht, Bollen, and Curran (2004) and Metha and West (2000) for further discussion of these important issues.

at age 55 (i.e., $a_{it} = age_{it} - 55$) so that that intercept of the trajectory was defined as the model–implied value of health status at age 55 (the youngest observed age in the sample at the initial assessment). As expected, the mean of the individual intercepts ($\hat{\mu}_\alpha = 1.74$) was significantly different from zero ($t(438) = 6.15$, $p < .0001$), indicating a significant level of health concerns even at age 55. The mean of the individual slopes ($\hat{\mu}_\beta = .143$) was also significantly different from zero ($t(540) = 9.90$, $p < .0001$) indicating that, on average, reported health problems increased linearly[3] between age 55 and 96. The model–implied mean trajectory is presented in Fig. 4.1. Further, there was significant variability in both the intercept and slope trajectory components indicating the presence of meaningful individual differences around the mean trajectory. Thus, although the mean trajectory of health problems is increasing over time, there is substantial individual variability around this trajectory over time. We would next like to move toward predicting this individual variability as a function of sex and social support to better understand the developmental process of perceived health problems.

Figure 4.1: Model–implied mean trajectory for entire group.

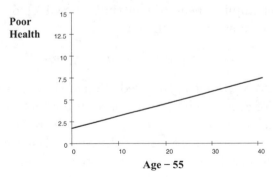

---

[3]We also tested for the presence of a nonlinear component by adding a quadratic term to our level 1 model, but the addition of this curvilinear effect did not result in a significant improvement in model fit. We thus focus on the linear model for the remainder of the analyses.

4.1.3   A Single Dichotomous Predictor of the Random Trajectories

We again consider the level 1 and level 2 model presented in Equations 4.1 and 4.2, but we now incorporate a single categorical predictor c within the level 2 equations where $c = 0$ denotes membership in group 1 (e.g., females) and $c = 1$ denotes membership in group 2 (e.g., males). The level 1 equation remains as before (e.g., Equation 4.1), but now we express the intercept and slope as a function of the categorical predictor c such that

$$\alpha_i = \mu_\alpha + \gamma_1 c_i + \zeta_{\alpha_i} \qquad (4.5)$$
$$\beta_i = \mu_\beta + \gamma_2 c_i + \zeta_{\beta_i}.$$

Here, c represents a direct effect in the prediction of the intercept and slope components. We can again create a reduced form expression of the model, and with simple rearrangement of terms, the relation between c and y can be expressed as an additive function of γ_1 and the product of $\gamma_2 a_{it}$.

$$y_{it} = [\mu_\alpha + a_{it}\mu_\beta] + [\gamma_1 + \gamma_2 a_{it}]c_i + [\zeta_{\alpha_i} + a_{it}\zeta_{\beta_i} + \varepsilon_{it}] \qquad (4.6)$$

We can factor our measure of time out of the equation to highlight that the model–implied mean of y at time t now includes information about group membership c such that

$$\mu_{y_t} = [\mu_\alpha + \gamma_1 c] + [\mu_\beta + \gamma_2 c]a_t. \qquad (4.7)$$

Here, c interacts with time in the prediction of the repeated measures. The influence of group membership c is seen both as an increment to the intercept of the trajectory (via γ_1) and an increment to the slope of the trajectory (via γ_2). To stress, although c is a *main effect* predictor of the intercept and the slope components (i.e., Equation 4.5), c *multiplicatively interacts* with time in the prediction of the repeated measures (i.e., Equation 4.7). Thus, the single dichotomous predictor c must be treated as a two–way interaction with time.

This is more clearly expressed by considering the model–implied mean of y at time t within each of two levels of c such that

$$\mu_{y_t}|_{c=0} = [\mu_\alpha] + [\mu_\beta]a_t \qquad (4.8)$$
$$\mu_{y_t}|_{c=1} = [\mu_\alpha + \gamma_1] + [\mu_\beta + \gamma_2]a_t.$$

Equation 4.8 highlights several important aspects of the conditional HLM. First, in the conditional HLM, μ_α and μ_β represent the mean intercept and mean slope of the trajectory when the predictor equals zero (i.e., the mean intercept and slope for group $c = 0$). Further, γ_1 reflects the difference between the mean intercept for group $c = 1$ compared to group $c = 0$, and γ_2 reflects the difference between the mean slope for group $c = 1$ compared to group $c = 0$. Although we have a formal test of the difference in mean slopes *between* the two groups, we do not yet have an estimate of the trajectory *within* group $c = 1$.

To highlight this, we regressed the intercept and slope parameters of the health trajectories onto the single dichotomous predictor, sex, where a value of 0 denotes female and a value of 1 denotes male. Of key interest is the finding that sex significantly predicted both the intercept parameter ($\hat{\gamma}_1 = -2.17$; $t(437) = -3.22$, $p = .0014$) and the slope parameter ($\hat{\gamma}_2 = .074$; $t(539) = 2.18$, $p = .0296$), indicating that women reported higher levels of health problems at age 55 and smaller slopes over the following 40 years when compared to men. Thus, the test of $\hat{\gamma}_2$ indicates that the magnitude of the rate of change of y over time varies as a function of participant sex. However, this test does not inform us about the characteristics of the trajectories *within* each of these two groups. For this, we turn to the estimation and testing of simple slopes.

Aiken and West (1991) defined a simple slope within the OLS regression model to be the conditional relation between a predictor x and a criterion y at a given value of a second predictor z. This same definition applies to the use of a single dichotomous predictor in HLM. However, we will refer to these conditional relations between the repeated dependent measures of y and time at a given value of the predictor as *simple trajectories*, given our interest in the model–implied trajectory within each group.

Why is consideration of the simple trajectories so important? Without considering simple trajectories within each group, we could easily find ourselves in a situation in which the simple trajectories between the two groups differ significantly from one another (i.e., the $\hat{\gamma}_1$ or $\hat{\gamma}_2$ is significantly different from zero), but one or even both simple trajectories within each group might itself not differ from zero. Figure 4.2 depicts three hypothetical situations in which there is precisely the same difference between model–implied intercepts and slopes for males versus females, but the simple trajectories reflect fundamentally different relations within each group. The top panel reflects that the two simple trajectories are both increasing over time; the middle panel reflects that the female simple trajectory is not changing, but the male simple trajectory is increasing over time; finally, the bottom panel reflects that the female simple trajectory is decreasing over time, whereas the male simple trajectory is not changing at all. It is important to stress that for all three of these conditions, precisely the same parameter estimates hold for the regression parameters relating subject sex to the random trajectories in the conditional HLM. That is, all three have the same difference between intercepts and the same difference between slopes, yet the simple trajectories within each group are fundamentally different. It is critically important that we probe these simple trajectories further in order to gain a full understanding of the relation between time and change in y as a function of group membership.

4.1.4   Probing Simple Trajectories with a Single Dichotomous Predictor

The conditional HLM with a single dichotomous predictor provides a formal test of the magnitude of the difference between mean intercept and mean slope for group $c = 1$ compared to group $c = 0$. Our goal here is to compute the point estimates and corresponding standard errors for the simple trajectory within group $c = 0$ and the simple trajectory within group $c = 1$. There are two ways in which we can accomplish this. First, we can derive the standard errors for the simple trajectories within each group as a quadratic weighted function of the standard errors of the regression parameters predicting the random trajectories (i.e., the standard errors of $\hat{\gamma}_1$ and $\hat{\gamma}_2$). Alternatively, we can estimate two models using any standard HLM software package, and by simply recoding group membership for the two analyses, we can obtain precisely the same point estimates and standard errors for the simple trajectories as would be derived analytically.

Figure 4.2: Three possible simple trajectories all corresponding to pre-
cisely the same $\hat{\gamma}_1$ and $\hat{\gamma}_2$ regression parameters predicting intercepts
and slopes.

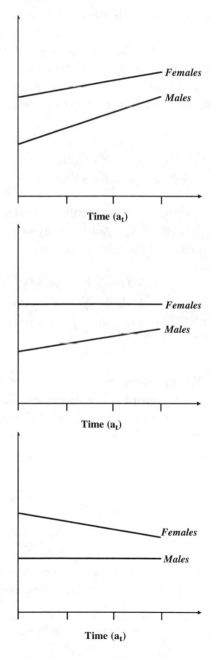

Computation of point estimates and standard errors for simple trajectories

To maintain notation consistent with that of more complicated models to be presented later, we will consider the simple trajectory between y and time at different conditional values of c, denoting the conditional values as cv_c. A value of $cv_c = 0$ denotes the simple trajectory conditioned on membership in group 1 and $cv_c = 1$ denotes the simple trajectory conditioned on membership in group 2. Thus, the intercept and slope of the simple trajectory for conditional value cv_c is

$$\hat{\alpha}|_{cv_c} = \hat{\mu}_\alpha + \hat{\gamma}_1 cv_c \qquad (4.9)$$
$$\hat{\beta}|_{cv_c} = \hat{\mu}_\beta + \hat{\gamma}_2 cv_c,$$

where $\hat{\alpha}|_{cv_c}$ and $\hat{\beta}|_{cv_c}$ represent the sample estimates of the population intercept and slope values of the simple trajectory at $c = cv_c$. The standard errors of these sample estimates are

$$SE(\hat{\alpha}|_{cv_c}) = [VAR(\hat{\mu}_\alpha) + 2cv_c COV(\hat{\mu}_\alpha, \hat{\gamma}_1) + \qquad (4.10)$$
$$cv_c^2 VAR(\hat{\gamma}_1)]^{1/2}$$
$$SE(\hat{\beta}|_{cv_c}) = [VAR(\hat{\mu}_\beta) + 2cv_c COV(\hat{\mu}_\beta, \hat{\gamma}_2) +$$
$$cv_c^2 VAR(\hat{\gamma}_2)]^{1/2},$$

where VAR and COV represent the appropriate variance and covariance elements from the asymptotic covariance matrix of parameter estimates (see Bauer & Curran, in press, and Curran et al., 2004, for further technical details).[4] The ratio of the sample estimate to the standard error follows a t distribution and allows for usual tests of significance. Note that for $cv_c = 0$, Equation 4.10 simplifies to

$$SE(\hat{\alpha}|_{cv_c}) = \sqrt{VAR(\hat{\mu}_\alpha)} \qquad (4.11)$$
$$SE(\hat{\beta}|_{cv_c}) = \sqrt{VAR(\hat{\mu}_\beta)},$$

which are simply the standard errors for the intercept terms of the intercept and slope trajectory equations when regressed on the di-

---

[4]All of the point estimates, standard errors, and regions of significance can be computed using online calculators at www.unc.edu/~curran.

chotomous predictor.[5] When $cv_c = 1$, the additional variance and covariance terms in Equation 4.10 are needed to compute the appropriate standard errors for the simple trajectories within group 2.

An equivalent method can be used to compute these same values using any standard HLM software package. Because Equation 4.10 simplifies to Equation 4.11 for $cv_c = 0$, the estimated intercept terms and associated standard errors of the intercept and slope trajectory equations from the conditional HLM represent the simple trajectory for group 1. The model can be re–estimated with group 2 coded as $cv_c = 0$ and group 1 coded as $cv_c = 1$, and the intercept terms of the intercept and slope equations now represent the simple trajectory for group 2. These point estimates and standard errors will be identical to those computed using equations 4.9 and 4.10.[6]

To demonstrate the estimation and testing of the simple trajectories, we probed the simple trajectories of health over time as a function of sex. The resulting simple trajectory for the women was $\hat{\mu}_{y_t} = 2.23 + .128a_t$ and for the men, $\hat{\mu}_{y_t} = .06 + .202a_t$. These model–implied trajectories are presented in Fig. 4.3. Importantly, only the intercept of the simple trajectory for women significantly differed from zero ($t(437) = 7.13$, $p < .0001$). The intercept for the male trajectory was nonsignificant ($t(437) = .10$, $p = .92$), implying that at age 55, men reported, on average, good overall health. The slopes from the female and male trajectories were both increasing at a significant rate ($p < .0001$). It is critical to note that only through the probing of the simple trajectories can we make these conclusions.

Regions of significance for simple slopes

Although we can explicitly test the simple trajectories within each of the two groups (i.e., $\hat{\alpha}|_{cv_c}$ and $\hat{\beta}|_{cv_c}$), this can be extended one step

---

[5]It is important to distinguish between the *intercept* of the random trajectory and the *intercept terms* of the equations that regress the random intercepts and slopes on the explanatory variable. When probing the simple trajectories across specific levels of the predictors, we are always referring to the intercept terms of the regression equations.

[6]There are other ways of testing these within software packages, including the use of two dummy vectors without an intercept term and the calculation of specific contrasts (e.g., the "estimate" command in MIXED). Here we only describe the method of multiple programs for maximal simplicity.

Figure 4.3: Model–implied simple trajectory of poor health as a function of gender.

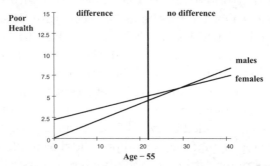

further to derive the precise point in time when the difference between the two simple trajectories is nonsignificant. To accomplish this, we used methods originally developed by Johnson and Neyman (1936) and extended by Pothoff (1964) and D. Rogosa (1980). The middle term of Equation 4.6 highlights that the difference in μ_{yt} (denoted Δ_y) as a function of c at any time point a_t is given as

$$\Delta_y = \gamma_1 + \gamma_2 a_t. \qquad (4.12)$$

We can test the magnitude of the sample estimate of this difference by calculating the ratio of the estimate to the corresponding standard error such that

$$t_{\hat{\Delta}_y} = \frac{\hat{\Delta}_y}{\sqrt{VAR(\hat{\gamma}_1) + 2a_t COV(\hat{\gamma}_1, \hat{\gamma}_2) + a_t^2 VAR(\hat{\gamma}_2)}}, \qquad (4.13)$$

in which this ratio follows a t distribution. As with t tests, an obtained value exceeding an absolute value of about 1.96 would imply a significant difference on the repeated measure y at time a_t as a function of group c (for large df). However, we can set the left side of Equation 4.13 to any desired critical t value (e.g., $t = 1.96$ to define $\alpha = .05$) and then solve for a_t. This will identify the specific points in time at which μ_{yt} does and does not significantly differ as a function of group membership c. This is called a *region of significance*.[7]

---

[7]Pothoff (1964)) distinguishes between *simultaneous* and *nonsimultaneous* regions of significance. For ease of presentation, we only focus on nonsimultaneous

Equation 4.13 is a quadratic expression, the solution of which involves two roots (see Curran et al., 2004, for further details). The lesser and greater roots reflect the lower and upper time points at which μ_{y_t} significantly differs as a function of c, respectively. (See D. Rogosa, 1981, for a clear discussion of these calculations and interpretations within the standard regression model.) Applying Equation 4.13 to our empirical data showed that the mean of y_t significantly varied ($p < .05$) as a function of membership c when $a_t < 21.88$ and $a_t > 129.84$. Because our coding of time ranges from 0 to 41 (corresponding to the age range of 55 to 96), these results imply that women report significantly worse health than men only between ages 55 and 76.88 and that there are no statistically significant sex differences thereafter.

4.1.5   A Single Continuous Predictor of the Random Trajectories

In the conditional trajectory model presented in Equation 4.7, the random intercepts and slopes are regressed onto a single dichotomous measure c in which values were equal to either 0 or 1. There are many situations, however, in which we would like to examine the relation between a continuously distributed predictor and the random trajectories. To accomplish this, we make a simple change to Equations 4.5, 4.6, and 4.7 to include a single continuous predictor x instead of the dichotomous predictor c used earlier. Specifically, we can express the model–implied mean of y_t at time a_t as a function of continuous predictor x as

$$\mu_{y_t} = [\mu_\alpha + \gamma_1 x] + [\mu_\beta + \gamma_2 x] a_t, \qquad (4.14)$$

in which all else holds as before, but now x is a continuously distributed predictor variable.[8]

Although the extension of the conditional HLM from a categorical to a continuous predictor is analytically trivial (i.e., Equation 4.7 vs.

---

regions here, although the computation of simultaneous regions are easily obtained (see Pothoff, 1964, Equation 3.1).

[8]Although we are focusing on predictors that are continuously distributed, just as in multiple regression, we are not concerned about the shape of these exogenous distributions.

4.14), the corresponding interpretations are not. Whereas we were able to express the conditional equations for the simple trajectories at each of the two discrete values $c = 0$ and $c = 1$, x encompasses a range of infinite potential values, with each value resulting in a uniquely different simple trajectory describing the relation between y_t and time. That is, there is an entire *family* of simple trajectories between y_t and time across all levels of x. Although choosing specific values of x on which to compute the simple trajectory is often arbitrary, it has been recommended in standard regression to select values at one standard deviation above and below the mean of x (Aiken & West, 1991, p. 13). We will utilize these same guidelines here, although we stress that any value of x might be chosen depending on the theoretical question of interest.

Recall from the dichotomous predictor model that the intercept terms in the regression of the random trajectories on the dichotomous measure c (i.e., μ_α and μ_β in Equation 4.7) represented the model–implied means of the random trajectories when the predictor variable was equal to zero. In the presence of a continuously distributed predictor, the intercept term similarly reflects the mean of the random trajectories when the predictor equals 0, although the value 0 may or may not be interpretable with respect to the raw metric of x (i.e., a value of 0 may lie outside the logical range of x). We can "center" our predictor x so that the mean of x is equal to 0, thus increasing the interpretability of several of our model parameters. By centering, we simply deviate each individual x from the mean of x, such that $x_i' = x_i - \bar{x}$ where x_i represents the measure on variable x for individual i, $\bar{x}$ represents the mean of x over all individuals, and x_i' is the centered x. Given $\Sigma x_i' = 0$, then $\bar{x}' = 0$. Because the mean of a centered variable is by definition zero, the intercept terms of the random trajectories when regressed on the centered x_i' represent the model–implied mean initial value and mean slope of y_{it} assessed at the mean of the predictor variable x_i'. There are interpretive and sometimes computational advantages to using centered predictors in conditional trajectory models. Because of this, we will assume that all continuous predictor variables are mean centered. For ease of notation, we will refer to the centered, continuous predictor as x_i.

To demonstrate these modeling strategies, we regressed the intercept and slope trajectory components of the perceived health problems on a single continuous measure of social support (from relatives) that had been centered around the mean. In contrast to our expectations, the effect of relative support was nonsignificant in the prediction of both intercepts ($\hat{\gamma}_1 = .01$; $t(437) = .17$, $p = .87$) and slopes ($\hat{\gamma}_2 = -.002$; $t(539) = -.81$, $p = .42$). Thus, there is no statistical evidence that social support provided by relatives meaningfully predicts either initial levels of health or changes in health over time.

Because no main effect of social support was found in the prediction of the random trajectories, there is of course no need to probe this effect further. If such a main effect had been identified, it could have been probed further in precisely the same way as with the dichotomous predictor. In the next section, we describe how such a main–effect predictor of the trajectories would be further probed, but we do not demonstrate these procedures given the lack of a significant effect associated with social support. However, at the risk of spoiling the surprise, we do find an effect associated with social support in the presence of gender, and we demonstrate how to probe this in greater detail later.

4.1.6 Probing Simple Trajectories with a Single Continuous Predictor

As we described earlier, regarding the simple trajectories of y_t regressed on time within discrete group c, we can analytically derive point estimates and standard errors for simple trajectories of y_t at specific values of x. Again, we can use standard HLM software packages to compute these estimates, and we can derive regions of significance for the simple trajectories across levels of x.

Computation of standard errors for simple slopes

Equation 4.14 expressed the model–implied mean of y_t as a function of x. If using a centered predictor, $x = 0$ represents the mean of x, and thus $\hat{\mu}_\alpha$ (the intercept term of the intercept equation) and $\hat{\mu}_\beta$ (the intercept term of the slope equation) in Equation 4.14 represent the model–implied simple trajectory at the mean of x. Although there is an infinite number of simple trajectories defined at every value of x, we will focus on the simple trajectories that exist for specific conditional values of x (denoted cv_x). The sample estimates of the model–implied intercept and slope of the simple trajectory at $x = cv_x$ is

$$\hat{\alpha}|_{cv_x} = \hat{\mu}_\alpha + \hat{\gamma}_1 cv_x \qquad (4.15)$$
$$\hat{\beta}|_{cv_x} = \hat{\mu}_\beta + \hat{\gamma}_2 cv_x$$

with standard errors

$$SE(\hat{\alpha}|_{cv_x}) = [VAR(\hat{\mu}_\alpha) + 2cv_x COV(\hat{\mu}_\alpha, \hat{\gamma}_1) + \qquad (4.16)$$
$$cv_x^2 VAR(\hat{\gamma}_1)]^{(1/2)}$$
$$SE(\hat{\beta}|_{cv_x}) = [VAR(\hat{\mu}_\beta) + 2cv_x COV(\hat{\mu}_\beta, \hat{\gamma}_2) +$$
$$cv_x^2 VAR(\hat{\gamma}_2)]^{(1/2)},$$

where VAR and COV again represent the appropriate variance and covariance elements from the asymptotic covariance matrix of sample parameter estimates. As before, the ratios of these point estimates to their corresponding standard errors follow a t distribution allowing for formal tests of significance of the intercept and slope of the simple trajectory at any given cv_x.

Using Equations 4.15 and 4.16, the sample estimates and corresponding standard errors for the simple trajectories can be computed for any desired cv_x. As in the dichotomous case, however, these same point estimates and standard errors can be obtained using any standard HLM software package. To accomplish this, we would create new variables based on our original x variable at each specific cv_x of interest such that $x_{new} = x - cv_x$. For example, when using centered predictors, our new measure of x at one standard deviation above the mean is $x_{high} = x - (1sd_x)$, at the mean is $x_{medium} = x - (0sd_x)$, and at one standard deviation below the mean is $x_{low} = x - (-1sd_x)$.[9] We then simply estimate three separate conditional HLMs, one regressing the random trajectories on x_{high}, one on x_{medium}, and one on x_{low}. As in OLS regression, each of these models will fit the data precisely the same, but the intercept terms and associated standard errors for

---

[9]Note that it is correct that one SD is subtracted to compute x_{high} and that one SD is added to compute x_{low}. This is because we take advantage of the fact that the intercepts of the regression equations predicting the intercept and slope factors represents the model–implied mean when all predictors are equal to zero. Thus, by *adding* one SD to all x scores, a value of zero on x represents one SD *below* the mean, and vice versa.

each of the trajectory equations represent the simple trajectory of y on time at the given level of x_{new}. As before, the resulting parameter estimates and standard errors are equal to the values that would be obtained using Equations 4.15 and 4.16.

Regions of significance for simple slopes

Just as we did for the dichotomous predictor, we can calculate regions of time over which the effect of the continuous predictor is or is not statistically significant. To demonstrate this, we can choose any arbitrary levels of the continuous predictor, say x_{high} and x_{low}, and determine the model–implied mean levels of y as a function of time:

$$\mu_{y_t}|_{x=x_{high}} = (\mu_\alpha + \gamma_1 x_{high}) + (\mu_\beta + \gamma_2 x_{high})a_t \quad (4.17)$$

$$\mu_{y_t}|_{x=x_{low}} = (\mu_\alpha + \gamma_1 x_{low}) + (\mu_\beta + \gamma_2 x_{low})a_t. \quad (4.18)$$

By simple subtraction, we can calculate the difference in these simple trajectories as

$$\Delta_y = (x_{high} - x_{low})(\gamma_1 + \gamma_2 a_t) \quad (4.19)$$

We can then test the magnitude of the sample estimate of this difference by calculating the ratio of the estimate to the corresponding standard error such that

$$t_{\hat{\Delta}_y} = \frac{(x_{high} - x_{low})(\hat{\gamma}_1 + \hat{\gamma}_2 a_t)}{\sqrt{(x_{high} - x_{low})^2(VAR(\hat{\gamma}_1) + 2a_t COV(\hat{\gamma}_1, \hat{\gamma}_2) + a_t^2 VAR(\hat{\gamma}_2))}},$$
$$(4.20)$$

which simplifies to

$$t_{\hat{\Delta}_y} = \frac{\hat{\gamma}_1 + \hat{\gamma}_2 a_t}{\sqrt{VAR(\hat{\gamma}_1) + 2a_t COV(\hat{\gamma}_1, \hat{\gamma}_2) + a_t^2 VAR(\hat{\gamma}_2)}}. \quad (4.21)$$

This is equivalent to Equation 4.13 and illustrates that the arbitrarily chosen values of the predictor (i.e., x_{high} and x_{low}) are unimportant for the test because they simply cancel out of the test of significance.

As before, we can set the left side of Equation 4.20 to any desired critical t value (e.g., $t = 1.96$ to define $\alpha = .05$) and then solve for a_t. This will identify the specific points in time at which the continuous predictor x does and does not significantly affect μ_{y_t}. Equation 4.13

is a quadratic expression, the solution of which involves two roots (see Curran et al., 2004, for further details). The lesser and greater roots reflect the lower and upper time points at which μ_{y_t} significantly differs as a function of x, respectively.

Again, because the interaction of social support with time was not significant in predicting health perceptions, we do not demonstrate these methods here. However, we will demonstrate these techniques in the next section when we probe the interaction of social support with gender in the prediction of health perceptions over time.

4.1.7   Categorical by Continuous Interactions in the Prediction of the Random Trajectories

Up to this point, we have only considered the estimation and testing of a single categorical or a single continuous predictor variable within the conditional HLM. We could easily extend this model to include two or more correlated predictor variables. The resulting regression parameters would be interpreted in precisely the same fashion as previously done, but these parameters would represent the unique effect of that predictor and *not* the influences of all other predictors. Our ultimate goal here, however, is not to simply estimate main effects in the prediction of the random trajectories, but to estimate higher–order interactions among our explanatory variables. We will begin by exploring the two–way interaction between a single dichotomous variable and a single continuous variable in the prediction of the random intercepts and slopes. Given that we just described how a main–effect predictor of random slopes should be treated as a two–way interaction with time, an interaction between two predictors of slopes should then logically be treated as a three–way interaction with time.

To estimate interactions between two level 2 exogenous variables in the prediction of the random intercepts and slopes, the level 1 equation (i.e., Equation 4.1) remains as before. Whereas we incorporated just main effects in the previous level 2 equations (Equation 4.7 for a dichotomous predictor and Equation 4.14 for a continuous predictor), we now add higher–order terms to represent these interactions. For example, say that we were interested in estimating the two–way interaction between a dichotomous measure c and a continuous measure x in the prediction of the random intercepts and slopes. We would ex-

pand the level 2 equations to contain these higher–order interactions
such that

$$\alpha_i = \mu_\alpha + \gamma_1 c_i + \gamma_2 x_i + \gamma_3 c_i x_i + \zeta_{\alpha_i} \qquad (4.22)$$
$$\beta_i = \mu_\beta + \gamma_4 c_i + \gamma_5 x_i + \gamma_6 c_i x_i + \zeta_{\beta_i},$$

Just as we substituted the level 2 equations into the level 1 equation to derive the reduced form expressions earlier, we can do this
same substitution here. The reduced form equation, however, is becoming an increasingly unwieldy expression in scalar terms, and we
will thus not present this here. The important point to recognize is
that although we are estimating a two–way interaction between c and
x in the prediction of β_i, we substitute this level 2 equation back into
the level 1 equation in the prediction of y. Thus, the entire equation
for β_i is multiplied by time, resulting in the three–way interaction
term $\gamma_6 c_i x_i a_{it}$. This, of course, is the standard cross–level interaction in general HLMs. It is important to remember, however, that the
two–way interaction between the level 2 variables in the prediction of
the random trajectories must be treated as a three–way interaction
between the level 2 variables and time.

As with our usual regression model, we test the interaction between our two predictors by examining the unique contribution of
the multiplicative term above and beyond the contribution of the
two corresponding main effects (see Cohen, 1978, for a detailed exposition on this). If the interaction between c and x is significant,
it must be probed to fully understand the nature of this relation.
Given that this two–way interaction itself interacts with time, we
must probe this effect as we would with a standard three–way interaction. The statistical question that we are asking is, "What is
the relation between y_t and a_t as a function of x within group c?"
The corresponding substantive question that we are asking is, "Do
trajectories of perceived health status vary over time as a function
of social support, and does the magnitude of this relation depend on
whether the individual is male or female?" To answer these questions, we must extend the methods for probing simple trajectories to
incorporate these higher–order interactions.

Conceptually, this extension involves probing the relation between
a continuous measure x and the random trajectories (as we discussed,
but did not demonstrate, earlier), but we are now going to probe

these effects within each group c. So, there will be one set of simple trajectories between y_t and a_t across levels of x for $c = 0$, and one set of simple trajectories between y_t and a_t across levels of x for $c = 1$. The model–implied mean of y at time t is thus

$$\mu_{y_t} = (\mu_\alpha + \gamma_1 c + \gamma_2 x + \gamma_3 cx) + (\mu_\beta + \gamma_4 c + \gamma_5 x + \gamma_6 cx)\, a_t. \quad (4.23)$$

Expansion and rearrangement of terms highlights that the simple trajectories between y_t and a_t as a function of x within group c are

$$
\begin{aligned}
\mu_{y_t}|_{c=0} &= (\mu_\alpha + \gamma_2 x) + (\mu_\beta + \gamma_5 x)\, a_t \qquad\qquad (4.24)\\
\mu_{y_t}|_{c=1} &= ((\mu_\alpha + \gamma_1) + (\gamma_2 + \gamma_3)\, x) + \\
&\quad\ ((\mu_\beta + \gamma_4) + (\gamma_5 + \gamma_6)\, x)\, a_t.
\end{aligned}
$$

Note that within group $c = 0$, the relation between y_t and a_t varies as a function of x in precisely the same way as expressed in Equation 4.14. However, in group $c = 1$, additional influences are incorporated (i.e., γ_1, γ_3, γ_4, and γ_6) to account for the interaction between x and time as a function of membership in group $c = 1$. In other words, there is a two–way interaction between x and time in the prediction of y_t, and this interaction itself interacts with group membership c. Our goal now is to test and probe this three–way interaction.

The formal test of the interaction is simply the test of γ_3 and γ_6. The significance of these terms implies that the relation between x and the growth trajectories depends, in part, on group membership c. To demonstrate this, we regressed the intercept and slope parameters of the health trajectories on three predictors: the dichotomous variable sex; the centered, continuous measure of social support from relatives; and the multiplicative interaction between these two measures. Importantly, the two–way interaction between sex and social support from relatives significantly predicted both the intercept and slope parameters ($p < .05$). These parameter estimates are presented in Table 4.1. We must now probe this interaction further to better understand the nature of this effect, bearing in mind that this two–way interaction itself interacts with time in the reduced form equation and must thus be treated as a three–way interaction.

To formally probe these effects, we need to compute the sample estimates for the intercept and the slope of the model–implied simple trajectories of y on a_t at the conditional level of x (i.e., cv_x) within the

Table 4.1: Parameter Estimates From the Main Effects and Two–Way Interaction Predicting the Random Intercepts and Slopes.

Predictor Variable	Random Intercept	Random Slope
Sex	−2.31	.082
Time 1 Support From Relatives	**.043**	**−.005**
Sex by Relative Support	−.342	.018
Intercept Term of the Prediction Equation	2.289	.124

Note: Model results are based on $n = 439$. All effects are significant at $p < .05$ except for the two parameters presented in bold.

conditional level of group c (i.e., cv_c). Re–expressing Equation 4.23, given conditional values of cv_x and cv_c, results in the sample estimates of the intercept and slope of the simple trajectory as

$$\hat{\alpha}|_{cv_x,cv_c} = \hat{\mu}_\alpha + \hat{\gamma}_1 cv_c + \hat{\gamma}_2 cv_x + \hat{\gamma}_3 cv_c cv_x \qquad (4.25)$$
$$\hat{\beta}|_{cv_x,cv_c} = \hat{\mu}_\beta + \hat{\gamma}_4 cv_c + \hat{\gamma}_5 cv_x + \hat{\gamma}_6 cv_c cv_x,$$

respectively. The standard errors for these point estimates are complex and are presented in Curran et al. (2004). As before, the ratio of the point estimate to standard error follows a t distribution allowing for the usual tests of significance.

We can also compute these point estimates and standard errors using the computer methods described earlier in this chapter. Specifically, to probe the simple trajectories of y_t at plus and minus 1 standard deviation around the mean of x within each of the two groups c, we would estimate a total of six conditional HLMs. Three HLMs would estimate the effect of x_{low}, x_{medium}, and x_{high} with group 1 coded as $cv_c = 0$, and three would repeat the process with group 2 coded as $cv_c = 0$. A model would be estimated for each combination of conditional main effects and their interaction (e.g., the main effect of cv_c, the main effect of cv_x, and the interaction between cv_c and cv_x). From each of these models, the sample estimates of the intercept terms of the random trajectory equations (i.e., $\hat{\mu}_\alpha$ and $\hat{\mu}_\beta$) represent the model–implied simple trajectory and appropriate standard error for each combination of conditional cv_c and cv_x values.

Using this technique, we probed the simple trajectories of health perceptions one standard deviation above and below the mean of social support from relatives within each sex. The simple trajectories for each combination are plotted in Fig. 4.4. Several interesting characteristics are evident. First, for women, we see that family support appears to have little effect either on intercepts or slopes. That is, trajectories of health problems are significantly increasing over time, but the starting point and rate of change does not appear to vary as a function of family support within females. In contrast, there is greater evidence that the trajectories of health problems in men do vary as a function of support from relatives. Specifically, men with higher levels of social support from relatives showed steeper increases in self–reported physical health problems than those with lower levels of social support.

Thus, although there was not evidence for an overall main effect of family support in the prediction of trajectories of health problems, evidence was found when considering the interactive effects of family support and gender. There are two interesting issues here, however. First, although nonsignificant, the intercepts of two of the simple trajectories for males are negative, which, given the scaling of the measure, are impossible values. This might imply some model misfit of the growth trajectory function for males or reflect unreliable estimation in this part of the trajectory; either way, these negative intercepts would not have been identified without the further probing of this relation. Second, it is potentially theoretically inconsistent to conclude that males reporting higher levels of social support also report greater increases in health problems when the opposite relation holds in females. To better understand both of these issues, we can probe this interaction one step further by computing regions of significance.

The computational formulae for the regions of significance are more complex with the additional terms involved, but represent a direct extension of Equation 4.20, so we do not present them here (see Curran et al., 2004, technical appendix, for further details). For females, the lower and upper boundaries of the region of significance are 21.10 and 35.35. Because our coding of time ranges from 0 to 41 (corresponding to the age range of 55 to 96), these results imply that relative support significantly reduces the perceived health

Figure 4.4: Model–implied simple trajectories for high, medium, and low values of social support as a function of gender.

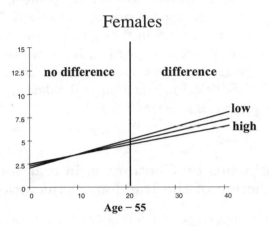

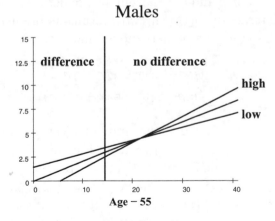

problems of women between ages 76.10 and 90.35 years of age. After this point, our estimate of the effect of social support is too imprecise (i.e., the standard error is too large) to be statistically significant. For males, the lower and upper boundaries of the region of significance are -447.09 and 13.14. Given our coding of time, these results imply that social support significantly reduces the perceived health problems of men between ages 55 and 68.14 years of age. This additional information helps us understand the earlier apparent contradiction. Specifically, higher levels of social support are associated with better overall health for women *later* in the aging process, whereas higher levels of social support are associated with better overall health for men *earlier* in the aging process. From the point of view of substantive theory, this is critical information that would not be available without these additional analyses.

4.1.8   Continuous by Continuous Interactions in the Prediction of the Random Trajectories

Whereas our previous discussion focused on the interaction between a continuous predictor x and a dichotomous predictor c, we can instead consider the interaction between two continuous predictors denoted x and w. In this case, the model–implied mean of y at time t is

$$
\begin{aligned}
\mu_{y_t} = {} & (\mu_\alpha + \gamma_1 w + \gamma_2 x + \gamma_3 wx) + \\
& (\mu_\beta + \gamma_4 w + \gamma_5 x + \gamma_6 wx)\, a_t.
\end{aligned} \tag{4.26}
$$

Whereas previously we probed the simple trajectories at conditional values of x_{low}, x_{medium}, and x_{high} within each of two groups cv_c, we now consider these same simple trajectories between y_t and time at conditional values of x (i.e., cv_x; namely, x_{low}, x_{medium}, x_{high}) across conditional values of w (i.e., cv_w; namely, w_{low}, w_{medium}, w_{high}). To accomplish this, we modify Equation 4.25 such that the sample estimates for the model–implied intercept and slope of the simple trajectory at a given conditional value of cv_x and cv_w is

$$
\begin{aligned}
\hat{\alpha}|_{cv_x, cv_w} &= \hat{\mu}_\alpha + \hat{\gamma}_1 cv_w + \hat{\gamma}_2 cv_x + \hat{\gamma}_3 cv_w cv_x \\
\hat{\beta}|_{cv_x, cv_w} &= \hat{\mu}_\beta + \hat{\gamma}_4 cv_w + \hat{\gamma}_5 cv_x + \hat{\gamma}_6 cv_w cv_x
\end{aligned} \tag{4.27}
$$

The standard errors for these sample estimates are similar to those with a dichotomous–by–continuous interaction and are presented in (Curran et al., 2004).

As with the earlier case, we can calculate these point estimates and standard errors using any standard HLM software package. Here, however, we must estimate nine separate conditional HLMs, three for each cv_x of interest evaluated at each cv_w of interest (e.g., x_{low} evaluated at w_{low}, w_{medium}, and w_{high}, etc.). The resulting sample estimates and standard errors for the simple trajectories will correspond to those derived in Curran et al. (2004).

We could extend the results from the two–way interaction in a number of interesting and straightforward ways. For example, we could again compute the regions of significance for the simple trajectory between y_t and time across values of x within each group membership c or across continuous values of w. To accomplish this, we would create the ratio of the point estimate of the simple trajectory to the appropriate standard error and solve for cv_x or cv_w. Further, we could test the equality of intercepts or slopes from any two simple trajectories taken at any conditional value of cv_x, cv_w, or cv_c. For example, we might like to formally test the equality of the slopes of the simple trajectory of perceived health at low levels of social support for males compared with females. We could easily include one or more control variables in the model, and all of these procedures could be directly applied to test and probe simple trajectories above and beyond the influence of covariates. Finally, all of these values can be computed using online calculators described in Preacher, Curran, and Bauer (in press).

4.2 Conclusion

Hierarchical linear modeling provides a powerful and flexible method for testing a variety of theoretical questions about individual differences in developmental trajectories over time. A set of particularly intriguing applications is the incorporation of one or more explanatory variables used to predict the random trajectory components. Of course, it has long been known in the HLM literature that the main–effect prediction of the random trajectories often involves a cross–level interaction with time. There is less evidence, however, that the presence of this interaction has been fully capitalized in HLM applications. Specifically, we are aware of no published literature that has drawn on classic methods to test and probe interactions in HLM that are commonly used in standard OLS regression. Here we have demonstrated that the methods used to probe interactions in OLS regression can be generalized directly to HLM as well. Further, our empirical example has highlighted what we believe to be significant advantages associated with the use of these techniques in practice. Indeed, based on our own experiences with these models, we recommend these methods be used anytime one or more explanatory variables are used in HLM growth models. This will not only enhance our ability to more fully understand complex models, but will also allow for the formal testing of additional types of research hypotheses in ways not possible without the use of such techniques.

4.3   Acknowledgments

This work was funded in part by grant DA13148 awarded to the first author, grant DA06062 to the second author, and grant MH12994 to the third author. We would like to thank Ken Bollen, Andrea Hussong, and the members of the Carolina Structural Equations Modeling Group for their valuable input throughout this project. We are also indebted to Cindy Bergeman for her generous provision of the LSOA data, which is supported in part by grant MH53895.

References

Aiken, L. S., & West, S. G. (1991). *Multiple regression: Testing and interpreting interactions.* Newbury Park, CA: Sage.

Bauer, D. J., & Curran, P. J. (in press). Probing interactions in fixed and multilevel regression: Inferential and graphical techniques. *Multivariate Behavioral Research.*

Biesanz, J., Deeb–Sossa, N., Aubrecht, A. M., Bollen, K. A., & Curran, P. J. (2004). The roll of coding time in estimating and interpreting growth curve models. *Psychological Methods, 9,* 30–52.

Bisconti, T. L., & Bergeman, C. S. (1999). Perceived social control as a mediator of the social support/successful aging relationship. *The Gerontologist*, *39*, 94–103.

Bryk, A., & Raudenbush, S. W. (1987). Application of hierarchical linear models to assessing change. *Psychological Bulletin*, *101*, 147–158.

Cohen, J. (1978). Partialled products are interactions; partialled vectors are curve components. *Psychological Bulletin*, *85*, 858–866.

Curran, P., Bauer, D., & Willoughby, M. (2004). Testing and probing main effects and interactions in latent curve analysis. *Psychological Methods*, *9*, 220–237.

Goldstein, H. (1986). Multilevel mixed linear model analysis using iterative generalized least squares. *Biometrika*, *73*, 43–56.

Gompertz, B. (1825). On the nature of the function expressive of the law of human mortality. *115*, 513–580. Philosophical Transactions of the Royal Society of London.

Johnson, P., & Neyman, J. (1936). Tests of certain linear hypotheses and their applications to some educational problems. *Statistical Research Memoirs*, *1*, 57–93.

MacCallum, R., Kim, C., Malarkey, W., & Kielcolt–Glaser, J. (1997). Studying multivariate change using multilevel models and latent curve models. *Multivariate Behavioral Research*, *32*, 215–253.

McArdle, J. (1988). Dynamic but structural equation modeling of repeated measures data. In J. Nesselroade & R. Cattell (Eds.), *Handbook of multivariate experimental psychology* (2nd ed.). New York: Plenum Press.

McArdle, J. (1989). Structural modeling experiments using multiple growth functions. In P. Ackerman, R. Kanfer, & R. Cudeck (Eds.), *Learning and individual differences: Abilities, motivation and methodology* (pp. 71–117). Hillsdale, NJ: Lawrence Erlbaum Associates.

McArdle, J. (1991). Structural models of developmental theory in psychology. In P. van Geert & L. Mos (Eds.), *Annals of theoretical psychology* (Vol. 7, pp. 139–160). New York: Plenum Press.

Meredith, W., & Tisak, J. (1984). *"Tuckerizing" curves*. Paper presented at the annual meeting of the Psychometric Society,

Santa Barbara, CA.

Meredith, W., & Tisak, J. (1990). Latent curve analysis. *Psychometrika, 55*, 107–122.

Metha, P. D., & West, S. G. (2000). Putting the individual back in individual growth curves. *Psychological Methods, 5*, 23–43.

Palmer, C., Kawakami, R., & Reed, L. (1937). Anthropometric studies of individual growth II. Age, weight, and rate of growth in weight, elementary school children. *Child Development, 8*, 47–61.

Pothoff, R. (1964). On the Johnson-Neyman technique and some extensions thereof. *Psychometrika, 29*, 241–256.

Preacher, K. J., Curran, P. J., & Bauer, D. J. (in press). Computational tools for probing interactions in multiple linear regression, multilevel modeling, and latent curve analysis. *Journal of Educational and Behavioral Statistics.*

Raudenbush, S. (2001). Toward a coherent framework for comparing trajectories of change. In L. M. Collins & A. G. Sayer (Eds.), *New methods for the analysis of change* (pp. 33–64). Washington, DC: American Psychological Association.

Raudenbush, S. W., & Bryk, A. (2002). *Hierarchical linear models: Applications and data analysis methods* (2nd ed.). Thousand Oaks, CA: Sage.

Rogosa, D. (1980). Comparing nonparallel regression lines. *Psychological Bulletin, 88*, 307–321.

Rogosa, D. (1981). On the relationship between the Johnson-Neyman region of significance and statistical tests of parallel within group regressions. *Educational and Psychological Measurement, 41*, 73–84.

Rogosa, D. R., & Willett, J. B. (1985). Understanding correlates of change by modeling individual differences in growth. *Psychometrika, 50*, 203–228.

Singer, J. (1998). Using SAS PROC MIXED to fit multilevel models, hierarchical models, and individual growth models. *Journal of Educational and Behavioral Statistics, 24*, 323–355.

Wallace, K. A., & Bergeman, C. S. (1997). Control and the elderly: Goodness-of-fit. *International Journal of Aging and Human Development, 45*, 323–339.

Willett, J., & Sayer, A. G. (1994). Using covariance structure analysis to detect correlates and predictors of individual change over time. *Psychological Bulletin, 116*, 363–381.

Willett, J., Singer, J., & Martin, N. (1998). The design and analysis of longitudinal studies of development and psychopathology in context: Statistical models and methodological recommendations. *Development and Psychopathology, 10*, 395–426.

Wishart, J. (1938). Growth rate determinations in nutrition studies with the bacon pig, and their analysis. *Biometrika, 30*, 16–28.

5

A Repeated Measures, Multilevel Rasch Model with Application to Self-Reported Criminal Behavior

Christopher Johnson and Stephen W. Raudenbush
University of Michigan

Repeated measures data generated from longitudinal designs are often used when studying correlates of individual change. Such studies pose several challenges: (1) The measurement scale must be invariant over time; (2) covariates of interest are often multilevel (e.g., measured at the person and neighborhood level); (3) some item-level missing data can be expected. To cope with these challenges, we propose a repeated measures, multilevel Rasch model with random effects. Under assumptions of conditional independence, additivity, and measurement invariance over time, the approach enables the investigator to calibrate the items and persons on an interval scale, incorporate covariates at each level, and accommodate data missing at random. Using data on eight items tapping violent crime from 2,842 adolescents ages 9 to 18 nested within 196 census tracts in Chicago, we illustrate how to test key assumptions, how to adjust the model in light of diagnostic analyses, and how to interpret parameter estimates.

5.1   Introduction

Longitudinal data enable us to repeatedly measure the status of individuals over a specified time period. We can then fit models to estimate the individual change taking place over that time. In fitting these models, we must assume that measurement invariance is present across our time points; that is, our items tap the same underlying latent trait at each time of measurement. We can test this assumption by assessing item behavior over time. This suggests application of a longitudinal item response theory (IRT) model, the focus of this chapter.

A second rationale for a longitudinal IRT model arises when the number of items is small and/or the item responses are highly skewed. Available methods for modeling growth typically assume a continuous outcome variable. Often this assumption will fail. For example, a scale score consisting of crime items with a low probability of endorsement would not approximate continuity even if it included a very large number of items. This is also the case for many other types of data that arise widely in studies of behavior, beliefs, attitudes, exposure to risk, and symptoms of disease. A longitudinal IRT model does not require that the outcome in growth studies be continuous or normally distributed.

Raudenbush, Johnson, and Sampson (2003) showed how to embed an IRT model in a hierarchical structural model using cross–sectional data. They also illustrated how to make this IRT model multivariate and multilevel. They found that this new methodology avoids problems such as negative predicted probabilities of the outcome variable and incorrect t statistics while providing a careful assessment of item functioning. In this chapter, we intend to extend their methodology to incorporate repeated measures data.

First, Raudenbush et al. extended the IRT model by making it multivariate. This allows for the simultaneous study of different types of crime, allowing assessments of the key model assumption of unidimensionality, which requires that each IRT measure taps a single interval scale. The multivariate approach enabled them to study whether covariates relate differently to different types of offending net effects of measurement error.

The second extension of the IRT model was made to make the model multilevel. This extension reflected the fact that many of the data collected within social settings are in a natural nested structure. For example, in the study of crime, we would like to take into account that the respondent is nested within a neighborhood, which is in turn nested within a city. Without taking this nested structure into account, the study of the variation and covariation of the propensity to offend might be biased due to the incorrect specification of the variance components. The multilevel approach is particularly important when explanatory variables are measured at higher levels, for example, at the neighborhood or city level.

The third extension of the IRT model had to do with accommodating the data missing at random. Data are missing at random when the probability of missing is independent of the missing data, given the observed data. This is a comparatively weak assumption that will be approximately correct when the observed data contain substantial information about the probability of missingness (Little & Rubin, 1987). To cope with this problem, the IRT model specifies the person effect as random rather than fixed. The fourth extension of the IRT model was to add covariates at different levels of the model in order to predict criminal behavior. Having set the model up in this way, Raudenbush et al. (2003) were able to determine whether covariates related differently to different scales of crime and whether covariates related differently to different items.

Raudenbush and colleagues opted for a one–parameter IRT or Rasch model. The Rasch model, which specifies a location parameter for each item, is simpler than a two–parameter model, which specifies a location parameter and a discrimination parameter for each item. This brings to light one of the strong assumptions of the Rasch model: Each item is equally discriminating. This assumption implies that the relative severity of the items is identical for all persons. This is a very appealing feature, allowing us to view items as more or less severe, anchoring the scale in a conceptually meaningful way.

In this chapter, we extend the Rasch model in a different way. While allowing the model to be a multilevel random effects model, we allow the model to encompass repeated measures on a set of items. This chapter is organized as follows: We begin with a brief review of the Rasch model, describing its application to self–reported criminal behavior. Second, we show how the Rasch model with random effects can be formulated as a special case of a two–level hierarchical logistic regression model. Third, we show how the two–level model formulation of the Rasch model readily extends to three levels incorporating multilevel data. Fourth, we extend the model to include repeated measures. Fifth, we illustrate an application of this model by analyzing data on 2,977 adolescents nested within 196 census tracks and interviewed at two time points. We show how to specify mean propensity and growth in propensity to commit violent crime and how to test hypotheses concerning person–level and neighborhood–level predictors of latent status and change in criminal propensity. We close with suggestions for future research.

5.2   The Rasch Model Applied to Self–Reported Crime

As mentioned, the easiest IRT model to interpret is the Rasch model. Consider a cross–sectional survey asking a series of questions about violent crime. For each question, the respondent indicates whether he or she has committed a specific act ("yes" or "no") during the past year. According to the Rasch model, the log–odds of a "yes" response depends on the severity of the act and the propensity of the respondent to commit violent crime. Key assumptions are that item severity and person propensity are additive in their effects and that item responses are conditionally independent given severity and propensity. These assumptions imply that the item set measures a unidimensional trait, for example, "propensity to commit violent crime." If these assumptions hold, the model estimates yield a readily interpretable ordering of items and persons on an interval scale (Rasch, 1980; Wright & Masters, 1982)

The additivity assumption of the Rasch model implies that each item is equally discriminating. When this assumption is true, the resulting scale has several appealing features. Item location can be interpreted as "severity," giving the scale a clear interpretation: Persons scoring higher on the scale display more severe levels of criminality than do persons scoring lower, and the relative severity of the items is identical for all persons.

More formally, when applied to binary items tapping acts of crime, the Rasch model locates item severities, ψ_m, and person propensities to offend, π_j, on a odds (logit) scale. For items $m = 1, ..., m$ and persons $j = 1, ..., J$, let $Y_{mj} = 1$ if person j responds affirmatively to item m and $Y_{mj} = 0$ if person j responds negatively to item j. Let $\mu_{mj} = Prob(Y_{mj} = 1|\psi_m\pi_j)$ denote the conditional probability that person j will respond affirmatively to item m, and let $\eta_{mj} = log[\frac{\mu_{mj}}{(1-\mu_{mj})}]$, the natural log–odds of responding affirmatively. Then, under the Rasch model,

$$\eta_{mj} = \pi_j - \psi_m. \tag{5.1}$$

In words, the log–odds of a "yes" response is the simple difference between person j's propensity to offend, π_j, and item m's severity, ψ_m. Key assumptions are:

1. *Local independence*: Conditional on item severity and person propensity, item responses Y_{mj} are independent Bernoulli random variables and thus have conditional mean μ_{mj} and conditional variance $\mu_{mj}(1-\mu_{mj})$.

2. *Additivity*: Item differences and person differences contribute additively to the log–odds of an affirmative response.

A key condition for local independence to hold is that the M items in a set tap a single underlying dimension of crime (unidimensionality). Suppose, for example, that unbeknownst to the researcher, a set of items assessing violent crime actually tapped two dimensions: for example, violence in service of robbery (armed robbery, purse–snatching) and interpersonal aggression (hitting a family member in anger, hitting a peer in anger). Then, local independence would fail because covariation would arise among the items of each subtype. Local independence would also fail if the ordering of items created an auto–correlation in the responses.

5.2.1   A Two–Parameter Model

If valid, assumption 2 gives credence to the idea that less frequently occurring acts of a given type are more severe. If assumption 2 fails, a two–parameter model might be formulated:

$$\eta_{mj} = \lambda_m(\pi_j - \psi_m). \qquad (5.2)$$

In Equation 5.2, item is characterized not only by a location parameter ψ_m, but also by the discrimination parameter, λ_m. Under Equation 5.2, item and person characteristics enter multiplicatively into the model, and the severity of the item depends on the propensity of the person to offend. This idea is depicted in Fig. 5.1a, which displays the item characteristic curves (ICC) of three items that follow a Rasch model (or one–parameter model) as contrasted to Fig. 5.1b, which displays three ICCs under the two–parameter model. The ICC expresses the probability of positive endorsement, that is, $Pr(Y_{mj} = 1)$, a function of the underlying latent propensity, to offend, π_j, of person j. The location parameter, ψ_m, is the point on the horizontal scale for which the probability of an affirmative response is .50. The slope, λ_m, is the slope of the ICC at that same point.

In Fig. 5.1a, item severities are, respectively, $\psi_1 = -2, \psi_2 = -1$, and $\psi_3 = 0$. Note that the Rasch model is a special case of the two–parameter model with $\lambda_1 = \lambda_2 = \lambda_3 = 1$. Under the Rasch model, a person with propensity of 0 is quite likely to respond affirmatively to the most frequently endorsed item (i.e., item 1) and somewhat unlikely to respond affirmatively to the least frequently endorsed item (item 3). Under the Rasch assumptions, the fact that only the most serious offenders are likely to respond affirmatively to the least frequently endorsed items leads to the interpretation of ψ_m as "item severity."

Under Fig. 5.1b, the Rasch assumptions fail. Here we have $\psi_1 = -2, \psi_2 = -1$, and $\psi_3 = 0$ as before, but now the discrimination parameters (or "slopes") are not all equal. Rather $\lambda_1 = .3, \lambda_2 = 1$, and $\lambda_3 = 1$. Though the item location parameters ψ_m are the same as in Fig. 5.1a, they cannot be interpreted unambiguously as item severities because now the relative likelihood of endorsement of the item depends on the criminality of the respondent. Those with very high propensities to offend are more likely to endorse item 2 than item 1, whereas those with lower propensities are more likely to endorse item 1 than item 2.

The parallelism of the curves in Fig. 5.1a reflects the additivity assumption. In contrast, the crossing of the item characteristic curves

Figure 5.1: Probability of an affirmative response (vertical axis) as a function of propensity to offend when (a) discrimination parameters are equal, and (b) when they are not. The location parameter, ψ_m, is the point on the horizontal scale for which the probability of an affirmative response is .50. The slope, λ_m, is the slope of the curve at that same point.

Figure 5.1a $\lambda_1 = \lambda_2 = \lambda_3 = 1, \psi_1 = -2, \psi_2 = -1, \psi_3 = 0$

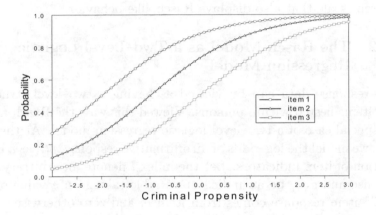

Figure 5.1b $\lambda_2 = \lambda_3 = 1, \lambda_1 = 0.3, \psi_1 = -2, \psi_2 = -1, \psi_3 = 0$

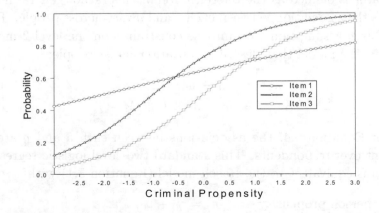

in Fig. 5.1b reflects the multiplicative relationship between items and persons and also undermines the notion that the item location parameters reflect severity.

Raudenbush et al. (2003) test the additivity assumption by studying a two–parameter model. They compared the fit of the two–parameter model to that of the Rasch model. They also checked item fit by examining item–total correlations and standardized residuals. Using the first wave of data we analyze in this chapter, they found that one item fit the scale poorly and also produced departures from the Rasch assumptions. Discarding that item created a more coherent scale that also displays Rasch–like behavior.

5.2.2 The Rasch Model as a Two–Level Logistic Regression Model

Item response data can be viewed as having a two–level structure with items nested within persons. Viewed this way, the Rasch model is a special case of a two–level logistic regression model. At the first level, we model the log–odds of an affirmative response, η_{ij}, as a linear function of item indicators. Let the index i denote an arbitrary item response and a_{mij} be an indicator variable taking on a value of 1 if the ith item response comes from item m and zero otherwise. Then we write

$$\eta_{ij} = \pi_j + \sum_{m=1}^{M-1} \alpha_{mj} a_{mij}. \tag{5.3}$$

Note that there are M - 1 item indicators and the item having no indicator is defined as the reference item. This rather general model allows the association between each a and η vary across people. To fit the Rasch assumptions, we impose constraints on the level 2 model, that is, the model that describes variation across people:

$$\begin{aligned} \pi_j &= \gamma_0 + u_{0j} \\ \alpha_{mj} &= \alpha_m, m = 1, ..., M - 1. \end{aligned} \tag{5.4}$$

Under Equation 5.4, the associations between each a and η are invariant over respondents. This standard two–level logistic regression model is equivalent to the Rasch model (Equation 5.1) with

$$\text{person propensity} \quad = \quad \pi_j = \gamma_0 + v_{0j}$$

$$\text{item severity} \;=\; 0 \text{ for the reference item}$$
$$\text{item severity} \;=\; -\alpha_m \text{ for items } m = 1, ..., M - 1.$$

5.2.3   The Rasch Model as a Multilevel Model

Our item response data can also be viewed as having a three–level structure with items nested within persons and persons nested within neighborhoods (or schools). At the first level, we model the log–odds of an affirmative response, η_{ijk}, as a linear function of item indicators. As before, let the index i denote an arbitrary item response and a_{mik} be an indicator variable taking on a value of 1 if the ith item response comes from item m and zero otherwise. Let j denote the person and k denote the neighborhood. Then we write

$$\eta_{ijk} = \pi_{jk} + \sum_{m=1}^{M-1} \alpha_{mjk} a_{mijk}. \tag{5.5}$$

The level 2 model describes variation across people within neighborhoods:

$$\begin{aligned}
\pi_{jk} &= \beta_{0k} + u_{0jk} \\
\alpha_{mjk} &= \alpha_{mk}, m = 1, ..., M - 1,
\end{aligned} \tag{5.6}$$

in which π_{jk} is the log–odds of an affirmative response by person j in neighborhood k; and u_{0jk} is a random person effect. At the third level (between neighborhoods), we allow the neighborhood mean propensities to vary randomly over neighborhoods, but fix the average item effects:

$$\begin{aligned}
\beta_{0k} &= \gamma_0 + v_{0k} \\
\alpha_{mk} &= \alpha_m
\end{aligned} \tag{5.7}$$

in which γ_0 is the population average log–odds of an affirmative response and u_{0k} is a random person effect. This standard three–level logistic regression model is equivalent to the Rasch model (Equation 5.1) with

$$\text{person propensity} = \pi_{jk} = \gamma_0 + v_{0k} + u_{ojk}, \tag{5.8}$$
$$\text{item severity} = 0 \text{ for the reference item,}$$
$$\text{and item severity} = -\alpha_m \text{for items m=1,...,M-1.}$$

In addition, this three–level model, which includes person and neighborhood effects (or school effects), allows contextual factors to contribute to individual propensities to offend. The correlation structure may differ at the person and neighborhood levels, and such differences can be studied using a multilevel approach. This multilevel approach naturally accommodates covariates measured on neighborhoods as well as persons, yielding standard errors that appropriately reflect the nested structure of the data and increase the efficiency of estimation.

5.2.4   The Rasch Model as a Repeated Measures Multilevel Model

We now extend the three–level model of the previous section to incorporate longitudinal data.[1] Here we add the index $t = 1, \ldots, T$ to allow for repeated measures. Our model for growth is a polynomial of degree P:

$$\eta_{tijk} = \pi_{0jk} + \pi_{1jk}d_{tijk} + \pi_{2jk}d_{tijk}^2 + \ldots + \pi_{pjk}d_{tijk}^P + \sum_{m=1}^{M-1} \alpha_{mjk}a_{mtijk}$$

$$(5.9)$$

where

$\eta_{tijk} = log[\mu_{tijk}/(1 - \mu_{tijk})]$ is the log–odds of the conditional probability μ_{tijk} that person j in neighborhood k will respond affirmatively to the ith item at time t;

$\mu_{tijk} = Prob(Y_{tijk} = 1|\pi_{jk})$, with conditioning on all fixed effects and predictors also implicit;

d_{tijk} is a measure of time or age;

π_{0jk} is a person–specific intercept, the log–odds of a 'yes,' at time $d_{tijk} = 0$, by person j in neighborhood k to the reference item;

$\pi_{pjk}, p > 0$ is the pth order polynomial effect (e.g. linear, quadratic, cubic, etc.) on the reference item;

---

[1]Note that we could also extend our model to incorporate multiple types of crime as shown in Raudenbush et al. (2003), but for simplicity we chose to examine a single type of crime.

$a_{mtijk} = 1$ if item i is the mth item at time t, 0 otherwise; and

α_{mjk} is the discrepancy between the log–odds of an affirmative response to the mth item for person j in neighborhood k at time t and the reference item, holding constant the changing propensity

$$\pi_{ojk} + \sum_{p=1}^{P} \pi_{pjk} d^p_{lijk}.$$

At the second level (between persons), we allow the person propensities to vary randomly within a neighborhood, but require the item effects to be invariant across persons:

$$\pi_{pjk} = \beta_{pk} + u_{pjk} \qquad (5.10)$$
$$\alpha_{mjk} = \alpha_{mk} m = 1, ..., M - 1$$

in which β_{pk} is the mean of the change parameter π_{pjk} within neighborhood k and u_{pjk} is a random person effect. The person–specific random effects are assumed independent across people, but correlated within people, having a multivariate normal distribution with means of zero and variance–covariance matrix T_π.

At the third level (between neighborhoods), we allow the neighborhood mean change parameters to vary randomly over neighborhoods, but fix the average item effects:

$$\beta_{pk} = \gamma_p + v_{pk} \qquad (5.11)$$
$$\alpha_{mk} = \alpha_m$$

in which γ_p is the population average change parameter of degree p. The neighborhood specific random effects v_{pk} are independent across neighborhoods, but correlated within neighborhoods, with a $P - 1$–variate normal distribution with means of zero and variance–covariance matrix T_β. The three–level model also accords the following definitions:

$$\text{item severity} = 0 \text{ for the reference item}$$
$$\text{item severity} = -\alpha_m \text{ for items } m = 1, \ldots, M - 1.$$

Person–level predictors of propensity to offend may be included in the level 2 model (Equation 5.10) and neighborhood–level predictors may be included in the level 3 model (Equation 5.11). In the following illustrative example, we consider a model with one type of crime: violent crime consisting of items measures at two different time points. With two different time points, the polynomial must be linear, that is, of the form $\pi_{0jk} + \pi_{1jk}d_{tijk}$, which is essentially Equation 5.9 with $p = 1$.

5.3   Illustrative Example

5.3.1   Sample and Data

The sample design involved two stages. In the first stage, Chicago's 343 neighborhood clusters (NCs) were cross–classified by seven levels of ethnic mix and three levels of socioeconomic status (SES).[2] Within the 21 strata so constructed, NCs were sampled with the aim of producing a nearly balanced design. The resulting sample is described in Table 5.1 with census tracts as units.[3] The number of tracts in each stratum is shown in parentheses. The table shows that the confounding of ethnic mix and neighborhood SES precludes study of certain combinations; there are no predominantly white and poor tracts, nor are there any predominantly Hispanic and high–SES tracts. Nevertheless, there is substantial variation with ethnic mix by SES (note the presence of low, medium, and high SES tracts that are predominantly black and many ethnically heterogeneous tracts that vary in SES). Table 5.1 confirms the racial and ethnic segregation in Chicago while rejecting the common stereotype that minority neighborhoods in the United States are homogeneous.

At the second stage, dwelling units were enumerated (listed) within each NC. In most instances, all dwelling units were listed, although for particularly large NCs, census blocks were selected for listing with probability proportional to size. Within listed blocks, dwelling units were selected systematically from a random start. Within selected

---

[2]See Sampson, Raudenbush, and Earls (1997) for a detailed description of the construction of the 343 NCs.

[3]Our analysis uses the census tract ($N = 196$) rather than the NC ($N = 80$) as the analytic unit to increase statistical power at the between–neighborhood level.

Table 5.1: Number of Census Tracts ($N = 196$) by Socioeconomic Status (SES) and Racial/Ethnic Composition in the PHDCN Design.

Racial/Ethnic Strata	SES							
	Low		Medium		High		Total	
75% Black	31	(9)	10	(4)	9	(4)	50	(17)
75% White	0	(0)	7	(4)	18	(8)	25	(12)
75% Latino	12	(4)	12	(4)	0	(0)	24	(8)
20% Latino and 20% White	11	(4)	14	(5)	10	(4)	35	(13)
20% Hispanic and 20% Black	7	(4)	7	(4)	0	(0)	14	(8)
20% Black and 20% White	3	(2)	4	(4)	10	(4)	17	(10)
NCs Not Classified Above	8	(4)	14	(4)	9	(4)	31	(12)
TOTAL	72	(27)	68	(29)	56	(24)	196	(80)

Note: The 80 sampled NCs are shown in parentheses. SES was defined by a six-item scale that summed standardized neighborhood-level measures of median income, percent college educated, percent with household income over $50,000, percent families below the poverty line, percent on public assistance, and percent with household income less than $50,000 based on the 1990 decennial census. In forming the scale, the last three items were reverse coded.

dwelling units, all households were enumerated. Age–eligible participants were selected with certainty. To be age–eligible, a household
member must have had an age within 6 months of one of seven ages:
0, 3, 6, 9, 12, 15, or 18 years of age. The analysis reported here used
cohorts 9, 12, 15, and 18. Each child was administered a Self–Report
of Offending questionnaire to determine participation in certain delin-
quent and criminal acts. Questions were of the form, "Have you ever
hit someone you lived with?" (Yes = 1 and No = 0), followed by
questions on prevalence and incidence during the past year.

Home–based interviews with parents and children in each cohort
were conducted in two waves over 54 months from 1994 to 99. On
average, approximately 2 years elapsed between waves. Though each
family was followed until 2002, we confine our attention in this paper
to wave 1 and wave 2 data. Approximately 50% of participants were
female; 45% were of Hispanic origin, 36% were black, and 15% were
white (Table 5.2). Frequencies for other ethnic groups were small.
To make use of all of the data, our analyses classified participants as
Hispanic, black, or other, with the understanding that "others" are
overwhelmingly white. At the neighborhood level, we are interested
in concentrated disadvantage, which is a weighted factor score constructed from the data of the 1990 decennial census of the population
to reflect differences in poverty, race and ethnicity, the labor market,
age composition, and family structure. Neighborhood–concentrated
disadvantage was created from five variables:

1. Percentage of population below the poverty line

2. Percentage of population that is on some form of
   public assistance

3. Percentage of population that is unemployed

4. Percentage of population that is less than 18 years of age

5. Percentage of population whose households are female headed.

Sampson et al. (1997) provides a detailed description of the construction of the scale.

For simplicity we will consider only the violent crime items presented in Raudenbush et al. (2003). The violent crime scale, dis-

Table 5.2: Descriptive Statistics

Person–Level Data (N = 2977)	
Age	$M = 13.28, SD = 3.33$
Female	$M = .500$
Hispanic	$M = .452$
Black	$M = .362$
White	$M = .146$
Asian	$M = .013$
Pacific Islander	$M = .002$
American Indian	$M = .010$
Other	$M = .014$
Neighborhood–Level Data (J = 196)	
Concentrated Disadvantage	$M = 0.04, SD = 0.82$

Note: Concentrated disadvantage is a weighted factor score constructed from the data of the 1990 decennial census of the population to reflect differences in poverty, the labor market, age composition, and family structure: (1) percent of population below the poverty line, (2) percent of population that is on some form of public assistance, (3) percent of population that is unemployed, (4) percent of population that is less than 18 years of age, and (5) percent of population whose households are female headed. Sampson et al. (1997) provides a detailed description of the construction of the scale.

played in Table 5.3, includes items self reported during personal interviews at waves 1 and 2. This scale indicates acts of physical aggression (hitting someone you did not live with in the past year with the intent of hurting them, throwing objects at others, robbery, purse snatching, pick pocketing, setting fires, gang fighting, and carrying a hidden weapon).

5.3.2   Checking Model Assumptions: The Additivity Assumption

We seek a model with Rasch properties; that is, with item location parameters interpreted as item severities and person propensities lying on the same scale. Under the Rasch assumptions, person propensity and item severity combine additively to determine the log–odds of item endorsement. We can check these assumptions by comparing results based on one–parameter and two–parameter models. Raudenbush et al. (2003) performed such a comparison using the wave 1 data, leading them to drop one ill–fitting item from the scale. We

Table 5.3: Item Responses for Violent Crime by Wave

Variable	Category	Frequency Wave 1	Wave 2
Hit someone with whom you did not live with in the past year with the idea of hurting them	0 = no	2129	1960
	1 = yes	685	451
Thrown objects such as bottles or rocks at people in the past year	0 = no	2495	2201
	1 = yes	333	210
Ever carried a hidden weapon in the last year	0 = no	2565	2221
	1 = yes	258	191
Ever maliciously set a fire in the last year	0 = no	2809	2402
	1 = yes	28	9
Ever snatched a purse/picked a pocket in the last year	0 = no	2821	2401
	1 = yes	18	10
Ever attacked with a weapon in the last year	0 = no	2739	2342
	1 = yes	95	69
Ever used a weapon to rob someone in the last year	0 = no	2822	2403
	1 = yes	10	8
Ever been in a gang fight in the last year	0 = no	2667	2307
	1 = yes	167	97

now examine item functioning of wave 2. Specifically, we estimated a Rasch model (Equation 5.1) using the program BILOG (Mislevy & Bock, 1997) and compared the results to those based on a two–parameter model (Equation 5.2), again using BILOG. The results appear in Table 5.4.

Note that all slopes are constant in the one–parameter (Rasch) results, but they are allowed to vary in the case of the two–parameter model.[4] Using a Bayesian information criterion (BIC) to compare models, the one–parameter model fits the data only slightly better than does the two–parameter model. That is to say, the BIC of the one–parameter model is higher than that of the two–parameter model. The results are similar for Wave 1 in that the one–parameter model has a better BIC.

We graphically display parameter estimates in Fig. 5.2. Note that all the ICCs are forced to be proportional in the case of the one–parameter model (Fig. 5.2a). Even in the case of the two–parameter model, however, (Fig. 5.2b), the ICCs tend to be nearly proportional. Within this scale, Rasch assumptions are reasonable; thus, we opted for using the Rasch model. Item location parameters can reasonably be interpreted as item severities, and items and persons arguably are calibrated on a common scale.

5.3.3   Checking Model Assumptions: The Local Independence Assumption

The Rasch model assumes that, given person propensity and item severity, item responses are independently sampled from a Bernoulli distribution. One way to test for violations of this assumption is to estimate a model with extra–binomial dispersion. If the within–participant variance is more or less than expected under an assumption of independent Bernoulli trials, we have evidence against the local independence assumption. This can be accomplished using the

---

[4]BILOG sets the slope in the one–parameter to a constant, not necessarily 1.0, and constrains the person propensities to have a mean of 0 and variance 1.0. An alternative and statistically equivalent parameterization would constrain the slope to 1.0 and allow the propensities to have a constant variance other than 1.0. See Mislevy and Bock (1997) and http://www.ssicentral.com/irt/bilog.htm for a copy of the BILOG program and users manual. To obtain the BILOG code used in our analysis, please contact the first author at cjque@umich.edu.

Figure 5.2: Graphical comparison of (a) one–parameter and (b) two–parameter models for violent crime at Wave 2.

Figure 5.2a

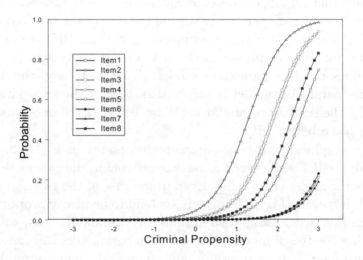

Figure 5.2b

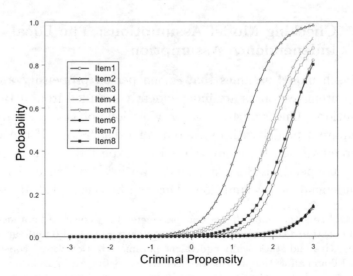

Table 5.4: Results for one-parameter and two-parameter models for violence at Wave 2

Item	Item Biserial Correlation	Violence					
		1 Parameter			2 Parameter		
		Threshold (SE)	Slope (SE)	Standardized Posterior Residual	Threshold (SE)	Slope (SE)	Standardized Posterior Residual
1 (attacked with weapon)	1.075	2.524 (0.089)	2.355 (0.104)	2.118	2.429 (0.124)	2.674 (0.348)	0.888
2 (hit someone you do not live with)	0.668	1.286 (0.049)	2.355 (0.104)	0.685	1.280 (0.059)	2.397 (0.258)	0.685
3 (thrown objects at someone)	0.756	1.846 (0.061)	2.355 (0.104)	1.893	1.995 (0.097)	1.958 (0.183)	1.143
4 (carried hidden weapon)	0.854	1.909 (0.064)	2.355 (0.104)	0.191	1.931 (0.087)	2.308 (0.229)	0.300
5 (set fire)	0.904	3.551 (0.161)	2.355 (0.104)	3.350	4.004 (0.591)	1.887 (0.551)	3.665
6 (snatched purse)	0.967	3.511 (0.162)	2.355 (0.104)	1.379	3.790 (0.457)	2.035 (0.471)	1.284
7 (used force to rob)	1.016	3.616 (0.177)	2.355 (0.104)	0.814	3.839 (0.509)	2.108 (0.566)	1.273
8 (been in a gang fight)	0.941	2.329 (0.078)	2.355 (0.104)	0.617	2.381 (0.121)	2.254 (0.242)	0.757
BIC (max BIC is best)		-3214.85			-3244.87		

HLM5 software (see Raudenbush et al., 2003).[5] We found that the conditional variance of the item responses is significantly lower than expected under a Bernoulli model. This result suggests that the local independence assumption may not hold. We therefore modified the Rasch model to allow for underdispersion in all subsequent analyses.

5.3.4   Assessing Item Invariance

A meaningful study of growth requires a constant metric over time. In the Rasch modeling framework, the item severities must be invariant across waves. To assess this assumption, we compared item severities estimated separately for the wave 1 and wave 2 data using BILOG. The results (Table 5.5) show quite remarkable agreement. Discrepancies between item severities are uniformly small relative to the estimated standard errors.

5.4   Fitting The Repeated Measures IRT Model

5.4.1   Setting Up the Data

In order to help us to understand the multilevel and repeated measures model, let us first look at the structure of the level 1 data, that is, the repeated measures data for each participant. Table 5.6 contains these repeated measures data for three persons residing in census tract $\neq$ 6109. The first column, labeled "Tract," gives the identification number of the census tract in which the participant resides. The second column, labeled "Person," is the personal identifier of the participant. The third column labeled "Dwave2" is a dummy variable taking on a value of 0 at wave 1 and 1 at wave 2. The fourth ("Age") column gives the age of the participant at each wave. "ΔAge," the fifth column, is the deviation of the participant's

---

[5]We estimated the three–level Rasch model using a very accurate approximation to maximum likelihood (ML) and also using penalized quasi–likelihood (PQL) with and without extra–binomial dispersion. Item severities were nearly perfectly correlated across the two analyses. The PQL results reveal evidence of substantial underdispersion. PQL with underdispersion produced slightly larger between–person variances than did the ML approach. Under this model the level 1 variance is $Var(Y_{ijk}|\eta_{ijk}) = \sigma^2 \mu_{ijk}(1 - \mu ijk), \sigma^2 > 0$. Under the Bernoulli model, $\sigma^2 = 1$.

Table 5.5: Results of the One–Parameter Model for Violence at Wave 1 and the One–Parameter Model for Violence at Wave 2

Item	Wave 1 Threshold (SE)	Wave 2 Threshold (SE)
1 (attacked with weapon)	2.627 (0.072)	2.524 (0.089)
2 (hit someone you do not live with)	1.240 (0.037)	1.286 (0.049)
3 (thrown objects at someone)	1.821 (0.046)	1.846 (0.061)
4 (carried hidden weapon)	2.001 (0.050)	1.909 (0.064)
5 (set fire)	3.298 (0.102)	3.561 (0.161)
6 (snatched purse)	3.482 (0.109)	3.511 (0.162)
7 (used force to rob)	3.812 (0.156)	3.616 (0.177)
8 (been in a gang fight)	2.301 (0.059)	2.329 (0.078)

Note: Wave 1 item severities were rescaled to have the same mean and standard deviation as the Wave 1 severities.

age from the mean of the two ages of that participant across the two waves (see note to Table 5.4 for an example on how to compute this). The sixth column contains the values of the outcome variable, Y, for each item at each wave. Columns 7 through 15 are dummy variables indicating the item with which each outcome Y is associated. Thus, for example, in the first row for participant 5081, we see that $Y = 1$ and $d1 = 1$, revealing that person 5081 said "yes" when asked if he or she had committed the crime of "ever carrying a hidden weapon in the last year," labeled "item 1" at wave 1. Similarly, we see that for the second row in the record of person 5081 that $Y = 0$ and $d2 = 1$, showing that, at wave 1, participant 5081 said "no" when asked if he or she had "ever hit someone you do not live with in the last year" (item 2).

Table 5.7a displays the level 2 data, that is, the person level data, for the same three participants. Just as in the level 1 data, the first two columns are labeled "Tract" and "Person." Thus, for example, we see that person 5081 in tract 6109 had a mean age of 16.29 (we can see from Table 5.6 that person 5081 was 15.19 at wave 1 and 17.39 at wave 2 so that mean age $= [15.19 + 17.39]/2 = 16.29$). In the analytic model, however, we work with mean age-16 and its square (columns 4 and 5) rather than working with the uncentered mean age. Centering age in this way sharply reduces collinearity between age and age–squared. It also defines the level 1 intercept, π_{0jk}, to be the propensity for violent crime at age 16, approximately the peak age of offending. Column 6 is an indicator for female gender, whereas columns 7 and 8 indicate ethnicity (column 7 indicates African–American ethnicity, whereas column 8 indicates white or other ethnicity). Column 9 contains the value for SES that is centered with a mean of zero. Thus, we see for example, that person 5081 is a black female having $SES = 0.074$.

Table 5.7b contains the level 3 data, which are the data that vary at the level of the census tract. In this case, there is just one variable of interest, concentrated disadvantage, that has a mean of zero. Thus, we see that tract 6109 has a value of 0.10 on concentrated disadvantage, just slightly above the overall mean.

Table 5.6: Level 1 Record for Subjects 4061, 5081, 5121

Tract	Person	Dwave2	Age	ΔAge	Y	d1	d2	d3	d4	d5	d6	d7	d8
6109	4601	0	12.45	-1.09	0	1	0	0	0	0	0	0	0
6109	4601	0	12.45	-1.09	0	0	1	0	0	0	0	0	0
6109	4601	0	12.45	-1.09	0	0	0	1	0	0	0	0	0
6109	4601	0	12.45	-1.09	0	0	0	0	1	0	0	0	0
6109	4601	0	12.45	-1.09	0	0	0	0	0	1	0	0	0
6109	4601	0	12.45	-1.09	0	0	0	0	0	0	1	0	0
6109	4601	0	12.45	-1.09	0	0	0	0	0	0	0	1	0
6109	4601	0	12.45	-1.09	0	0	0	0	0	0	0	0	1
6109	4601	1	14.63	-1.09	0	1	0	0	0	0	0	0	0
6109	4601	1	14.63	-1.09	0	0	1	0	0	0	0	0	0
6109	4601	1	14.63	-1.09	0	0	0	1	0	0	0	0	0
6109	4601	1	14.63	-1.09	0	0	0	0	1	0	0	0	0
6109	4601	1	14.63	-1.09	0	0	0	0	0	1	0	0	0
6109	4601	1	14.63	-1.09	0	0	0	0	0	0	1	0	0
6109	4601	1	14.63	-1.09	0	0	0	0	0	0	0	1	0
6109	4601	1	14.63	-1.09	0	0	0	0	0	0	0	0	1
6109	5081	0	15.19	-1.10	1	1	0	0	0	0	0	0	0
6109	5081	0	15.19	-1.10	0	0	1	0	0	0	0	0	0
6109	5081	0	15.19	-1.10	0	0	0	1	0	0	0	0	0
6109	5081	0	15.19	-1.10	0	0	0	0	1	0	0	0	0
6109	5081	0	15.19	-1.10	0	0	0	0	0	1	0	0	0
6109	5081	0	15.19	-1.10	0	0	0	0	0	0	1	0	0
6109	5081	0	15.19	-1.10	1	0	0	0	0	0	0	1	0
6109	5081	0	15.19	-1.10	0	0	0	0	0	0	0	0	1
6109	5081	1	17.39	1.10	1	1	0	0	0	0	0	0	0
6109	5081	1	17.39	1.10	0	0	1	0	0	0	0	0	0
6109	5081	1	17.39	1.10	0	0	0	1	0	0	0	0	0
6109	5081	1	17.39	1.10	1	0	0	0	1	0	0	0	0
6109	5081	1	17.39	1.10	0	0	0	0	0	1	0	0	0
6109	5081	1	17.39	1.10	0	0	0	0	0	0	1	0	0
6109	5081	1	17.39	1.10	0	0	0	0	0	0	0	1	0
6109	5081	1	17.39	1.10	0	0	0	0	0	0	0	0	1
6109	5121	0	18.32	-1.24	0	1	0	0	0	0	0	0	0
6109	5121	0	18.32	-1.24	0	0	1	0	0	0	0	0	0
6109	5121	0	18.32	-1.24	0	0	0	1	0	0	0	0	0
6109	5121	0	18.32	-1.24	0	0	0	0	1	0	0	0	0
6109	5121	0	18.32	-1.24	0	0	0	0	0	1	0	0	0
6109	5121	0	18.32	-1.24	0	0	0	0	0	0	1	0	0
6109	5121	0	18.32	-1.24	0	0	0	0	0	0	0	1	0
6109	5121	0	18.32	-1.24	0	0	0	0	0	0	0	0	1
6109	5121	1	20.80	1.24	0	1	0	0	0	0	0	0	0
6109	5121	1	20.80	1.24	0	0	1	0	0	0	0	0	0
6109	5121	1	20.80	1.24	0	0	0	1	0	0	0	0	0
6109	5121	1	20.80	1.24	0	0	0	0	1	0	0	0	0
6109	5121	1	20.80	1.24	0	0	0	0	0	1	0	0	0
6109	5121	1	20.80	1.24	0	0	0	0	0	0	1	0	0
6109	5121	1	20.80	1.24	0	0	0	0	0	0	0	1	0
6109	5121	1	20.80	1.24	0	0	0	0	0	0	0	0	1

Note:

ΔAge is defined as the difference between age and mean age where mean age = (age at time 1 + age at time 2) divided by 2. For example, in the case of person 5081 within tract 6109 (see above table) mean age = (15.19 + 17.39) / 2 = 16.29, and ΔAge = 15.19 16.29 = -1.10 at Wave 1 and 17.39 16.29 = 1.10 at Wave 2.

Table 5.7: Corresponding Level 2 and Level 3 Records for Subjects 4601, 5081, 5121

a. Level 2 Record for Subjects 4601, 5081, 5121

Tract	Person	Mean Age	Mean Age-16	$(MeanAge - 16)^2$	Female	Black	White & Other	SES
6109	4601	13.54	-2.46	6.04	1	0	1	1.00
6109	5081	16.29	0.29	0.08	1	1	0	-0.74
6109	5121	19.56	3.56	12.68	1	0	1	2.11

b. Level 3 Records for Subjects 4601, 5081, 5121

Tract	Concentrated Disadvantage
6109	0.10

5.4.2   Applying the Three–Level Model to the Data

We now estimate the three–level model (Equations 5.9, 5.10, and 5.11), expanded to include covariates. The level 1 model views the log–odds of endorsement on item i as depending on which item was endorsed. We now have

$$\eta_{tijk} = \pi_{0jk} + \pi_{1jk}d_{tijk} + \sum_{m=1}^{7} \alpha_{mjk}a_{mtijk} \qquad (5.12)$$

in which

a_{mtijk} is an indicator variable representing item;

π_{0jk} is the average log–odds of average criminal propensity of person j (averaged over wave 1 and wave 2; we will refer to this quantity as person mean propensity);

π_{1jk} is the rate of change per year in the log–odds of endorsing a crime for person j;

d_{tijk} is the change in age from wave 1 to wave 2 measured in years;

α_{mkj} represents the average item "severity" of crime item m over wave 1 and wave 2.

Note now that seven item indicators represent the eight violent crimes items. For the sake of parsimony, these item severities will again be fixed across the participants and across the tracts; that is, $\alpha_{mjk} = \alpha_m$ for all j, k.

Level 2 Model

The level 2 model accounts for variation between participants within tracts

$$\pi_{0jk} = \beta_{00k} + \sum_{s=1}^{5} \beta_{0sk}X_{sk} + u_{0jk} \qquad (5.13)$$

$$\pi_{1jk} = \beta_{10k} + \sum_{s=1}^{5} \beta_{1sk}X_{sk} + u_{1jk}$$

$$\alpha_{mjk} = \alpha_m \text{ all j,k}$$

on the measures of violent behaviors, in which β_{00k} and β_{10k} are the neighborhood intercepts for tract k of person status and change in person mean propensity, respectively. β_{0sk} and β_{1sk} are the effects of the indicator variables X_{sk}, $s = 1, \ldots, 5$ which are indicators for ethnicity, gender, the mean age of person j (mean–age), and mean person age centered squared (mean age $- 16)^2$. The random effects u_{0jk} and u_{1jk} are assumed to be bivariate normally distributed with means zero and person–level variance covariance matrix reflected by

$$\begin{bmatrix} \tau_{\pi 00} & \tau_{\pi 01} \\ \tau_{\pi 10} & \tau_{\pi 11} \end{bmatrix} \qquad (5.14)$$

Level 3 Model

The level 3 model accounts for variation between tracts on person mean propensity and the change in person mean propensity, respectively:

$$\begin{aligned} \beta_{00k} &= \gamma_{00} + \gamma_{01} W_k + \upsilon_{0k}, \qquad (5.15) \\ \beta_{10k} &= \gamma_{10} + \gamma_{11} W_k + \upsilon_{1k}, \\ \beta_{0sk} &= \gamma_{0s}, s > 1 \\ \beta_{1sk} &= \gamma_{1s}, s > 1 \end{aligned}$$

in which

γ_{00} and γ_{10} are the overall intercepts for status in propensity and the rate of change per year in propensity respectively;

W_k is the degree of neighborhood concentrated disadvantage in neighborhood k;

and the random effects υ_{0K} and υ_{1k} are assumed bivariate normally distributed with zero means and tract–level variance covariance matrix of

$$\begin{bmatrix} \tau_{\beta 00} & \tau_{\beta 01} \\ \tau_{\beta 10} & \tau_{\beta 11} \end{bmatrix} \qquad (5.16)$$

For simplicity we fixed β_{0sk} and β_{1sk}.

5.5   Results

5.5.1   Item Severities

Table 5.8 provides the severities of the items within each scale (note that these item severities are averaged over wave 1 and wave 2). As expected, we see that armed robbery, purse snatching, maliciously setting fire, and attacking someone with a weapon are among the rarest and therefore, under Rasch assumptions, the most severe crimes. In contrast, hitting someone you don't live with, throwing objects at someone, and carrying a hidden weapon are depicted as less severe.

5.5.2   Association Between Covariates and Mean Propensity

Our three–level model specifies mean propensity and change in propensity as depending on covariates measured at the level of the person and the neighborhood. Correlates of mean propensity appear in Table 5.9 (under "mean propensity"). We see a strong quadratic effect of age, to be discussed in more detail later (see "describing the age–crime curve"). Controlling for age and the other covariates, we find significant effects of ethnicity: African Americans display higher propensity than do Hispanics (coeff. $= 1.099$, odds ratio $= \exp 1.099 = 3.00, t = 10.54$). Whites also display higher propensity than do Hispanics (coeff $= 0.253$, odds ratio $= 1.29$, $t = 2.02$). We can deduce that the odds for African Americans, relative to whites is $3.00/1.29 = 2.33$. Similarly, females display lower propensity than do males (coeff. $= -.767$, odds ratio $= .46$, $t = -9.27$). Neighborhood concentrated disadvantage increases the risk of crime (coeff $= 0.214$, $t = 2.98$). Given the standard deviation of 0.82, a two standard deviation increase in concentrated disadvantage is associated with an increase of $2 \times (0.82) \times (0.21) = .351$, yielding an odds ratio of 1.42. Interestingly, personal SES is unassociated with violent crime after controlling for concentrated disadvantage.

Table 5.8: Model Fitting Results for Item Severity

Item	Coefficient Estimate
Intercept[a], γ_0	-1.92
Ever used a weapon to rob someone in the last year, α_1	-7.03
Ever snatched a purse/picked a pocket in the last year, α_2	-6.54
Ever maliciously set a fire in the last year, α_3	-6.23
Ever attacked someone with a weapon in the last year, α_4	-4.43
Ever been in a gang fight in the last year, α_5	-3.79
Ever carried a hidden weapon in the last year, α_6	-3.01
Ever thrown objects at someone in the last year, α_7	-2.71

Note a: The reference item is "ever hit someone you don't live with this year."

Table 5.9: Association Between Covariates and Crime

a) Fixed Effects

Predictor	Mean Propensity			Change in Propensity		
	Coeff.	SE	t ratio	Coeff.	SE	t ratio
Intercept	-1.919	0.090	-21.331	-0.133	0.065	-2.061
Concentrated						
Disadvantage	0.214	0.071	2.983	-0.003	0.055	-0.070
SES	0.031	0.035	0.896	-0.040	0.024	-1.660
African American	1.099	0.104	10.539	-0.039	0.077	-0.508
White and Other$_0$	0.253	0.125	2.020	-0.160	0.090	-1.775
Female	-0.767	0.083	-9.265	-0.067	0.058	-1.170
Mean Age-16	0.059	0.018	3.357	-0.041	0.011	-3.635
$(MeanAge - 16)^2$	-0.042	0.004	-9.688	0.002	0.003	0.743

b) Covariance Component

Variance component	
Level 1, σ^2	0.336
Level 2, τ_π	$\begin{bmatrix} 3.12 & 0.03 \\ 0.03 & 0.81 \end{bmatrix}$
Level 3, τ_β	$\begin{bmatrix} 0.009 & -0.013 \\ -0.013 & 0.019 \end{bmatrix}$

5.5.3 Association Between Covariates and Change in Crime

Table 5.9 shows an overall reduction in propensity per year of age, evaluated at the age of 16 (coeff. = -0.133, t = -2.06). The expected change, however, depends on age. Controlling for gender, ethnicity, and concentrated disadvantage, the expected change in propensity $= -0.133 - 0.041 \times (age - 16) + (.002) \times (age - 16)^2$. We can easily tabulate the expected change in propensity, therefore, for a typical participant in each of our four cohorts. Specifically, a typical person in the first cohort would have been 9 at wave 1 and 11 at wave 2. For the second, third, and fourth cohorts, the corresponding ages would be 12 and 14 for cohort 2; 15 and 17 for cohort 3; and 18 and 20 for cohort 4. Using the midpoint of each interval (e.g., using 10 for cohort 1, 13 for cohort 2, etc.), we can calculate the expected change for each "typical" cohort member.

The expected trajectories are graphed for four Hispanic males who are of typical age for their cohort (Figure 5.3a). The Y axis is

Cohort	Age at Wave 1	Age at Wave 2	Expected	Change/Year
1	9	11		1.85
2	12	14		0.01
3	15	17		-0.13
4	18	20		-0.24

the probability of committing violent crime, defined here in terms of the reference item ("ever hit someone you do not live with during the past year"). We see a rather sharp increase in the probability of committing crime for younger participants (those less than 13). The rate of increase, however, becomes negative thereafter and falls sharply for the oldest cohort.

5.5.4   Describing the Age–Crime Curve

The foregoing discussion suggests that our participants' rates of increase in committing violent crime tend to be large in early adolescence. These rates of increase eventually diminish as a function of age, reaching zero at about age 13, suggesting that the probability of violent crime is at its maximum at around 13. This seems to contradict conventional wisdom about the age–crime curve, suggesting that violent crime tends to peak later. We know, however, that Chicago and many other large cities experienced a sharp drop in the rate of violent crime during the years of our data collection, 1995 to 1999. In a longitudinal study, age and history are confounded. Presumably, the rates of change by age reflect combined effects of age and history. Figure 5.3b shows graphs of the expected age–crime curve for Hispanic males (of average SES and average neighborhood concentrated disadvantage) as a function of age in 1996 and 1998 (roughly the midpoints of waves 1 and 2, respectively).[6] Note that the age–crime curves have the "classic" forms at each wave. The wave 1 curve peaks at about age 17, whereas the wave 2 curve peaks at about age 16. Vertical distances between the curves at any age can be interpreted as com-

---

[6]The wave 1 curve is computed by substituting -1.0 for age–change in our model, allowing age to vary from 9 to 18 and setting other covariates to zero. The wave 2 curve is computed by setting age–change to 1.0, allowing age to vary from 11 to 20, again holding other covariates at zero.

Figure 5.3:

Figure 5.3a Change in the probability of offending of respondents
between Wave 1 and Wave 2

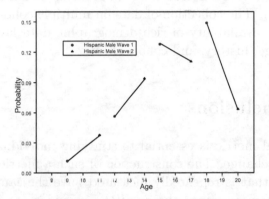

Figure 5.3b Change in the probability of offending of respondents
between Wave 1 and Wave 2 with cross–sectional age crime curves
superimposed for each wave.

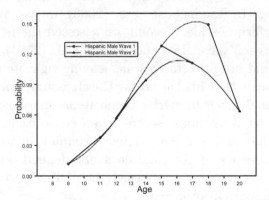

bined history and cohort effects. These effects are most pronounced at the later ages. Within each wave, the age–crime curves reflect cohort and age effects. To reduce cohort effects, we have controlled for ethnicity, gender, concentrated disadvantage, and SES. Increasingly precise control for demographic covariates would presumably eliminate most of the cohort effects, yielding graphical interpretations of history effects (vertical distances between the graphs at each age) and age effects (associations between cross–sectional age and crime at each wave). The collection of data on multiple cohorts at multiple ages plus the availability of rich demographic data lay the basis for separating age, history, and cohort effects.

5.6   Conclusions

A meaningful metric is essential to studying individual change and correlates of change. The construction of such a metric requires that the variable that is repeatedly measured have the same meaning at each age. Item response theory (IRT) provides a sensible way to create and assess metrics used to assess change.

Our approach to constructing such a metric has three distinct stages. First, we used available theory to tentatively assign items to common scales. In Raudenbush et al. (2003), we assigned nine items to the violent crime scale. Second, we assessed the fit of the Rasch model within each wave. In Raudenbush et al. (2003), we discarded an item that did not fit a Rasch scale, leaving eight items that did fit the scale. A scale that fits the strong Rasch assumption of additivity has an extremely nice property; crime items more rarely endorsed can be interpreted as more "severe" than crime items more readily endorsed in that only the most serious criminals endorse those rare items. The severity of the item does not depend on the criminal propensity of the person, an extremely helpful property when trying to measure changes in propensity.

Having scales within each wave that meet Rasch assumptions does not insure that the metric is invariant as a function of age. To assess this requirement, we scaled the items separately within waves. The results are encouraging (Table 5.5); the item severities show little evidence of dependence on age.

In taking the next step, it was tempting to create a single scale score for each participant at each wave, to view these scale scores as continuous, and to model correlates of change in a hierarchical model. We resisted this temptation because of the small number and skewed nature of our item responses. Many of our participants never endorsed a single item! To assign these participants a scale score would involve an extrapolation with large error. Moreover, the data would never approximate continuity. To model correlates of change, we therefore used a three–level logistic regression model, with item responses at level 1, persons at level 2, and neighborhoods at level 3. In essence, we modeled the probability of committing each of eight crimes as a function of covariates, but imposing the Rasch assumptions that the log–odds of each crime was equal apart from a constant. This can be viewed as a proportional odds assumption. Our checks on Rasch assumptions within each wave and across the two waves gives support to this constraint, and adds statistical power and ease of interpretation to the results.

Although longitudinal data afford many advantages, interpretation of results can nonetheless be quite ambiguous. In a longitudinal study of a single cohort, age and history are perfectly confounded. Cross–sectional studies, of course, confound age and cohort. Collecting data on multiple cohorts and multiple aspects of demography creates the possibility of separating age, period, and cohort effects. In our study, we know that young people were maturing at a time when the rate of violent crime was dropping in Chicago and many other cities. Thus, within–participant change confounds maturation and history effects. The age–crime curves at each wave give some indication of the magnitude of these history effects (see Fig. 5.3), though cohort effects are implicated as well. Precise control for participant demography in conjunction with data on multiple cohorts repeatedly observed over time creates potential, in principle, of separating age, history, and cohort effects in longitudinal studies.

5.7   Acknowledgments

The research reported here was funded by grants from the John D. and Catherine T. MacArthur Foundation and the National Institute of Justice to the Project on Human Development in Chicago Neighborhoods (Felton Earls, Principal Investigator). Previous versions were presented at the Johns Hopkins University and the American Society of Criminology annual meeting.

References

Little, R., & Rubin, D. (1987). *Statistical analysis with missing data.* New York: Wiley.

Mislevy, R. J., & Bock, R. D. (1997). *BILOG Version 3.11.* [Computer Software]. Chicago, IL: Scientific Software International.

Rasch, G. (1980). *Probabilistic models for some intelligence and attainment tests.* Chicago: University of Chicago.

Raudenbush, S. W., Johnson, C., & Sampson, R. (2003). A multivariate, multilevel rasch model with application to self–reported criminal behavior. *Sociological Methodology, 33,* 169–211.

Sampson, R. J., Raudenbush, S., & Earls, F. (1997). Neighborhoods and violent crime: A multilevel study of collective efficacy. *Science, 277,* 918–924.

Wright, B., & Masters, G. (1982). *Rating scale analysis: Rasch measurement.* Chicago: MESA Press.

6

Latent-Class Analysis Approaches to Determining the Reliability of Nominal Classifications: A Comparison Between the Response-Error and the Target-Type Approach

Christof Schuster
University of Notre Dame

Latent-class analysis can be used to analyze data obtained from multiple raters who independently assign the same set of targets to nominal categories. In this situation, the assessment of the degree to which raters agree is of considerable interest because it reflects the reliability of the classifications. Two different latent-class analysis approaches have been suggested for analyzing nominal rater agreement data. The first approach assumes that disagreement among raters occurs because of response error. The second approach distinguishes two different types of targets. I refer to the two approaches as the response-error approach and the target-type approach, respectively. I show that the response-error approach yields estimates of sensitivities as well as rater-specific and category-specific error rates. The response–error approach does not, however, yield a simple overall summary of the rater reliability. Although the target–type approach does not yield rater–specific or category–specific conclusions that ignore the target type, it yields an intuitively appealing reliability statistic that can be interpreted as the proportion of systematic agreement.

6.1   Introduction

The reliability with which psychological variables can be assessed has received considerable attention. Research on reliability for interval–scale data started almost a century ago (Brown, 1910; Spearman, 1910). This line of research developed rapidly, and an early comprehensive account of reliability in the context of mental tests was given by Gulliksen (1950).

Presumably because the assessment of nominal–scale reliability is considerably different from the assessment of interval–scale reliability, the development of reliability indices for nominal–scale data has received broader attention only after reliability theory for interval–scale data was well developed. The early reports on nominal–scale reliability included Bennett, Alpert, and Goldstein (1954); Cohen (1960); Goodman and Kruskal (1954); Guttman (1946), and Scott (1955).

As a simple example of a situation in which nominal–scale reliability is important, consider two psychiatrists who classify patients into categories such as (a) neurosis; (b) psychosis, and (c) other. Intuitively, it is clear that if both raters are highly reliable, then I can expect a high degree of agreement. Thus, it should be possible to assess rater reliability by focusing on the degree of agreement between the psychiatrists.

As a second example, consider the decline associated with Alzheimer's disease that has been categorized into three major clinical phases (Reisberg, Ferris, de Leon, & Crook, 1982). The *forgetfulness phase* is characterized by subjective memory deficit for which there is no objective evidence. Individuals do, however, display appropriate concern about the symptoms. In the *confusional phase*, there is memory deficit as well as concentration deficit. Patients can no longer perform complex tasks accurately and efficiently. Finally, in the *dementia phase*, patients may forget the name of their spouse and are largely unaware of all recent events and experiences in their lives. Each of these phases has been further subdivided into several stages. For instance, the dementia phase has been further subdivided into early, middle, and late dementia stages. For present purposes, however, it is sufficient to focus on the coarser phase classification of Alzheimer's disease. If two neurologists can reliably classify patients into these phases, a high degree of agreement between the neurologists is likely.

6.2 Nominal–Scale Reliability: Coefficients versus Models

Let A and B denote two different raters who classify the same n targets into one of r different categories. The frequency of each possible combination of ratings can be arranged in a so–called interrater contingency table. To each combination of ratings there belongs an unknown probability that underlies the corresponding observed frequency. Table 6.1 shows the interrater contingency table of probabilities, where for the sake of concreteness, three response categories have been assumed.

Specifically, the probability with which both raters agreed on the first category is π_{11}. The probability with which A classified the target into the first category, but B classified the target into the second category is denoted as π_{12}. The other probabilities in Table 6.1 are defined similarly. Note also that Table 6.1 contains the marginal probabilities π_i^A, $i = 1, \ldots, n$, which denote the probabilities with which rater A selects a particular category regardless of the category selected by rater B. The marginal probabilities for rater B, π_j^B, are defined similarly. The marginal probabilities are also referred to as *base rates*.

Table 6.1: Interrater Contingency Table of Probabilities Underlying the Observed Rating Frequencies

	B_1	B_2	B_3	
A_1	π_{11}	π_{12}	π_{13}	π_1^A
A_2	π_{21}	π_{22}	π_{23}	π_2^A
A_3	π_{31}	π_{32}	π_{33}	π_3^A
	π_1^B	π_2^B	π_3^B	

The proportion of observed agreement

$$\pi_0 = \sum_i \pi_{ii} \tag{6.1}$$

is an intuitively plausible measure of rater reliability because it has two desirable properties: It is easy to interpret, and it has the same range as interval–scale reliability statistics. Specifically, a value of zero indicates that raters never agreed, and a value of one indicates perfect agreement. Even if both raters randomly assign targets to categories, however, some amount of agreement should occur, although the ratings are obviously completely unreliable. As a result, the proportion of observed agreement will not be zero even if both raters behave randomly. Therefore, the proportion of observed agreement is positively biased in the sense of overestimating the reliability. In addition, in cases in which raters are able to assign a certain proportion of targets reliably, guessing about ambiguous targets may also lead to positive bias. Thus, regardless of the extent to which raters classify targets reliably, the proportion of observed agreement is likely to overestimate the rater reliability. To address this positive bias, essentially all reliability statistics that are based on the proportion of observed agreement implement a so–called correction for chance agreement.

The best known rater agreement statistic of this type is Cohen's kappa. It is defined as

$$\kappa = \frac{\pi_0 - \pi_e}{1 - \pi_e}, \tag{6.2}$$

in which π_e is the amount of chance agreement that can be expected if raters assign targets randomly in accordance with their respective base rates. Thus, chance agreement can be calculated as $\pi_e = \sum_i \pi_i^A \pi_i^B$. Kappa is interpreted by noting that it assesses the extent to which observed agreement exceeds chance agreement relative to the maximum possible amount of this difference. As a result, kappa ranges between zero and one. More specifically, kappa will only be equal to one in case of perfect agreement, and it will be zero in cases in which observed agreement does not exceed chance agreement.

In addition, kappa has three other desirable properties. First, it does not require the assumption of uniform margins as is necessary, for instance, for the reliability statistics proposed by Brennan and Prediger (1981) and Maxwell (1977). Second, it can be generalized to more than two raters (Conger, 1980; Fleiss, 1971), and third, it is easy to compute.

There has been a long debate, however, over the usefulness of Cohen's kappa (Brennan & Prediger, 1981; Feinstein & Cicchetti, 1990; Grove, Andreasen, McDonald-Scott, Keller, & Shapiro, 1981; Guggenmoos-Holzmann, 1993, 1996; Guggenmoos-Holzmann & Vonk, 1998; Perrault & Leigh, 1989; Shrout, Spitzer, & Fleiss, 1987; Spitznagel & Helzer, 1985). Typically, kappa has been criticized by presenting specific examples of interrater contingency tables for which the kappa statistic yields unintuitive values. Although kappa is defined without reference to a statistical model and therefore does not require assumptions in addition to rater independence, Zwick (1988) suggested that kappa is an appropriate agreement statistic only if rater margins are homogeneous. Thus, instead of voting unconditionally in favor or against kappa, Zwick established conditions under which kappa should not be used.

More generally, researchers may wonder how conditions can be established that guarantee the appropriateness of a particular agreement statistic in the sense of being a highly informative summary of the data. One way to establish such conditions is to incorporate the statistic into a probabilistic structure whose fit with the data can be quantitatively evaluated. If the model fits well, then conditions of appropriateness for its respective agreement parameter have been established. It is interesting that statistical models incorporating kappa as a model parameter confirm Zwick's claim for marginal homogeneity of the interrater contingency table in the sense that they satisfy marginal homogeneity (Agresti, 1989; Schuster, 2001). These models require even more stringent assumptions.

A modeling framework for interrater contingency tables that is quite flexible and in which rater reliability statistics can be defined is latent–class analysis. Before discussing latent–class models for rater agreement data, however, I review the general latent–class approach. For more detailed discussions of latent–class analysis, readers may want to consult Clogg (1995), Goodman (1974b), Goodman (1974a), Lazarsfeld and Henry (1968), or McCutcheon (1987).

6.3   Latent–Class Models for Categorical Variables

Consider three manifest categorical variables, A, B, and C. Let the number of levels of variables A, B, and C be denoted as I, J, K, respectively. The probability of observing a particular combination of levels of the three variables, $P(A = i, B = j, C = k)$, will also be denoted as π_{ijk}^{ABC}. In addition to the manifest variables, consider the categorical latent variable X. Each of the T levels of X represents a so–called latent–class.

Latent–class analysis is based on two fundamental assumptions about the relation between the latent and the manifest variables. First, the probabilities underlying the observed frequencies can be expressed as marginal probabilities of the joint distribution of the manifest and latent variables. In terms of a formula, this assumption is

$$\pi_{ijk}^{ABC} = \sum_{t=1}^{T} \pi_{ijkt}^{ABCX}. \tag{6.3}$$

The second assumption underlying latent–class models is that the joint probabilities of the manifest and latent variables satisfy the so–called local independence assumption (Lazarsfeld & Henry, 1968), that is, the manifest variables are independent given the level of the latent variable. This assumption implies that if the level of the latent variable is controlled, that is, statistically held constant, then the manifest variables display only residual variation. In this sense, the latent variable is said to explain the association among the manifest variables.

Applying the local independence assumption to the joint probabilities of the manifest and the latent variables yields the factorization

$$\pi_{ijkt}^{ABCX} = \pi_t^{X} \pi_{it}^{\bar{A}X} \pi_{jt}^{\bar{B}X} \pi_{kt}^{\bar{C}X}, \tag{6.4}$$

in which $\pi_{it}^{\bar{A}X} = P(A = i | X = t)$ and $\pi_{jt}^{\bar{B}X}$ and $\pi_{kt}^{\bar{C}X}$ are defined similarly.

An assumption similar to the local independence assumption is made in factor analysis for numerical data in which the latent factors account for the correlations among the observed variables (Harman, 1967). Thus, in factor analysis, zero partial correlations among

Figure 6.1: Illustration of the local independence assumption. The manifest variables A, B, and C are connected only via the latent variable X. Thus, controlling for X will allow the manifest variables to display only independent residual variation.

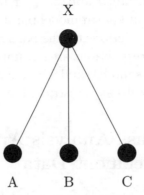

the manifest variables are assumed. This assumption is slightly less restrictive than the assumption of local independence. Figure 6.1 illustrates the local independence assumption graphically.

Combining the two fundamental assumptions underlying latent–class analysis yields

$$\pi_{ijk}^{ABC} = \sum_{t=1}^{T} \pi_t^X \pi_{it}^{\bar{A}X} \pi_{jt}^{\bar{B}X} \pi_{kt}^{\bar{C}X}. \tag{6.5}$$

This formula describes the probabilities underlying the observed frequencies, which are given on the left–hand side of Equation 6.5, in terms of the unobservable probabilities involving the latent variable, which are given on the right–hand side. All probabilities on the right–hand side of Equation 6.5 are considered model parameters. Fitting a latent–class model to data yields estimates of the model parameters based on estimates of the probabilities on the left–hand side of Equation 6.5. The latent–class model having three manifest variables is based on $IJK - (I + J + K - 2)T$ degrees of freedom.

A primary research question in latent–class analysis is the determination of the number of latent classes T. After the number of latent classes has been determined, the set of conditional response probabilities that pertain to the tth class, $\pi_{it}^{\bar{A}X}$, $i = 1, \ldots, I$, $\pi_{jt}^{\bar{B}X}$,

$j = 1, \ldots, J$ etc., then determines the substantive interpretation of this class. Again, this is analogous to factor analysis in which the interpretation of a factor is determined from the correlations between manifest variables and the factor, also referred to as factor loadings.

As the number of variables and/or the number of categories is increased, the number of unknown model parameters increases quickly. Therefore, imposing restrictions on the parameters is often desirable. A model in which such restrictions are not imposed is referred to as an unrestricted latent–class model, and a model in which the parameters are restricted is referred to as a restricted latent–class model.

6.4   Latent–Class Analysis Approaches to Rater Agreement Data

Two of the latent–class analysis approaches to reliability of nominal scales are (1) the response–error approach (Dillon & Mulani, 1984) and (2) the target–type approach (Schuster & Smith, 2002). In order to compare the two approaches, it will be helpful to consider a numerical example. Assume rater A, B, and C assign each of 194 Alzheimer patients to one of the phases briefly discussed at the beginning of this chapter: the forgetfulness phase, the confusional phase, or the dementia phase. Assume the frequencies given in Table 6.2 have been observed.

Table 6.2: Raw Frequencies

C_1	B_1	B_2	B_3	C_2	B_1	B_2	B_3	C_3	B_1	B_2	B_3
A_1	60	1	2	A_1	5	3	3	A_1	1	2	1
A_2	12	2	1	A_2	14	24	4	A_2	4	4	2
A_3	1	1	2	A_3	2	1	3	A_3	2	1	36

6.4.1   The Response–Error Approach

The response–error approach basically assumes the unrestricted latent–class model. The major difference to the unrestricted latent class model is that the response–error approach sets the number of latent classes equal to the number of rating categories. If this model fits well and there is a one–to–one correspondence between the latent classes and the manifest categories, then this model is very appealing because, in this case, the latent classes can be interpreted as the true target categories. If the response–error model fits well, the expected pattern of, say, rater A's response probability is expected to be

$$\pi_{11}^{\bar{A}X} = \text{high} \quad \pi_{21}^{\bar{A}X} = \text{low} \quad \pi_{31}^{\bar{A}X} = \text{low}$$

$$\pi_{12}^{\bar{A}X} = \text{low} \quad \pi_{22}^{\bar{A}X} = \text{high} \quad \pi_{32}^{\bar{A}X} = \text{low}$$

$$\pi_{13}^{\bar{A}X} = \text{low} \quad \pi_{23}^{\bar{A}X} = \text{low} \quad \pi_{33}^{\bar{A}X} = \text{high}.$$

For three raters, the response–error model is based on $df = r^3 - (3r - 2)r$. Fitting the response–error model to the data yields an excellent fit. The likelihood–ratio statistic has a value of 5.99, and the Pearson goodness–of–fit statistic is 6.92. Both statistics are based on $df - 6$. The fitted values of the response–error approach are given in Table 6.3. [1]

Table 6.3: Values From the Response–Error Approach Fitted to the Raw Frequencies in Table 6.2.

C_1	B_1	B_2	B_3	C_2	B_1	B_2	B_3
A_1	59.97	0.98	2.05	A_1	5.14	5.07	1.43
A_2	11.96	2.62	1.02	A_2	14.74	20.61	5.44
A_3	1.02	0.28	2.09	A_3	1.51	2.00	3.08

C_3	B_1	B_2	B_3
A_1	1.02	1.25	1.10
A_2	3.59	5.06	1.96
A_3	2.05	1.13	35.84

First, I can assume that each category's hit rate is constant within raters although it may vary across raters. The conditional probabilities of the latent–class model would satisfy the three restrictions

$$\pi_{11}^{\bar{A}X} = \pi_{22}^{\bar{A}X} = \pi_{33}^{\bar{A}X}$$
$$\pi_{11}^{\bar{B}X} = \pi_{22}^{\bar{B}X} = \pi_{33}^{\bar{B}X}$$
$$\pi_{11}^{\bar{C}X} = \pi_{22}^{\bar{C}X} = \pi_{33}^{\bar{C}X}.$$

[1]Although restricted response error models are not considered in this chapter, it should be pointed out that because of the relatively large number of model parameters, restrictions may lead to a simpler interpretation.

Second, I can assume that each category's hit–rate is constant across raters although it may vary within raters. The conditional probabilities of the latent–class model would satisfy the three restrictions

$$\begin{array}{ccc} \pi_{11}^{\bar{A}X} = & \pi_{11}^{\bar{B}X} = & \pi_{11}^{\bar{C}X} \\ \pi_{22}^{\bar{A}X} = & \pi_{22}^{\bar{B}X} = & \pi_{22}^{\bar{C}X} \\ \pi_{33}^{\bar{A}X} = & \pi_{33}^{\bar{B}X} = & \pi_{33}^{\bar{C}X}. \end{array}$$

Third, I can constrain the hit rates even further by imposing both constraints simultaneously, giving the single restriction

$$\begin{array}{ccc} \pi_{11}^{\bar{A}X} = & \pi_{22}^{\bar{A}X} = & \pi_{33}^{\bar{A}X} = \\ \pi_{11}^{\bar{B}X} = & \pi_{22}^{\bar{B}X} = & \pi_{33}^{\bar{B}X} = \\ \pi_{11}^{\bar{C}X} = & \pi_{22}^{\bar{C}X} = & \pi_{33}^{\bar{C}X}. \end{array}$$

6.4.2   Target–Type Approach

The target–type approach not only recognizes the latent variable X that represents a target's true category, but also the latent variable Y that indicates the target type. Only two types of targets will be assumed. First, targets can be obvious in the sense that raters readily identify the correct category. Second, targets can be ambiguous in the sense that raters essentially guess the category according to their category base rates.

To be able to express the probabilities with which each of the possible combinations of ratings occur, I assume local independence; that is, within each of the latent classes obtained from the factorial combination of the levels of X and Y, raters behave independently.[2] In this case, I obtain the latent–class model for two raters

$$\pi_{ij}^{AB} = \sum_{t=1}^{r} (\pi_{it0}^{\bar{A}XY} \pi_{jt0}^{\bar{B}XY} \pi_{t0}^{\bar{X}Y} \pi_0^{Y} + \pi_{it1}^{\bar{A}XY} \pi_{jt1}^{\bar{B}XY} \pi_{t1}^{\bar{X}Y} \pi_1^{Y}). \qquad (6.6)$$

The distinction between obvious and ambiguous targets is useful to justify restrictions on the conditional probabilities. Because for obvious cases, I expect both raters will likely identify the true category

---

[2]To avoid unnecessary complexity, the target–type approach will be presented for two raters. Generalizing the formulas to three raters is straightforward.

without problems, the hit rates for obvious targets are assumed to be equal to one for both raters, that is,

$$\pi_{it0}^{\bar{A}XY} = \begin{cases} 1 & \text{if } i = t,\ i = 1, \ldots, r \\ 0 & \text{else} \end{cases} \quad \text{and}$$

$$\pi_{jt0}^{\bar{B}XY} = \begin{cases} 1 & \text{if } j = t,\ j = 1, \ldots, r \\ 0 & \text{else} \end{cases}.$$

In addition, if raters are randomly classifying ambiguous targets, then the true category is irrelevant to the assignment process. Thus,

$$\pi_{it1}^{\bar{A}XY} = \pi_{i1}^{\bar{A}Y} \quad \text{and}$$
$$\pi_{jt1}^{\bar{B}XY} = \pi_{j1}^{\bar{B}Y}.$$

Incorporating these restrictions into the model equation yields

$$\pi_{ij}^{AB} = \delta_{ij}\gamma_0\tau_i + \gamma_1\phi_i^A\phi_j^B, \qquad (6.7)$$

in which $\delta_{ij} = 1$, if $i = j$ and $\delta_{ij} = 0$ as well as, $\gamma_0 = \pi_0^Y$, $\gamma_1 = \pi_1^Y$, $\tau_t = \pi_{t0}^{XY}$, $\phi_i^A = \pi_{i1}^{\bar{A}Y}$, and $\phi_j^B = \pi_{j1}^{\bar{B}Y}$.

The γ_0 parameter denotes the proportion of obvious targets for which raters readily identify the correct category and, therefore, necessarily agree. Therefore, γ_0 can be interpreted as the proportion of systematic agreement. Thus, the interpretation of γ_0 is as simple as the interpretation of the proportion of observed agreement, π_0. The proportion of systematic agreement, however, is not positively biased because it corrects for chance agreement. Thus, γ_0 is an attractive model–based reliability statistic. The τ_i parameters denote the proportions of obvious cases that belong to each of the categories.

The representation of a 3×3 interrater contingency table in Equation 6.8 may also be helpful in understanding how the probabilities are decomposed by the target–type model.

$$\begin{bmatrix} \pi_{11}^{AB} & \pi_{12}^{AB} & \pi_{13}^{AB} \\ \pi_{21}^{AB} & \pi_{22}^{AB} & \pi_{23}^{AB} \\ \pi_{31}^{AB} & \pi_{32}^{AB} & \pi_{33}^{AB} \end{bmatrix} = \gamma_0 \begin{bmatrix} \tau_1 & 0 & 0 \\ 0 & \tau_2 & 0 \\ 0 & 0 & \tau_3 \end{bmatrix} +$$

$$\gamma_1 \begin{bmatrix} \phi_1^A\phi_1^B & \phi_1^A\phi_2^B & \phi_1^A\phi_3^B \\ \phi_2^A\phi_1^B & \phi_2^A\phi_2^B & \phi_2^A\phi_3^B \\ \phi_3^A\phi_1^B & \phi_3^A\phi_2^B & \phi_3^A\phi_3^B \end{bmatrix} \quad (6.8)$$

For three raters, Equation 6.7 readily generalizes to

$$\pi_{ijk}^{ABC} = \delta_{ijk}\gamma_0\tau_i + \gamma_1\phi_i^A\phi_j^B\phi_k^C, \qquad (6.9)$$

in which $\delta_{ijk} = 1$ if $i = j = k$ and zero else.

Fitting the target–type model, Equation 6.9, to the data for three raters given in Table 6.2 yields an excellent fit. The likelihood–ratio statistic has a value of 13.30, and the value of Pearson's goodness–of–fit statistic is 13.21. Both statistics are based on $df = 17$. The fitted values of target–type approach are given in Table 6.4.

Table 6.4: Values From the Target–Type Approach Fitted to the Raw Frequencies in Table 6.2.

C_1	B_1	B_2	B_3	C_2	B_1	B_2	B_3
A_1	60.00	1.62	1.44	A_1	5.53	2.60	2.32
A_2	7.84	3.69	3.29	A_2	12.62	24.01	5.29
A_3	2.18	1.03	0.92	A_3	3.52	1.66	1.47

C_3	B_1	B_2	B_3
A_1	2.38	1.12	1.00
A_2	5.43	2.56	2.28
A_3	1.51	0.71	36.00

Before closing the presentation of the target–type model, I consider probability expressions that ignore the type of target. First, I consider the marginal probabilities with which a target truly belongs to the tth category. This probability can be expressed as

$$\begin{aligned} \pi_t^X &= \pi_{t0}^{\bar{X}Y}\pi_0^Y + \pi_{t1}^{\bar{X}Y}\pi_1^Y \\ &= \tau_t\gamma_0 + \pi_{t1}^{\bar{X}Y}\gamma_1. \end{aligned} \qquad (6.10)$$

Because the probabilities $\pi_{t1}^{\bar{X}Y}$ are unspecified in the target–type approach, the proportion of targets truly belonging to the tth category cannot be determined. Because probabilities necessarily are nonnegative, however, I can conclude that the second expression on the right–hand side of Equation 6.10 is nonnegative and therefore, $\pi_t^X \geq \tau_t\gamma_0$.

Second, I consider the conditional probabilities of the rater response at a particular level of the latent class ignoring the target type. This probability can be expressed as

$$\pi_{it}^{AX} = (\delta_{it}\tau_t\gamma_0 + \phi_i^A\pi_{t1}^{\bar{X}Y}\gamma_1)/\pi_t^X. \qquad (6.11)$$

In this expression, the probabilities π_t^X and $\pi_{t1}^{\bar{X}Y}$ are not available and therefore, $\pi_{it}^{\bar{A}X}$ cannot be determined from the target–type approach. Of course, the corresponding probabilities for the other raters are also not available.

6.5   Comparing the Response-Error Approach and the Target–Type Approach

Whereas both approaches distinguish between the latent and the manifest categories, only the target–type approach recognizes that targets may be either obvious or ambiguous. This conceptual difference renders the comparison of the two approaches more difficult because the information from the fitted models is only comparable if the distinction between obvious and ambiguous targets is ignored.

6.5.1   Parsimony

Model parsimony is a desirable characteristic because it limits the data requirements of the model. Of course, the model should also be sufficiently flexible to accommodate a wide variety of probabilistic structures that reflect the data–generating mechanism. Because a high degree of flexibility typically requires a high degree of model complexity, developing a flexible yet parsimonious model is hard to achieve. A particularly important aspect in the present context is whether a model can be used in the common situation in which classifications are available from only two judges.

The degree to which the response–error approach is more complex can be assessed by comparing the residual degrees of freedom of the two approaches. The response–error approach requires at least three raters assigning targets to three different categories. In case of three raters, the model has $r^3 - (3r - 2)r$ residual degrees of freedom. Thus, if $r = 3$, as is the case in this example, $df = 6$.

The target–type approach, however, requires only two raters assigning targets to three different categories. For two raters, the model is based on $df = (r - 1)^2 - r$; for three raters, the model has $r^3 - 4r + 2$ residual degrees of freedom. For this example, $df = 17$. As this example illustrates, the number of residual degrees of freedom is typically larger for the target–type approach, which reflects its greater parsimony.

6.5.2   Sensitivities

Sensitivity is an expression mainly used in medical research to denote the probability with which a test correctly identifies individuals that have the disease the test has been designed to detect. In other words, the sensitivity is the probability of a correct diagnosis among individuals who have the disease. Because the parameters $\pi_{ii}^{\bar{A}X}$, $\pi_{jj}^{\bar{B}X}$, and $\pi_{kk}^{\bar{C}X}$ indicate the probability with which the manifest category matches the latent class for targets belonging to this class, these probabilities are sometimes referred to as sensitivities. Alternatively, these probabilities can be referred to as hit rates. Clogg and Manning (1996) suggested that these probabilities can be used as reliability indices. The sensitivities, however, are not chance corrected in the sense of being zero if raters randomly guess.

For the response–error approach, the parameters $\pi_{ii}^{\bar{A}X}$, $\pi_{jj}^{\bar{B}X}$, and $\pi_{kk}^{\bar{C}X}$ belong to the standard output of computer programs that fit unrestricted latent–class models. For the data, example the sensitivities are

- For rater A: $\pi_{11}^{\bar{A}X} = 0.84, \pi_{22}^{\bar{A}X} = 0.75, \pi_{33}^{\bar{A}X} = 0.96$.

- For rater B: $\pi_{11}^{\bar{B}X} = 0.96, \pi_{22}^{\bar{B}X} = 0.51, \pi_{33}^{\bar{B}X} = 0.94$.

- For rater C: $\pi_{11}^{\bar{C}X} = 0.97, \pi_{22}^{\bar{C}X} = 0.73, \pi_{33}^{\bar{C}X} = 0.89$.

Note that these sensitivities are rater–specific as well as category–specific.

For the target–type approach, the sensitivities are not available because not all the relevant quantities on the right–hand side of Equation 6.11 can be determined.

6.5.3   Rater–specific Error Rates

Dillon and Mulani (1984) suggested that the overall error rate of, say, rater A should be determined as

$$\pi_1^X(\pi_{21}^{\bar{A}X} + \pi_{31}^{\bar{A}X}) + \pi_2^X(\pi_{12}^{\bar{A}X} + \pi_{32}^{\bar{A}X}) + \pi_3^X(\pi_{13}^{\bar{A}X} + \pi_{23}^{\bar{A}X}). \quad (6.12)$$

Note that this formula assumes three response categories. Generalizing this formula to more response categories is straightforward. The error rates for raters B and C are similarly defined.

To better understand this formula, consider the first of the three expressions that constitute Equation 6.12, that is, $\pi_1^X(\pi_{21}^{\bar{A}X} + \pi_{31}^{\bar{A}X})$. It is not difficult to see that this expression denotes the probability that given that target belongs to the first latent class, rater A will make an erroneous response, that is, classify the target into the second or third category. Similarly, the middle term in Equation 6.12 gives the probability that a target belonging to the second latent class will erroneously be classified, and the right–hand expression in Equation 6.12 gives the probability that a target belonging to the third latent class will erroneously be classified. Because the errors that pertain to each of these three probability expressions are mutually exclusive, the overall rater–specific error rate of rater A can be obtained from Equation 6.12.

For the response–error approach, calculating rater–specific error rates is simple. All relevant quantities are readily available from the standard output of a latent–class analysis program. For the data example, one obtains the error rates of rater A as 16.6%, of rater B as 21.6%, and of rater C as 14.0%.

For the target–type approach, calculating rater–specific error rates is not possible. Because the probabilities involved in Equation 6.12 all ignore the target type, they are not available from the target–type approach; see Equations 6.10 and 6.11.

6.5.4   Category–specific Error Rates

Category–specific error rates can be defined as the total probability with which at least one of the raters makes an erroneous classification. Using generic notation, this probability can be calculated from the addition rule of non–disjoint events (Arnold, 1990, p. 22) as

$$
\begin{aligned}
P\{(A=2, X=1) \text{ or } (B=2, X=1) \text{ or } (B=2, X=1)\} = \\
P(X=1)\{P(A=2|X=1) + P(B=2|X=1) + P(B=2|X=1) - \\
P(A=2, B=2|X=1) - P(A=2, C=2|X=1) - \\
P(B=2, C=2|X=1) + P(A=2, B=2, C=2|X=1)\},
\end{aligned}
$$

in which it has been assumed (for the sake of concreteness) that one is interested in the error rate of the second category given that the target truly belongs to the first category. Using the local independence assumption and switching to the previous notation shows that this probability is

$$\pi_1^X(\pi_{21}^{\bar{A}X}+\pi_{21}^{\bar{B}X}+\pi_{21}^{\bar{C}X}-\pi_{21}^{\bar{A}X}\pi_{21}^{\bar{B}X}-\pi_{21}^{\bar{A}X}\pi_{21}^{\bar{C}X}-\pi_{21}^{\bar{B}X}\pi_{21}^{\bar{C}X}+\pi_{21}^{\bar{A}X}\pi_{21}^{\bar{B}X}\pi_{21}^{\bar{C}X}).$$
$$(6.13)$$

Thus, the category–specific error rate, say, of the second category, is the total probability of an erroneous classifications into the second category given that it truly belongs to the first category. Of course, I can calculate such a category–specific error rate also for the case in which a target truly belongs to the third category.[3]

From application of the response–error approach, all relevant probabilities are readily available, and I obtain, the following error rates. Truly Stage 1 individuals are classified as Stage 2 in 6.6% of the cases and as Stage 3 in 1.6% of the cases. Individuals who are actually in Stage 2 are classified as Stage 1 in 20.2% of the cases and and as Stage 3 in 13.1% of the cases. Finally, Stage 3 individuals who are classified as in Stage 1 in 4.3% of the cases and as Stage Two in 3.7%.

Again, the target–type approach cannot be used to calculate the category–specific error rates because the relevant probabilities can not be expressed when ignoring the target type. Note, however, that the target–type approach offers category–specific information in terms of the τ_i parameters, which pertain to obvious cases only.

6.5.5   Overall Reliability Index

Although the response–error approach provides rater–specific and cate-gory–specific information, it does not provide an overall summary measure of the rating quality. The target–type approach, however, readily yields the reliability statistic γ_0. For the specific data set considered in this chapter, I obtain $\gamma_0 = 0.57$.

---

[3]Note that Dillon and Mulani (1984) appear to have applied the addition rule for mutually exclusive events when calculating the category–specific error rates. On p. 452, they calculate the probability given in Equation 6.13 as $\pi_1^X(\pi_{21}^{\bar{A}X} + \pi_{21}^{\bar{B}X} + \pi_{21}^{\bar{C}X})$.

Table 6.5: Feature Comparison of the Response–Error and the Target–Type Approaches

	Response–Error Approach	Target–Type Approach
Parsimony	no	yes
Sensitivity	yes	no
Rater–specific error rates	yes	no
Category–specific error rates	yes	no
Overall reliability	no	yes

6.6 Discussion

Table 6.5 gives a summary of the features of both latent–class approaches to analyzing rater agreement data. It is remarkable that both approaches provide mainly complementary information. The strength of the response–error approach lies in its potential to produce very specific information about the raters as well as the rating categories. This information can be very useful when developing or revising a classification system or when training raters.

The main virtue of the target–type approach is to provide an overall chance–corrected reliability statistic of the rating quality. The fact that the target–type approach can not produce very specific information about the raters or the categories is certainly related to its parsimony. Because of its parsimony, however, the target–type approach is applicable to all interrater contingency tables except for dichotomous classifications of two raters.

References

Agresti, A. (1989). An agreement model with kappa as parameter. *Statistics & Probability Letters*, *7*, 271–273.

Arnold, S. F. (1990). *Mathematical statistics*. Englewood Cliffs, NJ: Prentice Hall.

Bennett, E. M., Alpert, R., & Goldstein, A. C. (1954). Communications through limited response questioning. *Public Opinion Quaterly*, *18*, 303–308.

Brennan, R. L., & Prediger, J. D. (1981). Coefficient kappa: Some uses, misuses, and alternatives. *Educational and Psychological Measurement, 41*, 687–699.

Brown, W. (1910). Some experimental results in the correlation of mental abilities. *British Journal of Psychology, 3*, 296–322.

Clogg, C. C. (1995). Latent class models. In G. Arminger, C. C. Clogg, & E. Sobel (Eds.), *Handbook of statistical modeling for the social and behavioral sciences* (pp. 311–359). New York: Plenum Press.

Clogg, C. C., & Manning, W. D. (1996). Assessing reliability of categorical measurements using latent class models. In A. von Eye & C. C. Clogg (Eds.), *Categorical variables in developmental research* (pp. 169–182). San Diego, CA: Academic Press.

Cohen, J. (1960). A coefficient of agreement for nominal tables. *Educational and Psychological Measurement, 20*, 37–46.

Conger, A. J. (1980). Integration and generalization of kappas for multiple raters. *Psychological Bulletin, 88*, 322–328.

Dillon, W. R., & Mulani, N. (1984). A probabilistic latent class model for assessing inter-judge reliability. *Multivariate Behavioral Research, 19*, 438–458.

Feinstein, A. R., & Cicchetti, D. V. (1990). High agreement but low kappa: I. The problems of two paradoxes. *Journal of Clinical Epidemiology, 43*(6), 543–549.

Fleiss, J. L. (1971). Measuring nominal scale agreement among many raters. *Psychological Bulletin, 76*, 378–382.

Goodman, L. A. (1974a). The analysis of systems of qualitative variables when some of the variables are unobservable. Part I: A modified latent structure approach. *American Journal of Sociology, 79*(5), 281–361.

Goodman, L. A. (1974b). Exploratory latent structure analysis using both identifiable and unidentifiable models. *Biometrika, 61*(2), 215–231.

Goodman, L. A., & Kruskal, W. H. (1954). Measures of association for cross classifications. *Journal of the American Statistical Association, 49*, 732–764.

Grove, W. M., Andreasen, N. C., McDonald-Scott, P., Keller, M. B., & Shapiro, R. W. (1981). Reliability studies of psychiatric diagnosis: theory and practice. *Archives of General Psychiatry, 38*, 408–413.

Guggenmoos-Holzmann, I. (1993). How reliable are chance-corrected measures of agreement? *Statistics in Medicine, 12*, 2191–2205.

Guggenmoos-Holzmann, I. (1996). The meaning of kappa: probabilistic concepts of reliability and validity revisited. *Journal of Clinical Epidemiology, 49*(7), 775–782.

Guggenmoos-Holzmann, I., & Vonk, R. (1998). Kappa-like indices of observer agreement viewed from a latent class perspective. *Statistics in Medicine, 17*, 797–812.

Gulliksen, H. (1950). *Theory of mental tests.* New York: Wiley.

Guttman, L. (1946). The test-retest reliability of qualitative data. *Psychometrika, 11*(2), 81–95.

Harman, H. H. (1967). *Modern factor analysis* (2nd ed.). Chicago: University of Chicago Press.

Lazarsfeld, P. F., & Henry, N. W. (1968). *Latent structure analysis.* Boston: Houghton Mifflin.

Maxwell, A. E. (1977). Coefficients of agreement between observers and their interpretation. *British Journal of Psychiatry, 130*, 79–83.

McCutcheon, A. L. (1987). *Latent class analysis.* Newbury Park, CA: Sage.

Perrault, W. D., & Leigh, L. E. (1989). Reliability of nominal data based on qualitative judgments. *Journal of Marketing Research, 26*, 135–148.

Reisberg, B., Ferris, S. H., de Leon, M. J., & Crook, T. (1982). The global deterioration scale for assessment of primary degenerative dementia. *American Journal of Psychiatry, 139*(9), 1136–1139.

Schuster, C. (2001). Kappa as a parameter of a symmetry model for rater agreement. *Journal of Educational and Behavioral Statistics, 26*(3), 331–342.

Schuster, C., & Smith, D. A. (2002). Indexing systematic rater agreement with a latent class model. *Psychological Methods, 7*(3), 384–395.

Scott, W. A. (1955). Reliability of content analysis: The case of nominal scale coding. *Public Opinion Quarterly, 19*(3), 321–325.

Shrout, P. E., Spitzer, R. L., & Fleiss, J. L. (1987). Quantification of agreement in psychiatric diagnosis revisited. *Archives of*

General Psychiatry, *44*, 172–177.

Spearman, C. (1910). Correlation calculated from faulty data. *British Journal of Psychology, 3*, 271–295.

Spitznagel, E. L., & Helzer, J. E. (1985). A proposed solution to the base rate problem in the kappa statistic. *Archives of General Psychiatry, 42*, 725–728.

Zwick, R. (1988). Another look at interrater agreement. *Psychological Bulletin, 103*(3), 374–378.

7

Dynamical Systems Modeling in Aging Research

Steven M. Boker [1]
University of Notre Dame

Toni L. Bisconti
University of New Hampshire

Dynamical systems methods involve thinking about and modeling change in repeated observations data in such a way that deterministic relationships between the value of a variable and how rapidly it is changing can be estimated. These types of models test theories about the regularity of observed changes in such a way that independent contributions of self-regulation and exogenous influences can be differentiated. A central notion in dynamical systems is that of stable equilibrium: a particular value or set of values to which a system will return if an external influence pushes it away from that equilibrium. We illustrate some example dynamical systems models using physical analogs, discuss two specific methods for estimating model parameters, and perform an example analysis on a data set from an occasion–intensive study of bereavement in recent widows. Evidence is presented that supports a differentiation between long–term and short–term resiliency in self–regulation of an overall mental health construct in this sample of widows.

[1] Funding for this work was provided in part by NIH Grant No. 1R29 AG14983. Correspondence may be addressed to Steven M. Boker, Department of Psychology, The University of Notre Dame, Notre Dame, IN 46556, USA; e–mail sent to sboker@nd.edu; or browsers pointed to http://www.nd.edu/~sboker.

7.1   Introduction

The study of aging inherently involves the study of change. Functions
such as perceptual acuity, flexibility, and strength tend to decline
with age. Older adults tend to perform more poorly on cognitive
tests of problem solving and memory than do younger adults. However, the study of aging involves much more than just the study of
declining function within individual or sample mean differences between younger and older adults. For instance, the likelihood of some
life events, such as graduation from school, marriage, or the birth
of a child, is greater for younger adults. The likelihood of other life
events, such as retirement, birth of a grandchild, or death of a spouse,
is greater for older adults. How we adapt and regulate our behavior
in response to the changing nature of life events defines one aspect
of the aging process. Another question of interest involves how this
type of self–regulation in response to external events might be affected by slower term changes in physical, perceptual, and cognitive
performance. This question could be framed as one of age–related
changes in resilience.

Adaptation and regulation are in themselves types of change. But
these forms of change are not well suited to study using traditional
statistical methods such as ANOVA analysis of mean differences or
longitudinal techniques such as linear mixed effects models or mixed
effects growth curve analysis. ANOVA techniques are designed to
focus on mean differences between groups and, as a result, will not
separate intraindividual changes due to resilient adaptation from fluctuations due to unreliability of the measurement instrument. Linear
mixed effects models of longitudinal studies of adaptation are better
than ANOVA designs in that they allow for individual differences in
the way that people change. But the change that is assumed is linear
change. Thus, although individuals may differ from each other in the
way they change, an individual's change at any time t is exactly the
same as that individual's change at any other time. Linear intraindividual change over the long term is implausible, such that in the
absence of outside effects, it leads to unbounded outcomes. That is
to say if we were to be measuring happiness, an early life increase
in happiness would predict a lifelong increase in happiness. Psychological constructs are, as a rule, bounded. Thus, in the happiness

example, there is a practical upper and lower limit to how happy a person can be. The only bounded linear model is one in which the slope is zero; in other words, there is no predicted change.

Mixed effects growth curve models do an even better job of accounting for adaptation and regulation because they allow both interindividual differences in change as well as change in intraindividual change. Thus, mixed effects growth curve models allow for two types of differences in change. First, people may differ from one another in the way that they change. Second, people may be changing at one rate at time t and at another rate at a later time. Growth curves are theoretically more appealing than linear models because there are many simple curves that are unbounded. One curve that is commonly used is a negative exponential decay to asymptote: the curve implied by an autoregressive discrete time model with an autoregressive coefficient between 0 and 1. Similar curves have been used to model a variety of developmental phenomena, notably physical growth in height. Thus, models of this type have come to be known as growth curve models. But in general, curves may be formalized in a variety of different ways. For instance, polynomial curves have been used as an alternative to negative exponential curves. But polynomial models are plausible as growth curves for psychological phenomena only in the short term; in the long term, they are unbounded except in the uninteresting case when all parameters are zero.

A mixed effects growth curve can provide a useful method for modeling a process that evolves reasonably independently over a chosen time span and, like growth in height, starts at a known time and is expected to reach a steady asymptotic value after which there is little or no change. There are two assumptions in the previous sentence that reduce the desirability of growth curves as models of adaptation and self–regulation. The first assumption we will call the *assumption of equivalence of initial conditions*. That is, all individuals are assumed to start at a known time and state with respect to the evolution of the process in question. Modeling physical growth using mixed effects growth curves has an implied assumption that all individuals can be aligned to some reference time, typically birth or conception.

Although the assumption of equivalence of initial conditions poses a well–studied problem for modeling a developmental phenomenon that evolves slowly over a lifetime, it is often not clear how one should time–align data from measurements of short–term fluctuations presumed to be due to a self–regulatory process. Some individuals may enter an experiment "on an upswing" and others "on a downswing." Consider the data from 50 simulated individuals plotted in Fig. 7.1. At the first occasion of measurement, individuals differ in both the level and slope with which they enter the study. During the study, there are individual differences in the change in slope. Many individuals with a positive slope between Occasion 1 and Occasion 2 have a negative slope between Occasion 2 and Occasion 3. Others with a positive initial slope continue to have a positive slope. Many individuals with a negative slope in the first interval have a positive slope during the second interval. If we fit these data with a mixed effects polynomial growth curve, we would find large individual differences in intercepts, slopes, and curvatures. But the fixed effects, the mean between–subjects intercept, slope, and curvature would all be indistinguishable from zero.

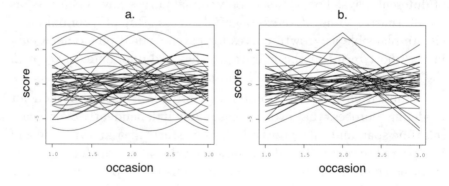

Figure 7.1: (a) Continuous data from 50 simulated self–regulating individuals and (b) a three–occasion panel study measuring those same individuals with perfect reliability.

In fact, all of the data in Fig. 7.1 are simulated from the same equation with no individual differences in parameters. The only differences between the individual curves in Fig. 7.1a are differences in initial conditions, that is, differences in the score and its instantaneous slope at the first occasion of measurement. Growth curves confound individual differences in initial conditions and individual differences in parameters. It is important to be able to distinguish between these two possible sources of individual differences if we cannot assume that observed individual differences in initial conditions come from equivalent portions of the hypothesized growth curve.

The second implicit assumption made when fitting a mixed effects growth curve model to longitudinal measurements is that the growth process in question evolves relatively independently from short–term changes in the environment. We will call this the *assumption of independence of evolution*. As an illustration of how violations of the assumption of independent evolution might affect a growth curve model, consider the simulated data presented in Fig. 7.2.

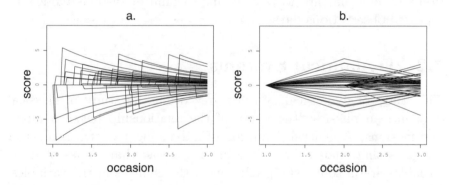

Figure 7.2: (a) Continuous data from 50 simulated self–regulating individuals who each had one random perturbation during the study and (b) a three–occasion panel study measuring those same individuals with perfect reliability.

The 50 simulated individuals' data shown in Fig. 7.2a all have exactly the same initial conditions and self–regulate according to the same simple negative exponential decay to equilibrium. There are no interindividual differences in either initial conditions or parameters. However, each individual experiences one perturbation during the study at a random time and of a random size. Once the data are sampled at three occasions of measurement and fit with a mixed effects polynomial model, we find that the fixed effects for level, slope, and curvature are all not significantly different than zero. However, this analysis does show significant individual differences in both slope and curvature. A violation of the assumption of independence of evolution again leads the mixed effects growth curve model to the wrong conclusion.

There are alternatives to growth curve modeling of longitudinal data in which one may relax both the assumption of equivalence of initial conditions and the assumption of independence of evolution. State–space time series modeling (Jones, 1993) and stochastic differential equations modeling (Singer, 1998; Oud & Jansen, 2000) represent two related methods for attacking this problem. This chapter focuses on a third alternative: continuous time differential equations modeling. All of these alternative methods are parameter estimation methods that are ways of fitting dynamical systems models to repeated observations data.

7.2   Dynamical Systems

The study of dynamical systems grew from the study of classical dynamics in physics: the study of the relationship between forces and motions. A general definition of a dynamical system is a set of variables that change over time in such a way that values of these variables are in some way predictive of the changes in the variables. Change can be usefully formulated as a derivative with respect to time: the instantaneous rate of change in a variable. If one plots the values of a variable x against time, then the instantaneous rate of change in x is the slope of the curve at a time t. The derivative of x with respect to t is sometimes written as dx/dt or alternatively as $\dot{x}$.

To understand the concept of a derivative, it is useful to consider a familiar dynamical system, for example, an automobile. If you are sitting in an automobile at rest, its position is not changing. The derivative of the automobile's position x with respect to time t is its velocity, $\dot{x}$. At rest, the velocity of the automobile is zero, $\dot{x} = 0$. If the automobile is traveling at some velocity, say 40 km per hour, one can read the instantaneous derivative of the automobile's position with respect to time from the convenient first derivative indicator on the dashboard: the speedometer.

Why do we speak of instantaneous derivatives? Because the velocity of the automobile may be changing from moment to moment. The change in velocity is acceleration (or deceleration), the second derivative of the position with respect to time, and is either written d^2x/dt^2 or $\ddot{x}$. The second derivative of a variable is the change with respect to time of the variable's change with respect to time. That is quite a mouthful, but if we substitute velocity and acceleration into the previous phrase, it might become more intuitive: The acceleration is the change in velocity with respect to time.

The accelerator and brake pedal provide means to change the velocity of the automobile. However, neither the accelerator nor the brake pedal is a direct linear control of acceleration the way that the speedometer is a direct linear readout of the first derivative of position with respect to time. The accelerator changes the equilibrium velocity of the car. That is, if the automobile is at a stop on a level road, depressing and holding the accelerator of the automobile will result in the car traveling at a fixed velocity, perhaps 40 km per hour, after some amount of time has passed. Before depressing the accelerator, the equilibrium velocity of the automobile is zero. Immediately after depressing the accelerator, the new equilibrium velocity is 40 km per hour. But the automobile's velocity doesn't instantaneously change to 40 km per hour. One can view the speedometer and see that it takes some time for the car's velocity to reach the new equilibrium. The automobile has a mechanism that regulates its velocity in response to the depression of the accelerator.

The analysis of repeated observations of a system from a dynamical systems perspective provides a way to understand the mechanical aspects of the automobile by observing its position over a repeated number of observations. If the automobile were always at rest, no matter how many measurements were taken of its position, we would be able to say nothing about its mechanisms. Similarly, repeatedly observing the automobile traveling exactly 40 km per hour tells us only that it is capable of traveling at this speed; it tells us nothing about the capabilities of its velocity regulation mechanism. However, if a driver is asked to press the accelerator all the way down while measurements of the automobile's position are taken, we may be able to infer important characteristics of the velocity regulation system of that automobile from analysis of changes in velocity with respect to time.

In general, repeated observations of a system at equilibrium are uninformative. To understand a self–regulating system, it is important to model repeated observations of the system as it is responding and adapting to an external change. For instance, from repeated observations of the system displayed in Fig. 7.2, it is possible to test the hypothesis that the individual curves are self–regulating according to the same mechanism. To understand a self–regulation phenomenon such as resilience in aging, it is necessary to have many observations of each individual and to time these observations to occur after a life event so that the adaptive response to the life event can be observed.

There are many metaphors, both explicit and implied, that are commonly applied to psychological phenomena and have their roots in intuitions derived from the dynamics of physical objects. Earlier in this chapter, we referred to participants entering an experiment on an upswing or on a downswing. The use of these phrases implies that the psychological variable of interest has properties like a swing. How well do such intuitive physical metaphors hold? One way to test them is to formalize the physical metaphor into a dynamical systems model and test how well that model's predictions fit empirical data. Dynamical systems models for physical systems are well known and widely studied. These models generally take the form of a differential equation, that is, an equation that formalizes predictions about the interrelationships between variables and their derivatives.

7.3   Modeling Dynamical Systems

Dynamical systems are often modeled as differential equations. Differential equations are simply equations that make predictions about instantaneous change. Thus, if we were to write a differential equation

$$\dot{y} = b_1 \tag{7.1}$$

for a chosen variable y and constant b_1, then the prediction is that change is constant. This is a model for a linear growth curve; the slope for any person does not change. If we integrate this equation, we would find the integral equation

$$y(t) = b_0 + b_1 t \tag{7.2}$$

where $y(t)$ is the value of y at time t and b_0 and b_1 are the familiar intercept and slope of the linear growth curve. The differential equation form has two differences from the integral equation form: (a) Change is explicitly modeled as the outcome variable in the differential form, and (b) there is a constant, b_0, representing the intercept in the integral form.

Explicitly modeling change can have advantages when building and interpreting models. For instance, consider the example of the automobile. The differential form, "We are currently traveling at 40 km per hour," is a different way of expressing the integral form, "We started at the stoplight at the intersection of Elm Street and in the intervening 10 min have traveled 4 km." Of course, sometimes it is important to phrase this model of travel so that the position when time is zero is made explicit. If we wish to know where we are with respect to Elm Street, the differential form doesn't help. But if we are less interested in where the car is than how the car works, the differential form focuses on information of use; Elm Street is literally neither here nor there when it comes to understanding the workings of the automobile engine.

In the automobile example of the differential form in Equation 7.1, Elm Street is considered to be an initial condition. That is, if we know how automobiles operate (our model predicts that they always travel at constant velocity b_1), then we can plug in Elm Street and integrate forward in time t minutes and find out what the trajectory is for a particular instance of automobile and position on the planet. These trajectories are what are estimated by growth curve models. Dynamical systems models are focused on classes of trajectories that share the same dynamic (in our example, "the class of cars that travel at a constant velocity of b_1 miles per hour"). In the case where the true dynamic is a linear trajectory, there is no difference in the parameters representing change (b_1) as estimated by growth curve modeling or differential equations modeling. Parameter differences between the two estimation procedures can become substantial in more complicated models when the appropriate reference time $t = 0$ is not known and may differ between individuals.

We discuss two types of linearity in this chapter. Most psychologists and gerontologists are familiar with linearity in the context of a growth curve (i.e., integral) model. That is to say, when the predicted trajectory is a straight line, then the model for growth is considered to be linear. But a differential equation may be linear, whereas its integral is not. Thus, a simple linear differential equation may produce complicated nonlinear trajectories. This is, from a practical model–fitting perspective, one of the advantages of linear differential models: Fitting an equivalent continuous time integral model will, in almost all cases, require nonlinear constraints on the parameters. The next example model illustrates how linearity in a differential equation does not necessarily imply linear trajectories.

7.3.1   Proportional Change

The constant change model shown in Equation 7.1 is a poor model for phenomena that involve adaptation or self–regulation; change occurs at the same rate regardless of the state of the system. The simplest model in which change is dependent on the state of the variables in the system is one in which the derivative of y with respect to time is proportional to the value of y, that is,

$$\dot{y} = b_1 y \tag{7.3}$$

where b_1 is a constant. This model will generate trajectories similar to those shown in Fig. 7.2a when b_1 is a negative number. At one randomly chosen time for each trajectory in Fig. 7.2a, a random number was added to the value of y, and then the dynamic of Equation 7.3 operated to cause the value of y to decay exponentially to zero. Although Equation 7.3 is linear, the trajectories it generates are nonlinear, that is, negative exponential curves. This is because the integral form of Equation 7.3 is nonlinear,

$$y(t) = b_0 e^{b_1 t} \tag{7.4}$$

where b_0 is the value of y when $t = 0$ and b_1 is a constant. The choice of exactly how to define the time $t = 0$ now becomes critical. One way that this problem has been attacked is by estimating only the short–term dynamics using what are called state–space models, models that estimate their parameters from short bursts of discrete observations. We return to state–space modeling in a moment, but first we consider Equation 7.3 in the context of the automobile example.

What type of automobile is described by Equation 7.3 when $b_1 <$ 0? If the position y is nonzero at some time t, then the velocity will be proportional to y and in the direction toward $y = 0$. As time goes on, the auto will approach $y = 0$. But as y becomes closer to zero, the velocity will also become closer to zero. We might name this automobile the "Homing Pigeon", because whenever it is taken from rest at $y = 0$, it adjusts its velocity in such a way that it smoothly comes back to rest at $y = 0$ after some time has elapsed. Differential equations of this type are said to have a fixed point attractor or, alternatively, a stable fixed point equilibrium.

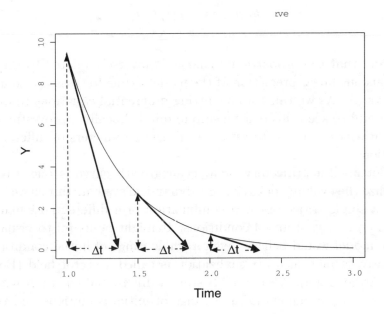

Figure 7.3: Negative exponential trajectory in which the slope of y at time t is proportional to the value of y at time t. Note that the linear prediction at each time t is that the trajectory will cross 0 after exactly the same elapsed time Δt, no matter what the value of y at time t.

A single trajectory generated from Equation 7.3 by giving an initial condition of $y(0) = 10$ is plotted in Fig. 7.3. It can be observed from this plot that the instantaneous slope at a chosen time t is re-

lated to the value of $y(t)$ by comparing the three right triangles in
the figure. The vertical side of each triangle is the value of $y(t)$, the
hypotenuse of the triangle has the slope of the trajectory at time t.
The horizontal side of each triangle is the interval of time that would
elapse before the trajectory would cross zero if the slope at time t was
constant over the interval Δt. Note that Δt is the same no matter
which time t is chosen. Since the slope at time t is

$$\dot{y}(t) = y(t)/\Delta t \tag{7.5}$$

and Δt is independent of t, we can substitute Equation 7.3 into Equation 7.5,

$$
\begin{aligned}
b_1 y(t) &= y(t)/\Delta t \\
b_1 &= 1/\Delta t
\end{aligned}
\tag{7.6}
$$

and find that the proportional change is inversely related to the instantaneous linear prediction of the model's time to cross the equilibrium value. As we think about fitting differential equations to data,
it is useful to keep this relationship in mind: Locally linear estimates
of derivatives can lead to estimates of the parameters of differential
equations.

Plotting the trajectory or a mean growth curve is one way to
visualize the evolving behavior of a dynamical system. But as we have
seen, a single trajectory is a combination of a differential equation
model and a set of initial conditions. It might be useful to visualize
how a model would behave given a whole range of initial conditions.
One way to plot such a visualization is called a vector field (Boker
& McArdle, 2005). Vector fields start a differential equation with a
given set of parameters using a range of initial conditions and then
allow it to evolve for a short interval of time.

An example vector field plot of Equation 7.3 is plotted in Fig. 7.4
for a range of initial conditions of y and time. The arrows within each
row are identical, so it is clear that the change in y is not dependent
on the value of t. On the other hand, the arrows in each column are
different from each other. Thus, the change in y is dependent on the
value of y. One may trace a variety of trajectories through this space
by simply following the arrows. At the base of each arrow is a new
initial condition, and at the head of the arrow is where the system is
expected to be a short interval of time later.

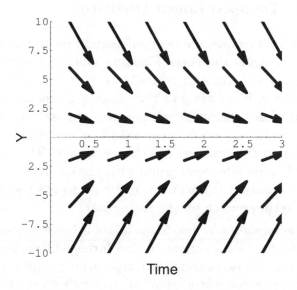

Figure 7.4: Vector field plot of Equation 7.3 under a range of initial conditions of time and y.

In the next section, we leave our metaphoric automobile behind, but before we do, let us consider how little control over the automobile we've modeled so far. One model for the automobile predicted a constant velocity b_1, and the other model returned home to an equilibrium. Both autos were traveling in only one dimension; there was a speed control, but no steering wheel to control turning on a two-dimensional plane. This chapter deals only with one-dimensional dynamics. Dynamical systems involving more than one dimension are interesting and can be fit by the modeling procedures we outline (see, e.g., Hubbard & West, 1991, 1995; Kaplan & Glass, 1995, for introductions to higher dimensional systems of differential equations). An example of a two-dimensional proportional change dynamical systems model applied to cognitive aging can be found in McArdle and Hamagami (chap. 3, this volume).

7.3.2   The Damped Linear Oscillator

One example of a simple, physical self–regulating system is the thermostat that controls the central heating and air conditioning in a house. The way a thermostat typically works is by the use of thresholds. Suppose it is winter and the weather is uncomfortably cold outside. Left alone, the house will lose heat through the walls to the environment until the indoor temperature is the same as outside in a way similar to the proportional change model. That is, the temperature will come into equilibrium with the environment. But the outdoors temperature is uncomfortably cold to the residents of the house, and so they switch on the thermostat.

When the temperature inside the house is below a predetermined threshold, the furnace is activated. The furnace blows warm air into the rooms of the house causing the temperature to quickly rise. Soon the temperature is too warm, above an upper threshold temperature, and the furnace is turned off. The house continues to lose heat to the environment, cooling off until the lower threshold is reached and the process begins again. Figure 7.5 plots the trajectory of the temperature over time. It is evident that this type of thermostat leads to cyclic changes in the temperature of the room, an oscillation.

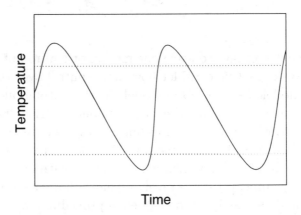

Figure 7.5: Oscillating trajectory of temperature over time for a thermostat with upper and lower thresholds controlling a furnace heating a house on a cold day.

If the thresholds are too far apart, the oscillation in the temperature will be uncomfortable for the residents of the house; first, it will be too warm and then too cold, and so forth. As the thresholds become close together, the frequency of oscillation increases, leading the furnace to be frequently turning on and off. Perhaps we can design a better thermostat by getting rid of the thresholds and instead using a differential equation model. From the perspective of creating and fitting models for psychological function, a move away from thresholds is also appealing because thresholds are inherently nonlinear and thus provide unwelcome complications when estimating parameters and evaluating model fit.

To design this thermostat, consider the temperature trajectory in Fig. 7.5. When the temperature is above or below threshold seems to be when the trajectory is most curved. This makes sense, since when the temperature is moving farther away from our preferred equilibrium, we would wish it to "turn around" and head back to equilibrium. We could rephrase this as wanting the slope of the trajectory to change sign; that is, a positive slope should change to negative when the temperature is greater than equilibrium, and a negative slope should change to positive when the temperature is below equilibrium. Thus, the change in the slope, in other words the second derivative of temperature, should be of opposite sign to the difference from equilibrium.

Now, let us formalize the preceding paragraph into a differential equations model and see what happens. If the difference between the temperature of the room and the desired equilibrium is y and the second derivative of the temperature is $\ddot{y}$, then suppose

$$\ddot{y} = \eta y \qquad (7.7)$$

where η is a constant such that $\eta < 0$. Then, the greater the difference is between equilibrium and the current temperature, the greater the curvature is in the trajectory of temperature. Also, because $\eta < 0$, the curvature will always bend the slope so that it moves back toward equilibrium. Figure 7.6 plots the result of this system. Although we are now using a simple one-parameter linear model for our thermostat instead of nonlinear thresholds, it is clear that we still have an oscillation. In fact, Equation 7.7 describes the behavior of an undamped linear oscillator. The oscillation is undamped, meaning that

given a set of initial conditions, the oscillation will continue indefi-
nitely. Note the initial conditions shown in Fig. 7.6; at time $t = 0$,
the starting value of the displacement from equilibrium is $y(0) = 0$,
but its first derivative is positive $\dot{y}(0) > 0$. This system requires two
initial conditions: a displacement and a slope.

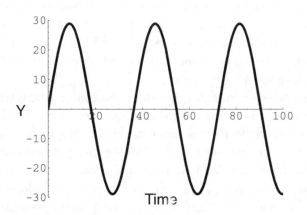

Figure 7.6: Oscillating trajectory of temperature over time for a thermostat controlling heating and air conditioning (Equation 7.7).

Figure 7.7 plots a vector field for the undamped linear oscillator
for a range of initial conditions of y and its first derivative $\dot{y}$. The
solid line in the form of a circle represents one trajectory through
this vector field. Note that there is a relationship between the value
of y and $\dot{y}$ such that when the value of y is near zero, the arrows are
nearly horizontal, and when the value of $\dot{y}$ is near zero, the arrows
are nearly vertical. If we consider what the arrows mean, this tells us
something important about the system. A horizontal arrow means
that when y is near zero, after the system has evolved for a short
time, the value of $\dot{y}$ hasn't changed. For that initial condition, there
is little change in the first derivative. Another way of saying this is
that when $y \approx 0$, the second derivative, $\ddot{y} \approx 0$. If we look back at the
plot of the trajectory over time in Fig. 7.6, we can verify this: When
y is near zero, there is little curvature in the trajectory. We can also
verify this in Equation 7.7. If $y = 0$, then $\ddot{y} = 0$.

Vertical arrows mean that there is little change in y over a short interval of time. If y doesn't change, then the slope of the trajectory must be near zero. In fact, the vertical arrows appear when $\dot{y}$ is near zero. Also note that there are two places where the circle in Fig. 7.7 crosses the horizontal axis (i.e. when $\dot{y}$ is zero), and these are when the value of y is at its maximum and its minimum. This can be verified in Fig. 7.6 by noting that the slope of the trajectory is zero when the value of y is at its maximum or minimum. Similarly, the value of $\dot{y}$ is at its maximum and minimum when $y = 0$.

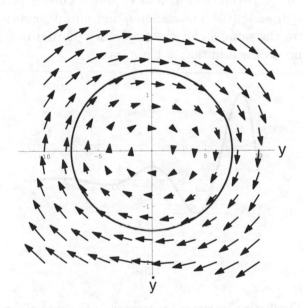

Figure 7.7: Vector field of Equation 7.7 for a range of initial conditions of y and $\dot{y}$. The circle plots the values of y and $\dot{y}$ for one trajectory. A trajectory plot of the relationship of the derivatives of a curve to one another is called a *phase portrait*.

Returning to our task of building a self–regulating thermostat, let us attempt to damp the oscillations so that the system tends toward a stable, fixed-point equilibrium after some time has elapsed. Consider that slope of the trajectory of the oscillation in Fig. 7.6 is at a maximum and the curvature is at a minimum when the trajectory is near the desired equilibrium ($y = 0$). Perhaps we can use this fact to reduce the change in temperature when the temperature is near the desired equilibrium. We can modify Equation 7.7 to make the second derivative of y also proportional to the first derivative of y,

$$\ddot{y} = \eta y + \zeta \dot{y} \tag{7.8}$$

where ζ is a constant such that $\zeta < 0$. Since the slope is high when y is near zero, this damping will have the maximum effect near the desired equilibrium. Figure 7.8 plots the trajectory resulting from a chosen pair of parameters η and ζ and a chosen pair of initial conditions $y(0)$ and $\dot{y}(0)$. The chosen η and initial conditions for this trajectory are the same as for the trajectory plotted in Fig. 7.6; the only difference is the addition of damping.

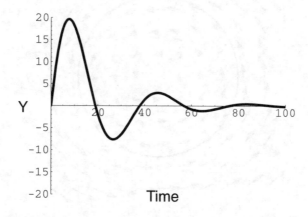

Figure 7.8: Oscillating trajectory of temperature over time for a thermostat controlling heating and air conditioning according to Equation 7.8.

Figure 7.9 plots a vector field over a range of initial conditions for the damped linear oscillator from Equation 7.8. Note that the solid line phase portrait trajectory no longer traces a circle, but now traces a spiral in to the equilibrium value of $y = 0$ and $\dot{y} = 0$. If some external momentary influence suddenly changed the temperature in the room to be something other than equilibrium, we could think of this as moving to a new, nonzero, spot on this vector field. If the system were then left alone, it would come back to equilibrium after a few oscillations.

We have successfully modeled a simple thermostat that exhibits behavior similar to a nonlinear threshold thermostat and also has the desirable characteristic of approaching a chosen equilibrium temperature. The purpose of this exercise was twofold: (a) to demonstrate the process of thinking about and designing models for change from a dynamical systems perspective, and (b) to familiarize the reader with the simplest forms of linear differential equations. It is important to remember that these simple models are not the only dynamical systems models for self–regulation or developmental change. The characteristics of the model should fit the researcher's theoretical reasoning about how and why change occurs within an individual.

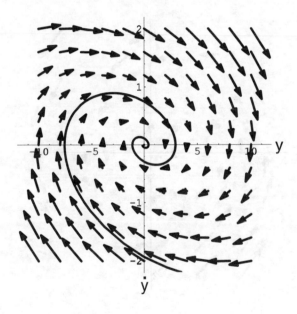

Figure 7.9: Vector field of Equation 7.8 for a range of initial conditions of y and $\dot{y}$.

The metaphors we have used, an automobile and a thermostat, are systems with active control mechanisms. However, the damped linear oscillator is also a model for a pendulum with friction in a gravitational field. It is important to recall that a self–regulating dynamical system might have an active control mechanism, or it might be passively responding to the effects of a field (Boker, 2002). There may be theoretic reasons to prefer active or passive mechanisms as explanations for a particular chosen gerontological or developmental system, but the dynamical systems model in and of itself will generally not distinguish between active and passive mechanistic interpretations.

If we construct a dynamical systems model for change, how might data from aging research be fit and model parameters be estimated? Three basic methods are available: state-space discrete time methods, state-space continuous time methods, and continuous time differential methods. We focus on the third alternative and examine how and why a dynamical systems model might help solve some problems in longitudinal analysis.

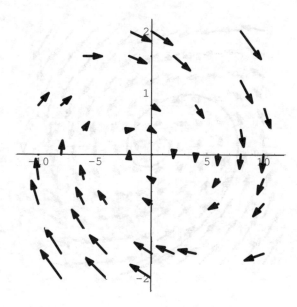

Figure 7.10: Random sample of initial conditions of y and $\dot{y}$ from a vector field of Equation 7.8.

7.4   Data Analysis for Dynamical Systems

The vector fields in Figs. 7.4, 7.7 and, 7.9 plot the short–term behavior of their respective models for a range of initial conditions. Suppose we possessed data on short–term outcomes for a particular system from a random sample of initial conditions as shown in Fig. 7.10. To construct an empirical vector field plot from these data, we would need to estimate initial level and slope, as well as the change in slope, after a short interval of time. With a few assumptions, these estimated values could also be used to find out how well a chosen dynamical systems model fit the data. To perform this type of analysis, we construct what is called an embedded state space, composed of many short sequences of longitudinal data. From this, we estimate the phase space of the system, that is, the form of the relationship between the derivatives of the system as plotted in Fig. 7.10.

An embedded state space data set (also sometimes called a state space embedding) is constructed by lagging a time series against itself. If we were to have a set of repeated observations

$$\{y_1, y_2, y_3, y_4, \ldots y_{n-2}, y_{n-1}, y_n\}$$

spaced at equal intervals t (called the *sampling interval*), then we could produce a three–dimensional embedded state space by rearranging the data vector into a data matrix of the form

$$\begin{bmatrix} y_1 & y_{1+\tau} & y_{1+2\tau} \\ y_2 & y_{2+\tau} & y_{2+2\tau} \\ y_3 & y_{3+\tau} & y_{3+2\tau} \\ \vdots & \vdots & \vdots \\ y_{n-2\tau} & y_{n-\tau} & y_n \end{bmatrix} \tag{7.9}$$

where τ is an integer value called the *analysis interval* (also known as the *embedding lag*). Embedded state spaces don't need to be only three columns; sometimes four, five, or more are used.

Why are embedded state spaces used? The most basic answer is that this provides us with information about how the system co-varies with itself over time so that we can estimate the parameters of a dynamical model. We turn to how this can be accomplished in a moment, but first let us consider measuring the behavior of our "Homing Pigeon" model automobile.

Suppose that we measure the position of the automobile at regular intervals, perhaps 15 sec apart. We start the automobile 5 km from home and, over the course of 80 measurements (20 min), it returns to close to equilibrium, as shown in the trajectory plot in Fig 7.11a.

Now suppose there is a giant who can pick the car up and move it arbitrarily. At random intervals, the giant comes along and moves the car a random amount. Now our measurements look something like those plotted in Fig. 7.11b. Whereas a growth curve model would work well in fitting the data from Fig. 7.11a, the data in Fig. 7.11b violate the assumption of independence of evolution.

Dynamical systems models that estimate their parameters from some form of embedded state space can still recover the coefficients of the differential equation underlying the behavior of our "Homing Pigeon" automobile. Why? One reason is that in the current example, most of the rows in the embedded state space are not influenced by the random shocks to the system provided by the giant. That is to say, the sampled vector field is still largely intact except for some noisy arrows exactly at the points where the shocks occurred. It turns out that even when there are small shocks happening all the time, it is often still possible to accurately estimate the parameters of the differential equation using methods that begin by forming a state space embedding. This is because methods that rely on a state space embedding separate initial conditions from the parameters of the dynamical system because there is essentially a new set of initial conditions for each row of the embedded state space matrix. Thus, random shocks, in other words random changes in initial conditions, are not propagated systematically into the estimation of the model parameters.

Once an embedded state space data set has been constructed, there are two main categories of methods used to estimate parameters of a hypothesized differential model for change. One category of methods uses the integral of the proposed differential model and fits a forward prediction form of the integral in either discrete time (autoregressive models) or continuous time (the *exact discrete* method). Another category of methods uses interpolative or smoothing techniques to provide estimates of derivatives and then fits the differential equation model to those derivatives. The remainder of this chapter discusses two methods from the second category: (a) a two-step manifest variable method, *local linear approximation* (LLA), that first explicitly estimates derivatives and then fits the model to those estimates; and (b) an approach that simultaneously estimates derivatives as latent variables and models the covariances between them, *latent differential equations* (LDE). We then provide an example of the use of the LLA method in a study of the grieving process in recent widows.

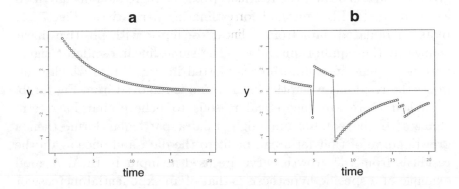

Figure 7.11: Two trajectories that conform to Equation 7.3. (a) The system starts at an initial condition of $y = 5$ and evolves independently. (b) The trajectory has random shocks (changes in initial conditions) that occur at random intervals.

7.4.1 Local Linear Approximation

A simple and effective method for recovering parameters of differential equations from repeated measures of a variable is to estimate derivatives for the second column of a three-dimensional state space embedding and then fit a multiple regression or structural model to find regression coefficients for the model-predicted relationship between the estimated derivatives. To apply this method, the data must first be centered so that the centroid of the hypothesized equilibrium for the data is at zero and is not time dependent. For dynamical models that have fixed-point attractors, such as the models we have discussed so far, this means that the data must be centered so that the value of the fixed-point attractor is at zero for all of the occasions of measurement in the data set.

The reason for this centering step is to remove long–term changes in the value of the equilibrium fixed point and to allow the value of the variable, say y, to indicate the displacement from equilibrium. When there is no theoretical reason that the equilibrium should be any particular value, frequently the assumption is made that any long–term changes in equilibrium can be modeled linearly, and so a straight line growth model is fit and the residuals from the regression line are used as input to the LLA method for estimating derivatives. Fig. 7.12b plots a simulated data from a linear oscillator with positive linear change in the equilibrium value. The same linear oscillator signal with no change in equilibrium is plotted in Fig. 7.12a, which comprises the residuals when the linear trend is removed from Fig 7.12b.

When there are theoretical reasons to believe that long–term changes to the equilibrium might take a particular form, then a growth curve of that form can be fit to the data and once again the residuals from the growth curve are used as input to LLA. A good example of a specific hypothesis is that of an exponential increase or decrease to some asymptotic value. For instance, one might hypothesize that recovery after some major life event involves a long–term process resulting in a negative exponential return to some pre–event state, but that during the recovery process there might be short–term variability with an oscillatory pattern. Fig. 7.12c plots simulated error–free data that conform to one possible realization of this hypothesis; measured values oscillate more after the event at $t = 0$, and oscillations are damped as the system approaches an equilibrium asymptote.

Once the residuals have been obtained from the model of the equilibrium change over time, a three-dimensional embedded state space $\mathbf{X}$ is constructed, where the lag offset between the columns is τ. LLA is a transformation that operates on the $N \times 3$ matrix $\mathbf{X}$ as follows: If $\mathbf{x}_0$, $\mathbf{x}_1$, and $\mathbf{x}_2$ are the three column vectors of $\mathbf{X}$ and s is the sampling interval (the time between successive occasions of measurement), then an $(N + 1 - 2\tau) \times 3$ estimated derivative matrix $\mathbf{D}$ can be calculated such that the column vectors of $\mathbf{D}$ are

$$\mathbf{d}_0 = \mathbf{x}_1 \tag{7.10}$$

$$\mathbf{d}_1 = \frac{\mathbf{x}_2 - \mathbf{x}_0}{2\tau s}$$

$$\mathbf{d}_2 = \frac{\mathbf{x}_2 + \mathbf{x}_0 - 2\mathbf{x}_1}{2\tau^2 s^2} .$$

Now, a differential equations model can be estimated from these transformed data. For instance, the parameters of a linear oscillator

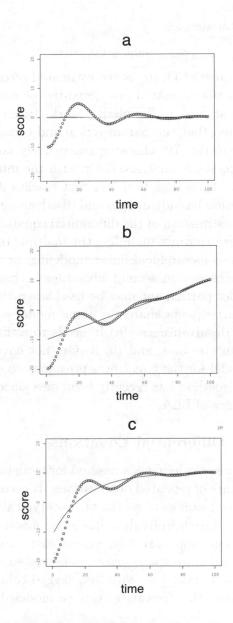

Figure 7.12: Simulated measurements of oscillations (plotted as circles) around equilibrium values as a function of time (plotted as solid lines). (a) Linear oscillator with no time–related change in equilibrium. (b) Linear oscillator with positive linear change equilibrium. (c) Linear oscillator with negative exponential change in equilibrium approaching a positive asymptote.

model can be estimated as

$$d_{i2} = \eta d_{i0} + \zeta d_{i1} + e_i \qquad (7.11)$$

where for the ith row of $\mathbf{D}$, d_{i2} is the estimated second derivative of x_t at time t, d_{i1} is the estimated first derivative of x at time t, and d_{i0} is the value of x at time t. Simulation work (Boker & Nesselroade, 2002) has indicated that the parameters η and ζ may be biased if τ is not chosen correctly. By choosing successively larger values of τ and rerunning the above analysis, the τ with the minimum bias will occur when the r^2 from Equation 7.11 first reaches its asymptote.

The LLA method has advantages and disadvantages. The method allows for simple estimation of the differential equation model parameters with standard routines including the multiple regression, mixed model regression or hierarchical linear modeling, or structural equations modeling packages. A second advantage is that small numbers of observations per participant may be used when the assumption is made that all participants share the same model parameters. The method has two disadvantages: (a) It needs to estimate a value for τ in order to minimize bias, and (b) it does not have a multivariate measurement model for the constructs presumed to exhibit dynamic behavior. A new method has recently been developed that addresses these disadvantages of LLA.

7.4.2   Latent Differential Equations

Latent growth curve modeling is a method for modeling the intercept, slope, and curvature of repeated observations. It accomplishes this by constraining factor loadings to represent prototypical functions (basis functions) of which each individual has some amount. By choosing these basis functions appropriately, we can extract derivatives from an $N \times 4$ embedded state space matrix constructed in the same way as in the previous section, but with four lagged columns. Then, the covariances between the derivatives can be modeled as a regression model.

For instance, consider the damped linear oscillator version of the latent differential equations (LDE) model shown in Fig. 7.13. All of the "factor loadings" are completely constrained so as to estimate derivatives as opposed to intercept, slope, and curvature. A time located halfway between x_2 and x_3 is the time for which the intercept,

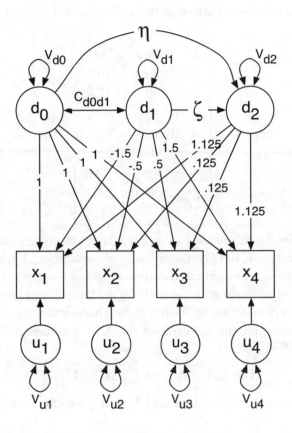

Figure 7.13: Latent differential equations (LDE) model for the damped linear oscillator using a four–dimensional embedded state space (i.e., a four–column lagged data matrix).

first derivative, and second derivative are estimated. But these estimates are never directly observed. Instead, the covariances between these latent variables (d_0, d_1 and d_2) are used to estimate regression parameters that are in turn estimates of the η and ζ parameters from the damped linear oscillator model shown in Equation 7.8.

Three structural equation matrices $\mathbf{L}$, $\mathbf{A}$, and $\mathbf{S}$ can be defined as

$$\mathbf{L} = \begin{bmatrix} 1 & -1.5\tau s & (-1.5\tau s)^2/2 \\ 1 & -0.5\tau s & (-0.5\tau s)^2/2 \\ 1 & 0.5\tau s & (0.5\tau s)^2/2 \\ 1 & 1.5\tau s & (1.5\tau s)^2/2 \end{bmatrix} \tag{7.12}$$

$$\mathbf{A} = \begin{bmatrix} 0 & 0 & 0 \\ 0 & 0 & 0 \\ \eta & \zeta & 0 \end{bmatrix} \tag{7.13}$$

$$\mathbf{S} = \begin{bmatrix} V_{d0} & C_{d0d1} & 0 \\ C_{d0d1} & V_{d1} & 0 \\ 0 & 0 & V_{d2} \end{bmatrix} \tag{7.14}$$

where τ is the lag offset used in constructing the state space matrix, s is the time interval between successive observations, V_{d0} and V_{d1} are the variances of the estimated latent scores $d0$ and $d1$, C_{d0d1} is the covariance between $d0$ and $d1$, and V_{d2} is the residual variance of the latent second derivative $d2$. Given these three matrices, the expected covariance between the columns of the $N \times 4$ embedded state space $\mathbf{X}$ can be calculated as

$$\mathbf{R} = \mathbf{L}(\mathbf{I} - \mathbf{A})^{-1}\mathbf{S}(\mathbf{I} - \mathbf{A})^{-1'}\mathbf{L}' + \mathbf{U} \tag{7.15}$$

where $\mathbf{I}$ is the identity matrix and $\mathbf{U}$ is a diagonal matrix of unique variances.

The LDE method has been tested in simulations and has shown itself to provide reasonably low bias estimates of model parameters when there are more than eight occasions within a single cycle of oscillation with little or no dependence on the value of τ. However, simulations using the form of the LDE model discussed here have shown that (a) fewer than eight observations per cycle reliably results in the model not converging, and (b) the estimates of ζ tend to have wider confidence intervals than those from LLA. Thus, both LLA and LDE have their place in the arsenal of methods for use by researchers in aging.

7.5 Dynamical Systems and Aging

There are many candidates for self–regulating psychological systems that might be theoretically cast as a dynamical system and modeled using differential equations (e.g., Cummings & Davies, 2002; Donaldson & Horn, 1992; Gottschalk, Bauer, & Whybrow, 1995; Sarrias, Artigas, & Martínez, 1989). For instance, consider daily changes in mood and affect. Some changes in mood might be linked to external events. Yet an event, such as a pleasant meal, that induces a positive change in affect does not have a long–term effect. Instead, the short–term positive change in affect tends to diminish over time. It is as if there is a preferred equilibrium in affect to which the system returns after some interval of time, in some sense similar to the previously described "Homing Pigeon" automobile.

In aging, this return to equilibrium has sometimes been termed *resilience*, a term that highlights the positive effect it might have on long–term consequences of negative life events such as death of a spouse (McCrae & Costa, 1988). For those that experience it, loss of a spouse is likely to be one of the major traumas associated with aging. There are likely to be individual differences in how large the impact of the trauma may be: Some deaths are sudden and shocking, whereas others may come after a long painful illness and may be perceived as a relief. There are also likely to be individual differences in how self–regulation brings the widow or widower's system back into equilibrium.

Just as the dynamic mechanisms of the physical systems we have discussed can only be understood by measuring the system when it is not at equilibrium, so too are self–regulating psychological systems likely to be best measured as the system returns to equilibrium after the effect of some external event. The example data presented here comes from an intensive longitudinal study of mood and affect in recent widows (Bisconti, 2001).

7.6   An Example — Bereavement

7.6.1   Participants

Recent widows ($N = 49$) who met the inclusion criteria (having recently lost a husband at least 60 years of age and not being involved in a subsequent romantic relationship), were recruited into the study beginning approximately one week after the death of the spouse. Participants ages ranged from 57 to 82 (M = 72.23; SD = 6.13), 34 were widows of their first marriage, and length of marriage ranged from 14 to 63 years (M = 49.93; SD = 10.97). The sample was split into two groups, a target and control group; the target group ($N = 28$) participating in the full longitudinal daily assessments and the control group only participating in initial and follow–up interviews.

7.6.2   Procedure

The target group participants were first given an initial 90–minute interview and were then asked to complete a daily questionnaire, including items related to emotional affect and well–being, to be completed each evening for a total of 12 weeks. The questionnaire was reported to take between 5 and 10 minutes a day to complete. If the participant missed a day, they were instructed to leave it blank and not fill it in retrospectively. Participants were instructed to not look back at previous questionnaires after answering. Packets of questionnaires sufficient to last 2 weeks were mailed at 2-week intervals, and participants were phoned to remind them to mail back each 2-week packet of questionnaires after they were completed.

Daily assessments included the 36–item Mental Health Inventory (MHI; Veit & Ware, 1983). Items from the MHI assess anxiety (Today I felt anxious, worried), depressive affect (Today I felt downhearted and blue), emotional ties (Today I felt loved and wanted), positive affect (Today I felt cheerful, lighthearted), and behavioral/emotional control (Today I felt emotionally stable). The response format of each item was a scale ranging from 1 (completely true) to 4 (not at all true); negatively worded items were reflected and all items summed. In previously reported samples of college students, the internal consistency of the summed MHI ranged from .92 to .96 (Veit & Ware, 1983).

In addition to understanding the process of adaptation, it is important to identify factors that contribute to individual differences in adjustment trajectories. The loss of a spouse is a negative life event that directly induces a loss of social connectedness, and as such, may affect well–being through its impact on protective resources, such as components of the social support process. The social support process can be viewed as having four components including both individual and environmental protective factors. Environmental factors include network size from both family and friends, whereas individual factors include perceived control over the networks utilization and the actual mobilization of the support system in the face of a stressor, either with emotion–focused or problem–focused social coping. The current example focuses on the individual factors a widow possesses that may help to ameliorate the stress of losing a spouse.

The characteristic vulnerabilities of support networks in old age suggest that it may be important for an individual to try to impose some degree of control over his or her social support network (Hansson & Remondet, 1988). Much research has indicated that control is an important predictor of psychological and physical functioning (Gatz, 1991; Heckhausen & Schulz, 1995; Skinner, 1996), particularly in the face of a stressor. Similarly, social coping strategies have been found to be necessary in well–being outcomes in older adulthood. Two types of coping have been identified: problem–focused, defined as responses aimed at eliminating or modifying the conditions that give rise to the problem, and emotion–focused, which are responses geared toward the management of the emotional consequences of the stressor and the maintenance of emotional equilibrium (for a more complete discussion, see Lazarus & Folkman, 1984). Although most people appear to use both emotional– and problem–focused strategies, contextual differences have been found in their use (deKeijser & Schut, 1990); therefore, these strategies need to be examined separately in relation to an individuals utilization of his or her social network.

As part of the initial and follow–up interviews, participants were asked to complete a packet of questionnaires, which included standard measures of control and coping. Perceived social control is a 13–item subscale of the Desire for Control measure created by Reid and Ziegler (1981) that was designed specifically for the elderly. Examples of perceived social control statements include, "I can rarely find people who will listen closely to me," and "I find that if I ask my family (or friends) to visit me, they come." A higher score indicates more perceived social control. In the current sample, Cronbach's alpha is .85.

Coping was assessed using two subscales of the COPE (Carver, Scheier, & Weintraub, 1989), including seeking emotional support and seeking instrumental support. Seeking emotional support is a four–item assessment that is designed to measure emotion–focused coping. Sample items include, "I talk to someone about how I feel," and "I get sympathy and understanding from someone." Seeking instrumental support is a four–item assessment that is designed to measure problem–focused coping. Sample items include, "I ask people who have had similar experiences what they did," and "I try to get advice from someone about what to do." A higher score indicates a greater amount of coping by way of seeking social support for either emotional or instrumental (problem–focused) purposes. In the present study, Cronbach's alpha is .80 for problem–focused coping and .81 for emotion–focused coping.

7.6.3 Modeling

We fit widows' MHI scores as the sum of two models, one governing the long–term behavior of the short–term equilibrium and the other governing the fluctuations about the short–term equilibrium. We fit the long–term dynamic using three competing growth curves: an intercept–only model, a linear trend with slope and intercept, and a negative exponential growth curve. We thereby sought to compare the results of three hypotheses about how the long–term equilibrium shifts during recovery from loss of a spouse. The first hypothesis is that the long–term equilibrium stays constant during bereavement, and changes in reported MHI are simply a self–regulated return to that equilibrium. The second hypothesis is that there are changes in long–term equilibrium, and these changes are linear. The third hypothesis is there is a long–term negative exponential change in equilibrium returning to some asymptotic value. For each of these hypotheses, we fit a growth curve model to individuals' repeated observations and use the residuals from that analysis to model short–term variability as a self–regulating dynamical system using a second–order differential equation.

We chose to fit long–term changes with continuous time growth curves because (a) each of the proposed long–term processes are monotonic and thus do not exhibit individual differences in phase and (b) because the date of death of spouse is known and thus all of the widows can be placed on time metric with a known zero. These models are not directly nested, and thus, we do not make exact statistical comparisons between them but rather describe the results of predicting individual differences in their parameters and results of a differential equations model of short–term variability of the residuals of each of these analyses. We also present the results of predicting the individual differences parameters of each of the long–term equilibrium models and differential models from three variables: perceived control, emotion–focused coping and problem–focused coping.

We modeled the hypothesis of constant long–term equilibrium by fitting a random coefficients intercept–only model to the final 20 observations from each widow, thus giving an estimate of the central tendency of widows' MHI scores near the end of the experiment,

$$m_{it} = b_{i0} + \epsilon_{it} \tag{7.16}$$

where m_{it} is the MHI score for widow i at time t expressed in days since the loss of spouse and b_{i0} is the predicted MHI score at the end of the experiment for widow i. The individual differences in parameters were predicted by a second–level model

$$b_{i0} = c_1 + x_i + y_i + z_i + u_{1i} \tag{7.17}$$

where c_1 is the overall mean values of b_{i0}; and x_i is perceived control, y_i is emotion–focused coping, and z_i is problem–focused coping for widow i.

We expressed the hypothesis of linear trend change in long–term equilibrium as a linear random coefficients model

$$m_{it} = b_{i0} + b_{i1}t + \epsilon_{it} \tag{7.18}$$

where m_{it} is the MHI score for widow i at time t expressed in days since the loss of spouse, b_{i0} is the predicted MHI score at the time of loss of the spouse ($t = 0$), b_{i1} is the expected daily change in MHI score and ϵ_{it} is the residual for widow i at time t. The individual differences in parameters were predicted by a second–level model

$$b_{i0} = c_1 + x_i + y_i + z_i + u_{1i}$$
$$b_{i1} = c_2 + x_i + y_i + z_i + u_{2i} \tag{7.19}$$

where c_1 and c_2 are the overall mean values of b_{i0} and b_{i1} respectively, x_i is perceived control, y_i is emotion–focused coping, and z_i is problem–focused coping for widow i.

The third hypothesis of negative exponential return of equilibrium to a positive asymptote was modeled as

$$m_{it} = b_{i0} + b_{i1}e^{-b_{i2}t} + \epsilon_{it} \tag{7.20}$$

where m_{it} is the MHI score for widow i at time t, b_{i0} is the long–term asymptote, b_{i1} is the difference from long–term equilibrium at $t = 0$, and b_{i2} is the amount of exponential curvature for person i. In this model, b_{i0} can be considered to be the long–term equilibrium to which person i is expected to return, b_{i1} is an estimate of the effect of the death of the spouse on the widow on the day of death, and b_{i2} can be considered as an estimate of the long–term resiliency of the widow.

The residual, ϵ_{it}, from Equations 7.16, 7.18, and 7.20 is not necessarily error. It represents the part of the daily MHI score that is not accounted for by the long–term return to overall equilibrium. We chose to model this residual from each of the hypothesized long–term equilibrium equations as a second–order differential equation to account for shorter term fluctuations in mood:

$$\ddot{\epsilon}_{it} = \eta_i \epsilon_{it} + \zeta_i \dot{\epsilon}_{it} + \varepsilon_{it} \tag{7.21}$$

where ϵ_{it}, $\dot{\epsilon}_{it}$, and $\ddot{\epsilon}_{it}$ are the residual MHI score and its first and second derivatives respectively for person i at time t. The parameter η_i is related to the frequency of the oscillation for widow i and ζ_i is related to the damping, or short–term resilience of widow i. We chose to use local linear approximation to explicitly calculate these derivatives prior to fitting Equation 7.21 as part of a multilevel model such that

$$\eta_i = c_1 + x_i + y_i + z_i + w_{1i}$$
$$\zeta_i = c_2 + x_i + y_i + z_i + w_{2i} \tag{7.22}$$

where c_1 and c_2 are the mean values of η and ζ respectively, x_i is perceived control, y_i is emotion–focused coping, and z_i is problem–focused coping for widow i. A r^2 was constructed for each individual widow as

$$r^2 = 1 - \frac{\varepsilon_{it}}{\ddot{\epsilon}_{it}} , \qquad (7.23)$$

the proportion of the variance in the second derivative $\ddot{\epsilon}_{it}$ accounted for by Equation 7.21.

7.6.4   Results

Figure 7.14 plots raw time series for four example widows. Figure 7.14a exhibits a pattern that is strikingly similar to that of the damped linear oscillator shown in Fig. 7.12a. Note that there is also apparent evidence of periodicity in Fig. 7.14c, but that these data are also highly variable. Figures 7.14a and 7.14c do not appear to exhibit much, if any, long–term change in equilibrium. On the other hand, Figs. 7.12b and 7.12d are examples that appear to exhibit a long–term negative exponential change in equilibrium, as there appears to be more variability around that exponential trajectory in the first part of the experiment than there is later on.

Fitting the constant long–term equilibrium model from Equation 7.16 to the data resulted in an overall mean long–term equilibrium of 121.3 $(SE = 2.9)$. Individual differences in the long–term equilibrium were not reliably predicted by perceived control, emotion–focused coping, or problem–focused coping as shown in Table 7.1.

Table 7.1: Constant Equilibrium Coefficient Predicted by Perceived Control, Emotion–Focused, and Problem–Focused Coping

Coefficient	Value	SE	t Value	$p(< |t|)$
Perceived Control $\rightarrow$ Intercept	0.2247	0.6783	0.33	0.743
Emotion–Focused Coping $\rightarrow$ Intercept	1.6980	1.4259	1.19	0.247
Problem–Focused Coping $\rightarrow$ Intercept	-0.8077	1.1505	-0.70	0.490

The linear trend hypothesis of change in long–term equilibrium resulted in an overall mean slope of 0.069 $(SE = 0.021)$ and overall

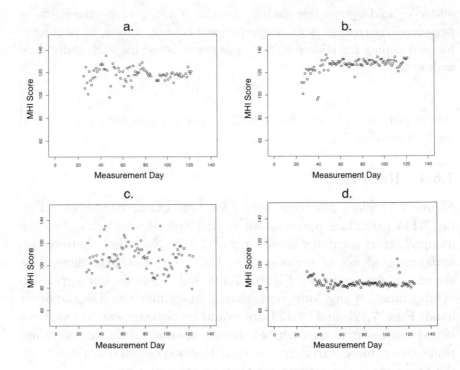

Figure 7.14: Time series of MHI scores over 12 weeks of daily self–report for four example widows.

mean intercept of 115.8 ($SE = 2.4$). Individual differences in the linear trend slope were reliably predicted by perceived control, emotion–focused coping, and problem–focused coping as shown in Table 7.2. In addition, perceived control reliably predicted individual differences in the intercept of the trend line.

The hypothesis of long–term equilibrium change in the form of a negative exponential approach to asymptote were fit using the nonlinear least squares (nls) algorithm in R. This procedure needed to be performed on a case–by–case basis as the nls algorithm was sensitive to starting values and cases where the curvature was near zero. The results of predicting the individual differences in coefficients of this model for long–term equilibrium change are presented in Table 7.3. Perceived control and emotion–focused coping were predictors of the

Table 7.2: Linear Trend Equilibrium Coefficients Predicted by Perceived Control, Emotion–Focused Coping, and Problem–Focused Coping

Coefficient	Value	SE	t Value	p($< |t|$)
Perceived Control → Slope	-0.0128	0.0041	-3.10	0.005
Emotion–Focused Coping → Slope	0.0335	0.0086	3.86	< 0.001
Problem–Focused Coping → Slope	-0.0149	0.0070	-2.12	0.045
Perceived Control → Intercept	1.4215	0.5597	2.54	0.019
Emotion–Focused Coping → Intercept	-1.1688	1.1766	-0.99	0.332
Problem–Focused Coping → Intercept	0.5067	0.9494	0.53	0.599

curvature coefficient (b_{i2} in Equation 7.20). Greater values of Perceived Control were associated with slower return to equilibrium, that is, smaller values of long–term resiliency. Greater values of emotion–focused coping were associated with faster return to equilibrium, that is, greater long–term resiliency, and with smaller differences between initial MHI and long–term equilibrium MHI.

Table 7.3: Exponential Trend Coefficients Predicted by Control, Emotion–Focused Coping, and Problem–Focused Coping

Coefficient	Value	SE	t value	p($< |t|$)
Perceived Control → Asymptote	-0.0578	0.7513	-0.077	0.939
Emotion–Focused Coping → Asymptote	2.5578	1.5792	1.620	0.121
Problem–Focused Coping → Asymptote	-0.7046	1.2742	-0.553	0.586
Perceived Control → Curvature	-0.0146	0.0055	-2.646	0.015
Emotion–Focused Coping → Curvature	0.0243	0.0116	2.086	0.050
Problem–Focused Coping → Curvature	0.0043	0.0094	0.462	0.649
Perceived Control → Initial Value	0.9005	0.6592	1.366	0.187
Emotion–Focused Coping → Initial Value	-2.5528	1.3857	-1.842	0.080
Perceived Control → Initial Value	0.6270	1.1181	0.561	0.581

In the second part of the analysis, local linear approximation was used to explicitly calculate derivatives using the residuals from the long–term equilibrium analysis. Since the lag (τ) used to calculate the LLA derivatives can affect the estimated coefficients of differential models (Boker & Nesselroade, 2002), a range of lags ($1 \leq \tau \leq 15$) were used in the calculations. The second–order linear differential

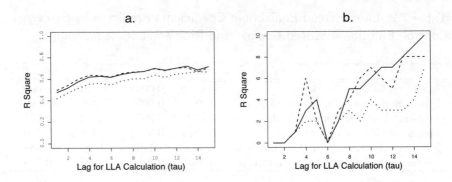

Figure 7.15: Proportion of second derivative variance accounted for by linear oscillator LLA model fit to residuals from long–term equilibrium equations for a range of LLA lags ($1 \leq \tau \leq 15$). (a) Mean r^2 for constant equilbrium residuals (dotted line), linear trend residuals (solid line), and exponential residuals (dashed line). (b) Number of r^2s greater than 0.76 for constant equilibrium residuals (dotted line), linear trend residuals (solid line), and exponential residuals (dashed line).

equation from Equation 7.21 was fit to the LLA derivatives calculated with each lag using a mixed effects routine (the lme function from R; Pinheiro & Bates, 2000) and r^2s were calculated using Equation 7.23. The mean r^2 for each lag for the residuals from each of the three hypothesized changes in long–term equilibrium are plotted in Fig. 7.15a. Note the positive trend in the r^2 which is particularly pronounced from lags 1 to 5 for all three curves. Also note that the mean r^2 is similar for the linear trend and exponential residuals, but the r^2 is somewhat smaller for the constant equilibrium residuals. One possible explanation for this difference is that the residuals from the constant equilibrium model are confounding two sources of variability: long–term and short–term variability.

Although the mean r^2s appear to be high, one must take into account the fact that high r^2s are possible even when fitting this differential equation to normally distributed random numbers. From a previous simulation, an empirical estimate of the upper 95% confidence interval for the r^2 from fitting this model to 100 normally

distributed random numbers is 0.76. Thus, another way to consider
the fit of Equation 7.21 is to plot the number of individuals whose
individual r^2 is greater than 0.76, as is plotted in Fig. 7.15b. There
is a peak in the number of such individuals at $\tau = 4$ for the exponential model and at $\tau = 5$ for the linear trend model. Since we
are interested in short–term variability, and shorter values of the lag
allow us to examine shorter cycles, we have chosen to examine the
second–level predictions of individual differences in coefficients of the
differential equation from derivatives calculated at a lag of $\tau = 4$.
We exclude the constant long–term equilibrium residuals from further analysis due to the consistently lower values of r^2 and lower
numbers of individuals with r^2s greater than 0.76.

Table 7.4 contains the results of the mixed effects model from
Equations 7.21 and 7.22, fit to derivatives calculated with LLA using
a lag of 4 on the residuals from the linear trend model. While the
overall mean values of η and ζ are significant, it does not appear
that any of the second–level variables provide a reliable prediction of
individual differences in η and ζ.

Table 7.4: Residuals From Linear Trend Fit With Linear Oscillator Random Coefficients Model ($\tau = 4$, $AIC = 3446$, $BIC = 3510$)

Coefficient	Value	SE	DF	t Value	p value
Intercept η	-0.0427	0.0141	1563	-3.03	0.002
Perceived Control $\rightarrow \eta$	-0.0047	0.0034	1563	-1.38	0.165
Emotion–Focused Coping $\rightarrow \eta$	-0.0023	0.0051	1563	-0.44	0.653
Problem–Focused Coping $\rightarrow \eta$	-0.0060	0.0043	1563	-1.39	0.163
Intercept ζ	-0.1119	0.0047	1563	-23.62	< 0.001
Perceived Control $\rightarrow \zeta$	-0.0008	0.0011	1563	-0.71	0.476
Emotion–Focused Coping $\rightarrow \zeta$	0.0021	0.0021	1563	0.99	0.319
Problem–Focused Coping $\rightarrow \zeta$	-0.0014	0.0017	1563	-0.82	0.412

On the other hand, when the mixed effects differential equations
model is fit to the residuals from the exponential equilibrium change
model, the results are strikingly different. Table 7.5 contains the results of a mixed effects linear model fit to derivatives calculated with
LLA using a lag of $\tau = 4$ on the residuals after removing an exponential long–term change in equilibrium. Emotion–focused coping has a

positive effect on ζ, suggesting that higher values of Emotion–focused coping are associated with slower damping of short–term variability. Conversely, higher values of problem–focused coping appear to be associated with quicker damping of short–term variability, that is, greater short–term resilience. Perceived control is near the 0.05 cut-off for being declared to have a positive association with short–term resilience.

Table 7.5: Residuals From Exponential Fit With Linear Oscillator Random Coefficients Model ($\tau = 4$, $AIC = 3452$, $BIC = 3516$)

Coefficient	Value	SE	DF	t Value	p Value
Intercept η	-0.0304	0.0139	1563	-2.18	0.029
Perceived Control $\rightarrow \eta$	-0.0044	0.0034	1563	-1.31	0.189
Emotion–Focused Coping $\rightarrow \eta$	-0.0021	0.0050	1563	-0.41	0.675
Problem–Focused Coping $\rightarrow \eta$	-0.0048	0.0043	1563	-1.11	0.264
Intercept ζ	-0.1150	0.0046	1563	-24.90	< 0.001
Perceived Control $\rightarrow \zeta$	-0.0021	0.0011	1563	-1.93	0.053
Emotion–Focused Coping $\rightarrow \zeta$	0.0048	0.0020	1563	2.39	0.016
Problem–Focused Coping $\rightarrow \zeta$	-0.0038	0.0017	1563	-2.25	0.024

7.6.5 Example Summary

The intercept–only model for no long–term change in equilibrium performed poorly in comparison to the other two models. If we were uninterested in the process of adaptation and were to fit only this model, we might have been satisfied with the results: The intercept term was significant, and the residuals did not exhibit much evidence of correlational structure. But the results from the other two models for long–term change in equilibrium demonstrate that much is being missed by such a simplified view of self–regulation.

The linear trend model for long–term change in equilibrium performed better than the intercept–only model in three regards. First, there was evidence that the three chosen variables — perceived control, emotion–focused coping, and problem–focused coping — were associated with changes in long–term equilibrium. Greater values of perceived control and problem–focused coping were associated with faster increases in MHI equilibrium, whereas greater values of emotion–

focused coping were associated with slower increases in MHI equilibrium. In addition, greater values of perceived control were associated with higher intercepts. Second, there was evidence that the residuals from the linear trend model fit a linear oscillator model better than would be expected by chance.

However, the linear trend model was unsatisfying in three ways. First, while trends might be linear within a span of a few months, it is unrealistic that the MHI equilibrium would continue to increase or decrease in a straight line over a longer time span. Second, while the three chosen predictor variables were associated with slopes, a slope is sensitive to changes near the beginning of the time span (i.e., effect on the widow at the time of death of spouse) and at the end of the time span (i.e., value of the overall equilibrium). The linear trend model does not explicitly separate these two ideas from the notion of resiliency. Finally, while the residuals from the linear trend analysis did show evidence of patterned variability, the coefficients of a second–order differential equations model were not reliably associated with the three chosen predictor variables.

The exponential trend model for long–term equilibrium was the most satisfying model for four reasons. First, the initial value and final asymptote were separated from an independent assessment of curvature corresponding to an estimate of long–term resiliency. Second, greater values of perceived control were associated with less curvature (lower long–term resiliency), and greater values of emotion–focused coping were associated with greater curvature (greater long–term resiliency). The three predictor variables were not associated with the initial value (i.e., effect at time of death of spouse) or with the long–term asymptotic value of the equilibrium. Third, the residuals from the exponential trend model exhibited the greatest amount of patterned variability as judged by number of r^2s greater than 0.76. Fourth, individual differences in the damping parameter ζ from the differential equation model, an estimate of short–term resiliency, were associated with the three predictor variables. Greater values of perceived control and problem–focused coping were associated with quicker damping of short–term variability, that is, greater short–term resilience. Greater values of emotion–focused coping were associated with slower damping and thus lower short–term resiliency.

The exponential trend model provided an interesting look at a potential differences between short–term and long–term resiliency. For instance, emotion–focused coping predicted greater long–term resiliency but lower short–term resiliency. Perceived control predicted lower long–term resiliency but greater short–term resiliency. We expect that the efficacy of separating resiliency into these two time scales may have a impact on how we conceive of resiliency in aging.

7.7   Conclusions

One of the most important implications is in this example's empirical addition to more recent conceptualizations of bereavement. More specifically, the current study is a strong first-step in validating "guideposts" to describe the normal bereavement process that corresponds with theoretical underpinnings. For example, the findings from the present study complement a recent model of coping with bereavement (Stroebe & Schut, 1999). The dual process model of coping includes the stressors related to loss, the cognitive strategies that assist in adjustment to the event, and the "dynamic process of oscillation" (Stroebe & Schut, 1999, p. 212) that distinguishes this conceptualization from more traditional models of adjustment. More specifically, the dual process is described as a loss- and restoration-oriented coping. Loss orientation refers to concentrating on, dealing with, and/or processing some aspect of the loss itself. It has been suggested that loss orientation is the dominant process early on in bereavement. Restoration orientation focuses on what situations need to be dealt with and how one goes about dealing with them.

According to Stroebe and Schut (1999), the dynamic process of oscillation refers to the alternation between loss- and restoration-oriented coping. More specifically, at various points in the bereavement process, the widow will confront her loss (i.e., loss orientation), whereas at other times, she will actively avoid thinking about it by doing new things or distracting herself from the grief (i.e., restoration orientation). This cognitive process is a regulatory mechanism, which is specified as dynamic, and oscillation is hypothesized as being necessary for successful adjustment to take place. Finally, across time, loss orientation is replaced more fully with restoration, leading to habituation to the loss (Stroebe & Schut, 1999).

The analysis of data from a dynamical systems perspective enables researchers to develop and test hypotheses in a somewhat different way than most methods for the analysis of change. Thoughtful model construction can lead to parameters whose interpretation is intuitively appealing and map onto theoretical constructs that can be reasonably communicated to a broad audience. While the modeling is relatively straightforward, it does require conceptual understanding that is not commonly taught in statistics for the behavioral and social sciences. The field of dynamical systems data analysis is relatively young and there are, as yet, no automatic routines for these analyses built in to popular statistical analysis packages such as SAS and SPSS. However, if the field of aging is to come to grips with process–oriented notions of development, we believe that methods similar to those presented in this chapter will need to be implemented and mastered.

References

Bisconti, T. L. (2001). *Widowhood in later life: A dynamical systems approach to emotion regulation.* Unpublished doctoral dissertation, University of Notre Dame, Notre Dame, IN.

Boker, S. M. (2002). Consequences of continuity: The hunt for intrinsic properties within parameters of dynamics in psychological processes. *Multivariate Behavioral Research, 37*(3), 405–422.

Boker, S. M., & McArdle, J. J. (2005). Vector field plots. In P. Armitage & T. Colton (Eds.), *Encyclopedia of biostatistics (2nd edition)* (Vol. 8, p. 5700-5704). Chichester, UK: Wiley.

Boker, S. M., & Nesselroade, J. R. (2002). A method for modeling the intrinsic dynamics of intraindividual variability: Recovering the parameters of simulated oscillators in multi–wave panel data. *Multivariate Behavioral Research, 37*(1), 127–160.

Carver, C. S., Scheier, M. F., & Weintraub, J. K. (1989). Assessing coping strategies: A theoretically based approach. *Journal of Personality and Social Psychology, 56*(2), 267–283.

Cummings, E. M., & Davies, P. T. (2002). Effects of marital conflict on children: Recent advances and emerging themes in process–oriented research. *Journal of Child Psychology and Psychiatry, 43*(1), 31–63.

deKeijser, J., & Schut, H. (1990). Perceived support and coping with loss. In K. C. P. M. Knipscheer & T. C. Antonucci (Eds.), *Social network research: Substantive issues and methodological questions* (pp. 67–82). Amsterdam: Swets & Zeitlinger.

Donaldson, G., & Horn, J. L. (1992). Age, cohort and time developmental muddles: Easy in practice, hard in theory. *Experimental Aging Research, 18*, 213–222.

Gatz, M. (1991). Stress, control, and psychological interventions. In M. L. Wykle, E. Kahana, & J. Kowal (Eds.), *Stress and health among the elderly* (pp. 209–222). New York: Springer.

Gottschalk, A., Bauer, M. S., & Whybrow, P. C. (1995). Evidence of chaotic mood variation in bipolar disorder. *Archives of General Psychiatry, 52*, 947–959.

Hansson, R. O., & Remondet, J. H. (1988). Old age and widowhood: Issues of personal control and independence. *Journal of Social Issues, 44*, 158–174.

Heckhausen, J., & Schulz, R. (1995). A life-span theory of control. *Psychological Review, 102*(2), 284–304.

Hubbard, J. H., & West, B. H. (1991). *Differential equations: A dynamical systems approach.* New York: Springer–Verlag.

Hubbard, J. H., & West, B. H. (1995). *Differential equations: A dynamical systems approach, higher dimensional systems.* New York: Springer–Verlag.

Jones, R. H. (1993). *Longitudinal data with serial correlation: A state–space approach.* Boca Raton, FL: Chapman & Hall/CRC.

Kaplan, D., & Glass, L. (1995). *Understanding nonlinear dynamics.* New York: Springer–Verlag.

Lazarus, R. S., & Folkman, S. (1984). *Stress, appraisal, and coping.* New York: Springer.

McCrae, R. R., & Costa, P. T. (1988). Psychological resilience among widowed men and women: A 10-year follow-up of a national sample. *Journal of Social Issues, 44*(3), 129-142.

Oud, J. H. L., & Jansen, R. A. R. G. (2000). Continuous time state space modeling of panel data by means of SEM. *Psychometrica, 65*(2), 199–215.

Pinheiro, J. C., & Bates, D. M. (2000). *Mixed–Effects Models in S and S–Plus.* New York: Springer–Verlag.

Reid, D. W., & Ziegler, M. (1981). The desired control measure and adjustment among the elderly. In H. M. Lefcourt (Ed.),

Research with the locus of control construct: Vol. 1, assessment methods (pp. 127–158). New York: Academic Press.

Sarrias, M. J., Artigas, F., & Martínez, E. (1989). Seasonal changes of plasma serotonin and related parameters: Correlation with environmental measures. *Biological Psychiatry, 26*, 695–706.

Singer, H. (1998). Continuous panel models with time dependent parameters. *Journal of Mathematical Sociology, 23*(2), 77–98.

Skinner, E. A. (1996). A guide to constructs of control. *Journal of Personality and Social Psychology, 71*(3), 549–570.

Stroebe, M. S., & Schut, H. (1999). The dual process model of coping with bereavement: Rationale and description. *Death Studies, 23*, 197–224.

Veit, C. T., & Ware, J. E. (1983). The structure of psychological distress and well-being in general populations. *Journal of Consulting and Clinical Psychology, 51*(5), 730–742.

8

Applying Proportional Hazards Models to Response Time Data

Michael J. Wenger and Christof Schuster
University of Notre Dame

Lindsay E. Petersen and Ronald C. Petersen
Mayo Clinic Alzheimer's Disease Research Center

Response time (RT) data are widely used in studies of cognitive abilities, both in typical college-aged populations and (increasingly) in aging populations. Although many of these studies focus on aspects of processing capacity (as it is affected, e.g., by variations in stimulus conditions, cuing conditions, etc.), the typical analyses of RT data do not map well onto the construct of capacity. We suggest (following Townsend & Ashby, 1978) that hypotheses framed at the level of the hazard function of the RT distribution do map well onto the notion of capacity. We then consider, in a set of simulations, the extent to which a set of well–known models for the hazard function—proportional hazards models—can be applied to data that possess the properties of typical RT distributions. We find that the models are sensitive to the presence of true orderings on hazard functions, but are consistently conservative in their estimates of the magnitude of the ordering. We illustrate the use of these models on a data set from a free and cued recall task administered to a set of older adults.

8.1   Introduction

Interest in the changes associated with both normal aging (Petersen,
1995; Petersen, Smith, Kokmen, Ivnik, & Tangalos, 1992) and a range
of disease states (Petersen, Smith, Kokmen, Ivnik, & Tangalos, 1994;
Petersen et al., 1999) has led researchers to focus on the real–time information processing requirements placed on individuals in daily life
(e.g., directing attention, recalling information, recognizing and identifying objects and individuals, etc.). The ability to respond to these
requirements is based on a range of fundamental perceptual and cognitive abilities that have been shown to undergo reliable changes with
increasing age (Petersen, 1995). Numerous measures of these abilities
have been explored in the cognitive literature (see Payne & Wenger,
1998, for an overview), many of them based on measurements of the
latency of an observer to respond to stimuli in an experimental task.

In this chapter, we argue that the standard approaches to sum-
marizing and analyzing these response time (RT) data are not well–
suited to the fundamental constructs that researchers desire to assess.
Specifically, we argue that although researchers are interested in measuring levels of and changes in the real–time *capacity* of individuals
to process external and internal information, typical analyses only
provide information about the average speed with which experimental tasks are performed. Further, we suggest that a set of reasonably
well–known statistical techniques can be applied to RT data to allow
direct inferences about real–time information processing capacity.

8.2   Background

We begin by providing some context for the argument, considering
first some of the history of the use of RT data in studying human performance, and second, some of the basic characteristics of RT data.
These characteristics can pose some appreciable challenges for statistical modeling, and these challenges provide important motivations
for the particular modeling approach we suggest here.

The use of RTs as dependent measures in psychology has a long
and interesting history.[1] The basic logic of the use of RTs was first

---

[1] Readers interested in comprehensive treatments of the historical and technical
issues associated with RTs should consult (in alphabetical order) Luce (1986),

summarized by Jastrow (1890): If we begin with the assumption that mental information processing is structured in some regular way, then it is safe to assume that there are various and regular ways in which information can pass through this structure. Differences among the paths required by different types of stimulus information should then be reflected in differences in the time required to accomplish the processing. This was the logic that Wundt and his colleague von Tchisch applied almost 30 years before Jastrow's summary, in studying the simultaneous perception of auditory and visual stimuli (a "complication" in the theoretical language of the time; see Townsend & Ashby, 1983).

Beginning with Wundt, almost all of the central figures in psychology — from von Helmholtz to Cattell to Skinner to Estes to Stevens to the Gibsons to the contemporary leaders in cognitive science—have had an association with RT data. For example, the Dutch psychologist Donders used RT data as the basis for his "method of subtraction" (see discussion in Townsend & Ashby, 1983). This simple and creative idea took as its starting point the logic of Jastrow, in the following way. For any task, of any given complexity, our measures of RT include (roughly speaking) the time required to process the information and the time required to make an observable response (such as a button press). If we can get measures of the time required to make the observable motor response *without* the requirement to encode and process the task information, and if we can get measures of the time required to complete the entire task (including making the observable response), then it should be possible to estimate the duration of the mental processes by subtracting the first measure from the second. This basic idea was compelling enough to allow the method of subtraction to remain (in various forms) a part of the cognitive psychologists' "toolbox" well into the 20th century (Ashby & Townsend, 1980).

While psychology in the early 20th century was dominated by behaviorist approaches, time was still an important, though subsidiary, dependent variable, in the form of response rates (as epitomized by Ferster & Skinner, 1957). Time reappeared as a central concern in the middle of the century with the cumulative revolutionary influ-

---

Townsend (1992), Townsend and Ashby (1983), and Zandt (2000, 2002).

ences of mathematical learning theory, cybernetics and communication theory, automata theory, and information theory. An example from these influences that foreshadow the arguments we pursue in this chapter was the notion of channel capacity, as it was considered in information theory (Shannon, 1948; Shannon & Weaver, 1963).[2] Close on the heels of these intellectual developments was a set of developments that allowed the technology required to make precise measurements of RTs to become more widely available and usable. Included here are the computer, the voice switches required for various psycholinguistic tasks, and the refined response boxes required by psychophysicists. By the 1960s and 1970s, RTs were held to be the dependent variable of choice for testing hypotheses about some of the most fundamental characteristics of human thought (Sternberg, 1966, 1969; Townsend, 1974).

The contemporary literature in cognitive psychology reflects a continuing reliance on RT data. By example, Zandt (2002) reports that 63% of all the published papers in one year's edition of a prominent journal in cognitive psychology used RTs as one form of experimental evidence. RT data have also become critical in studying aspects of the changes in attention and memory associated with aspects of both normal aging and age–related disease states (Faust, Balota, & Spieler, 2001; Fisher & Glaser, 1996; Salthouse, 2000; Spieler, Balota, & Faust, 2000). Unfortunately, the development of the statistical treatment of RT data has not kept pace with the development of technology and theory. For the most part, RT data are analyzed, at the level of the mean, with statistical models (usually the general linear model) that bear no a priori relationship to the theoretical model(s) or constructs of interest. Although there have recently been attempts to model entire RT distributions (see discussions in Spieler et al., 2000; Zandt, 2000, 2002), many of these attempts have used specific distributional forms without any strong theoretical justification (e.g., as is the case in Ratcliff, 1978).

---

[2]Though it is worth noting that the formal characterization of capacity that we will present does differ in a fundamental way from the approach suggested by information theory. See Townsend and Ashby (1978) for a complete discussion of this issue.

8.2.1   Important Characteristics of RT data

RT data possess some characteristics that have some important implications for statistical modeling. At a minimum, a number of these characteristics serve as bounds on the types of assumptions that can be justified in selecting statistical tools. This is of particular importance for models of the RT distribution.

A basic characteristic of RT distributions is that they have a positive lower bound. Since von Helmholtz's work on the speed of neural conduction (see, e.g., Cahan, 1993), it has been apparent that no mental state (or observable response indicative of a mental state) is instantaneous: Even the simplest perceptual experience lags physical reality by an often appreciable amount of time (see Massaro & Loftus, 1996). Time is required for the transmission of information from the sensory receptors through the afferent pathways, through the neural networks, then back through the efferent pathways, in order to execute an observable response. Generally, this lower bound is taken to be somewhere between 100 and 200 ms (Pachella, 1974).

In addition, RT distributions have finite upper bounds. In almost all known uses of RT data, values beyond some limit are assumed to be representative of processing or actions that have no relation to the psychological processes of interest. A common and compelling example is the tendency of observers in some experimental tasks to "nod off" in the middle of an experimental session, generating exceptionally long RTs on some trials. In practice, the upper bound on allowable RTs is set on the basis of the experimenter's experience with the particular paradigm. In some basic perceptual or attentional tasks, for example, the upper bound may be set at 2000 ms, while in some tasks requiring more complex activities (such as complex problem solving), the upper limit may be much higher. The combination of the positive lower bound and the finite upper bound suggests the need for methods of censoring any sample of RT observations (e.g., as discussed in Allison, 1995; Collett, 1994).

Another critical characteristic of RT distributions is that they tend to be nonnormal, possessing long positive tails (see Luce, 1986; Zandt, 2000, 2002). This characteristic skew suggests that RT distributions are best characterized (at a theoretical level) by random variables such as the Rayleigh, Weibull, or ex–Gaussian (the convolution of the exponential and Gaussian, e.g., Ratcliff, 1978), a distribution that has seen recent application in studies of cognitive aging (Spieler et al., 2000). The distributions, however they are characterized, are also, strictly speaking, conditional distributions. That is, the entry of any one observation into the sample of RTs is usually conditional on the categorical state of the response. For example, typical practice is to include only those latencies that are associated with correct responses, although there have been suggestions that RTs for incorrect responses may, in some cases, represent an important source of additional evidence for hypothesis testing (e.g., Ratcliff & Rouder, 1998).

Two types of sequential effects also need to be considered when characterizing RT data. The first is associated with the effects of practice on the experimental task. Even in somewhat simple cognitive tasks, repeated exposure can lead to systematic changes (typically reductions) in latencies (Logan, 1992). When this practice extends across a number of experimental sessions, two other effects can be noted. The first is a slowing near the end of any one session, an effect usually attributed to fatigue. The second is a brief period of slowing at the beginning of session $n + 1$, relative to, for example, the mean latency in session n; this is sometimes referred to as a "warm–up decrement." These sequential effects are associated with correct responses, but a second type of sequential effect is associated with errors, particular when, as is common, observers are presented with feedback on each trial. For example, it is often the case that responses following errors will be systematically slowed relative to responses following correct responses (Kornblum, 1969).

A final set of issues is associated with the need, in many experimental contexts, to estimate aspects of the RT distribution by aggregating repeated observations across a set of participants. The statistical issues in this case are complicated by the fact that individual differences (in terms of, e.g., measures of central tendency and dispersion, and even in terms of distributional shape) can be quite profound (Hecht, 1999; Luce, 1986; Wenger & McKinzie, 1996). A number of techniques for dealing with this situation have been suggested (see important discussions in Zandt, 2000, 2002), with an approach known as "Vincentizing" being perhaps the most common. This is an approach, adapted from the treatment of cumulative response records in the learning literature (Vincent, 1912), that (roughly speaking) aligns estimates of the quantiles of individual observers' distributions in order to produce an estimate of the aggregate distribution (see, in particular Ratcliff, 1979). Although the approach is used in a rather wide range of applications (Spieler & Balota, 1997; Spieler et al., 2000; Theeuwes, 1994), there are problems with the approach (discussed in Zandt, 2000) that suggest some caution in its application.

Figure 8.1: Example histogram for a sample of RTs, illustrating many of the typical characteristics of RT distributions.

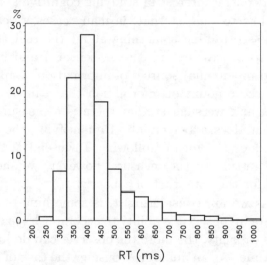

Figure 8.1 shows an example histogram for a sample of RTs collected in a recent experiment in our laboratory (Ingvalson & Wenger, 2005), and this example illustrates a number of the characteristics just discussed. In this study, the lower bound of the distribution was truncated at 100 ms, and the upper bound was set to 2000 ms. (As can be seen in Fig. 8.1, all of the observed RTs took on values far below this upper bound.) All RTs in this distribution were associated with correct responses (from a two–alternative forced–choice response task, modeled on Townsend & Nozawa, 1995; Wenger & Townsend, 2001).

8.3   RTs and a Specific Hypothesis: Capacity

By far, the majority of the published papers that use RT as a dependent measure summarize the results in terms of the central tendency (the mean or the median) of the RT distribution. The sample mean is an unbiased estimate of the expected value of a random variable (Cox & Hinkley, 1974; Papoulis, 1991). Thus, the mean RT is an estimate of what one should typically expect for the average time required to complete the processing involved in an experimental task. Although completely justifiable as a summary measure, focusing on the mean may not be optimal for analyzing the theoretical construct that is often of central interest in studying cognitive abilities.

We would like to suggest that, in many cases, researchers' true interest lies in ascertaining something about the real–time capacity of individuals to process external (e.g., sensory) and internal (e.g., attentional and mnemonic) sources of information. Capacity, in this case, refers to the amount of information that can be processed in a unit of time, and we suggest that there is a measure on the RT distribution that does a better job of quantifying the construct of capacity than does the mean (following Townsend & Ashby, 1978, 1983). Before getting to the measure, however, we should develop some intuition for the construct of capacity.

Capacity, as we are considering it, is something of an instantaneous measure of an observer's ability to accomplish (cognitive) work. The higher the capacity, the more the observer can do in a unit (e.g., an instant) of time. As an analogy,[3] consider the task of boiling a pot of water. Imagine that we have two stoves available for this task: a small backpacking stove and a professional–grade cooktop. We place a pot of water on each stove and turn each to its highest level of heat. We would have two expectations for this situation. First, we would expect the average time required to boil the water on the professional cooktop to be less than the average time required to boil the water on the backpacking stove. Second, if we were to check the water on each cooking surface at some time between when we start the process and the instant at which the water in one of the pots comes to a boil, there would be a higher likelihood of the water beginning to boil while we were checking it on the professional cooktop than there would be

---

[3]We thank Lael Schooler for suggesting this analogy.

on the backpacking stove. This second expectation is the one we suggest is captured by the notion of capacity: The professional cooktop has a higher capacity for completing its task (boiling the water) in an instant of time (that instant associated with the time required to check the water) than does the backpacking stove.

Capacity is a construct with a long history in psychology, dating back to the notion of "span of apprehension" as it was studied in the 1860s by the philosopher Hamilton and later by Cattell (see Townsend & Ashby, 1983). It would seem to be of fundamental importance in understanding a range of cognitive abilities, including the ability of various types of cues to orient selective attention, the effectiveness of various types of stimulus organization to aid perception, and the effectiveness of various types of cues for recollective performance. Although the construct is discussed frequently in a range of literatures, it has taken on a set of meanings, many of them ambiguous and only loosely related to the notion we are developing here. These include the notions of channel capacity (borrowed, as noted earlier, from information theory, e.g., Shannon, 1948; Shannon & Weaver, 1963), the capacity of the short–term memory buffer (Atkinson & Shiffrin, 1968; Shiffrin, 1975, 1976), and a variety of perspectives on the idea of working–memory capacity (Engle, 2001).

8.3.1 Formalizing the Notion of Capacity

The approach taken here is modeled directly on an idea first proposed by Townsend and Ashby (1978). Consider that we have at our disposal a sample of RT data and that we wish to test, using these data, some hypothesis regarding cognitive capacity. Following from the example we presented earlier, we desire a measure of the instantaneous likelihood that an individual in the experiment completed the task, as it would be measured *prior* to their completion of the task. This is essentially a conditional measure, one assessing the likelihood (at any given point in time) of completing the task in the next instant of time, given that it has not been completed yet.

This measure is one that is familiar in applications as diverse as reliability engineering (e.g., Cooper & McGillem, 1999) and epidemiology (e.g., Collett, 1994), where it is known as the hazard or intensity function. Mathematically, the hazard function is defined as

$$h(t) = \lim_{\Delta t \to 0} \frac{P(t \leq T \leq t + \Delta t | T \geq t)}{\Delta t}$$

$$= \frac{f(t)}{S(t)},$$

in which $f(t)$ is the probability density function (in our case, for task completion times), and $S(t) = 1 - F(t)$ is the survivor function. Because the survivor function is the complement of the cumulative distribution function $F(t) = P(T \leq t)$, it gives the probability that the task has not been completed by time t, that is, $P(T > t)$. Using the hazard function, hypotheses regarding capacity would take the form of hypothesized orderings on hazard functions in two or more conditions. For example, imagine that we have the hypothesis that older adults in the early stages of Alzheimer's disease show a decline in their capacity to process memory information, relative to an age–matched healthy control group. We can state this hypothesis as

$$h_A(t) < h_C(t)$$

for all $t > 0$, where the subscripts A and C indicate the Alzheimer's and control samples, respectively. Note that this hypothesis, by extension, implies that

$$\frac{h_A(t)}{h_C(t)} < 1$$

with the corresponding null hypothesis being

$$H_0 : \frac{h_A(t)}{h_C(t)} = 1$$

for all $t > 0$.

8.3.2   An Option for Testing Capacity Hypotheses

The formalization of the notion of capacity we have presented is one that follows from the suggestion of Townsend and Ashby (1978). These authors, however, did not address the statistical questions associated with use of the hazard function (those issues being quite tangential to the purposes of that chapter). The conventional wisdom on these issues, both at the time of Townsend and Ashby's proposal and in the published literature since, has been that the options for working with hazard functions were very limited. The handful of isolated contributions that were known in the RT literature (e.g., Bloxom, 1984, 1985; Miller & Singpurwalla, 1977) further suggested numerous technical challenges. For example, Luce (1986) emphasized these technical difficulties, noting only two approaches that might be viable, neither of which had been applied to RT data at the time. The recent treatment of RT distributions by Zandt (2000) echoed these sentiments, and an even more recent review of work with RT distributions (Zandt, 2002) considered a variety of estimators for the hazard function, including some robust kernel estimators. Application of these estimators, however, was limited to consideration of individual hazard functions, with only limited applicability to tests of hypotheses such as the one just suggested.

During this same period, there was a developing literature on a set of statistical methods designed explicitly to deal with the hazard function. In particular, in the early 1970s a highly influential paper was published by the British statistician Cox (1972). By some estimates (Garfield, 1990), this paper has become one of the 100 most–cited papers in all of science (as cited in Allison, 1995, who contends this is actually an underestimate). The basic approach outlined in this paper has come to be referred to as proportional hazards (or Cox) modeling and possesses a set of properties that are well suited to RT data.

Assume an experimental setting task involving a set of k covariates or independent variables. The modeling then begins with the assumption that the hazard function for individual i in this setting can be written as

$$h_i(t) = \lambda_0(t) \exp\left[\beta_1 x_{i1} + \ldots + \beta_k x_{ik}\right],$$

in which $\lambda_0(t)$ is some underlying *but unspecified* baseline hazard. Because this model leaves the baseline hazard $\lambda_0(t)$ unspecified, it is not necessary to make any type of assumption about the parametric form of the baseline hazard (thus getting past some of the technical concerns discussed by Luce, 1986; Zandt, 2000, 2002, in estimating the form of individual hazard functions). For this reason, proportional hazards models are sometimes referred to as "semi–parametric" (Allison, 1995; Collett, 1994). All that is required of this baseline hazard is that it not be negative.

If it can be assumed that the hazard functions for any two individuals i and j are proportional, then the model for the effects of the covariates (or independent variables) can be simplified as follows:

$$\frac{h_i(t)}{h_j(t)} = \frac{\lambda_0(t) \exp\left[\beta_1 x_{i1} + \ldots + \beta_k x_{ik}\right]}{\lambda_0(t) \exp\left[\beta_1 x_{j1} + \ldots + \beta_k x_{jk}\right]}$$

$$= \exp\left[\beta_i(x_{i1} - x_{j1}) + \ldots + \beta_k(x_{ik} - x_{jk})\right].$$

Further, taking the log of this relationship results in a linear model.

The only other critical assumption is that the hazard functions for any two individuals be proportional, an assumption that can be verified empirically. Specifically, if the hazard functions are proportional, then

$$h_{1j}(t) = \gamma h_{2j}(t)$$

for individuals 1 and 2 in condition j (Allison, 1995, p. 169). If this basic condition holds, then it can be shown (Allison, 1995) that

$$\ln\left\{-\ln\left[S_{1j}(t)\right]\right\} = \ln \gamma + \ln\left\{-\ln\left[S_{2j}(t)\right]\right\}.$$

This implies that, if one plots $\ln\left\{-\ln\left[S(t)\right]\right\}$ against t for each of the conditions, the curves should be parallel (i.e., separated by the constant distance $\ln \gamma$) if the proportionality assumption holds.

8.4   Proportional Hazards Models and RT Data

In spite of these rather weak assumptions, we are aware of only one application of the Cox models to RT data (Wenger, Schuster, & Townsend, 2002). Much of this may be due to the fact that little is known about how well proportional hazards models perform when applied to RT data. In this section, we consider the performance of these models by simulating conditions typical of RT studies. We do this for two different contexts. The first is typical of detailed studies of cognitive processes (Townsend & Nozawa, 1995; Wenger &

Townsend, 2001). In such studies, small numbers of individuals are observed over extended periods, and all analyses (including distributional analyses) are conducted at the level of the individual. The second context is used much more often and involves less–intense observation of larger numbers of individuals. For both of these situations, we create data sets in which proportionality of the hazard functions holds, with variations in the magnitude of the proportionality. We do this for sample sizes that are commonly used in RT studies, and we investigate the extent to which the proportional hazards models can both detect the proportional differences and recover an accurate estimate of the proportionality.

8.4.1   Simulating Individual Observers

When extensive amounts of data are taken from individual observers, it is typically assumed that the RTs in any one of the experimental conditions represent independent samples from the same "population" (or independent observations of an invariant generating mechanism). The sequential effects discussed in the introduction are typically dealt with in a number of ways. First, data from an initial set of sessions are discarded prior to analyses, to minimize the effects associated with practice (Wenger & Townsend, 2001). Second, a variety of "data cleaning" procedures are used to deal with the sequential effects associated with errors (Kornblum, 1969). Many of these types of RT studies, however, involve performance involving very few (e.g., less than 3%) errors, so this second type of sequential effect is assumed to exert very little influence on the obtained data.

In order to generate data for the simulation of individual observers, we began with the assumption that the overall process times (including the residual or base times required to generate the observable response) can be modeled using a two–parameter Weibull (1951) distribution. The probability density function for this distribution is given by

$$f(t) \;=\; \frac{\gamma t^{\gamma-1}}{\lambda^{\gamma}} \exp\left[-\left(\frac{t}{\lambda}\right)^{\gamma}\right], \qquad (8.1)$$

in which λ is a location parameter, and γ is a shape parameter. The Weibull distribution has been used in a number of applications to RT

data (Colonius, 1990, 1995; Logan, 1988, 1992, 1995), in part because
it is easy to use in analytic work, and in part because variations
in the shape parameter allows the Weibull to approximate a set of
important distributional forms. Both properties are relevant to the
work presented here.

Figure 8.2: Weibull density functions that are equated on their median
values and differ in shape, approximating exponential, ex–Gaussian, and
Gaussian densities.

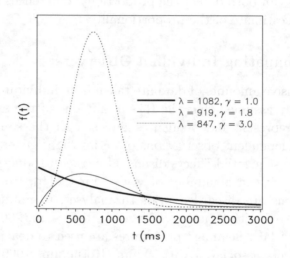

The flexibility of the Weibull distribution, in terms of its shape,
is illustrated in Figure 8.2. This figure shows three Weibull distributions, all possessing the same median value (750 ms), but varying
in terms of their shapes. When $\gamma = 1.0$, the density approximates
the shape of an exponential distribution. When $\gamma = 1.8$, the density
possesses the long tail associated with the ex–Gaussian distribution.
And when $\gamma = 3.0$, the Weibull approximates the Gaussian distribution. The hazard functions corresponding to each of these densities
are presented in Figure 8.3.

With respect to analytic work, basic descriptive statistics—the
mean, median, and variance—can be obtained from the following:

$$\text{Mean} \;=\; \frac{\beta}{\gamma}\Gamma\left(\frac{1}{\gamma}\right)$$

$$\text{Median} \;=\; \beta \left[\ln(2)\right]^{1/\gamma}$$

$$\text{Variance} \;=\; \frac{\beta^2}{\gamma} \left[2\Gamma\left(\frac{2}{\gamma}\right) - \frac{1}{\gamma}\left(\Gamma\left(\frac{1}{\gamma}\right)\right)^2 \right],$$

where Γ is the gamma function (S. Ross, 1994). The cumulative distribution and survivor functions for this form of the Weibull are given by

$$F(t) \;=\; 1 - \exp\left[-\left(\frac{t}{\beta}\right)^{\gamma}\right] \tag{8.2}$$

and

$$S(t) \;=\; \exp\left[-\left(\frac{t}{\beta}\right)^{\gamma}\right], \tag{8.3}$$

respectively. These functions are important in generating data that possess a specific proportionality relationship in their hazard functions. Specifically, assume that the hazard functions from two experimental conditions are related by the proportionality constant k:

$$h_1(t) = k h_2(t).$$

Then, from the relationship between the hazard and survivor functions,

$$S_1(t) \;=\; [S_2(t)]^k, \tag{8.4}$$

when the expression in Equation 8.3 is used in Equation 8.4, and with the complementary relationship between the hazard function and the cumulative distribution function, it becomes possible (using inverse methods, e.g., S. M. Ross, 1997) to generate distributions (for any value of λ and γ) that possess a known proportionality k in their hazard functions.

Table 8.1 presents the parameters that were used to perform the simulations of single–observer data. The critical variations were the value of the shape parameter for the Weibull distribution, the magnitude of the proportionality relationship for two hazard functions, and the number of trials simulated for the two hazard functions.

Figure 8.3: Hazard functions corresponding to the three density functions presented in Fig. 8.2.

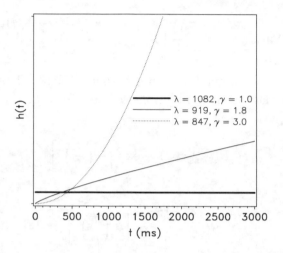

The range of values for the number of trials per condition represents the typical lower and upper values used in experiments of this type (Townsend & Nozawa, 1995; Wenger & Townsend, 2001). In the simulations that we report next, the hazard function with the higher values represented the baseline or "control" condition, whereas the hazard function with the lower values represented the "experimental" condition. Thus, all estimates of the proportionality relationship returned by the model estimation procedures were in terms of the inverse of the proportionality relationship given by k, with the expected value of the parameter estimate being $\ln[1/k]$.

For all of the possible combinations of Weibull shape parameter, proportionality, and sample size, we performed 1,000 replications, obtaining the estimate of the proportionality relationship for each replication. All data were generated using SAS 8.2, and all parameter estimates were obtained using proc phreg in SAS 8.2. Having the data and parameter estimates obtained from the simulations, we were in a position to both estimate the overall probability that the null hypothesis of equal hazards (i.e., $k = 1$) was rejected and examine the extent to which the parameter estimates returned by the model–

Table 8.1: Parameters for the Simulations of the Single–Observer Data

Parmameter	Role	Values
	Lower bound, RT distribution	100
	Upper bound, RT distribution	3000
γ	Distributional shape	1.0, 1.8, 3.0
k	Proportionality	1.05, 1.30, 1.55, 1.80, 2.05
β	$\ln[1/k]$	-.05, -.26, -.44, -.59, -.72
n	Trials/condition	50, 150, 250
N_R	Replications	1000

fitting procedure accurately captured the actual proportionality in the data.

Figure 8.4 presents the proportion of the total replications in which the null hypothesis was rejected, for each combination of sample size and proportionality. Data in this figure are for the simulations in which the shape parameter of the Weibull was set to 1.8 (approximating the long–tailed ex–Gaussian distribution); results for the other two values of the shape parameter were essentially identical.[4] As can be seen in Fig. 8.4, once the value of the proportionality parameter k was beyond 1.55, the probability of rejecting the null hypothesis was reasonably high (above 50%), even for the smallest sample size. Although there were sizable differences in the probability of rejecting the null hypothesis across the three sample sizes at all but the highest value of the proportionality parameter, these results suggest that, given standard practices (in terms of sample sizes, e.g., Townsend & Nozawa, 1995; Wenger & Townsend, 2001), investigators can have a reasonable degree of confidence in being able to detect true proportional differences.

Figure 8.5 presents the mean values of the obtained parameter estimates, as a function of the proportionality parameter (expressed, as explained earlier, as $\ln(1/k)$) and the sample size. Again, we present results only for the simulations in which the shape parameter of the Weibull was set to allow the distribution to approximate the long–

---

[4]Plots of all of the results for the other two values of the shape parameter are available on request from M. J. Wenger, Department of Psychology, The Pennsylvania State University, mjw19@psu.edu.

Figure 8.4: Estimated probability of rejecting the null hypothesis of equality in the hazards, as a function of the magnitude of the proportionality parameter and sample size, assuming a Weibull distribution with $\gamma = 1.8$ (see Equation 8.1).

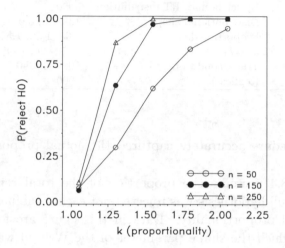

tailed ex–Gaussian distribution. The error bars in this figure give the 95% confidence intervals for each of the sample sizes, estimated as range of values between the 2.5th and 97.5th percentile of the 1,000 replications. The line running from the origin to the lower right corner of the figure gives the expectation for what should have been obtained had the model returned veridical estimates of proportionality.

A first point of note in these results is that there is very little evidence suggesting any effects of sample size across this range of values. A second point of note is that the model estimation procedure appears to be quite good at estimating the true proportionality in the data. Figure 8.6 presents another view of these results, this time in terms of the magnitude of the difference between the true and the estimated values of the parameter for the proportionality. The results in Fig. 8.6 suggest a slight underestimate of the true proportionality, but the magnitude of the underestimate diminishes as sample size increases.

Figure 8.5: Estimated parameters for the proportional hazards model, as a function of the actual proportionality parameter and sample size, for the simulations involving the Weibull distribution with $\gamma = 1.8$ (see Equation 8.1). Error bars represent the 95% confidence intervals for each of the sample sizes.

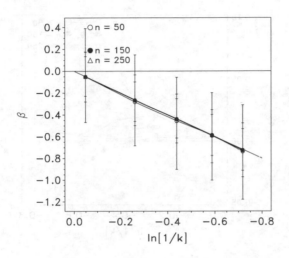

The results for the simulations of the single–observer data are quite encouraging. Specifically, it appears that, for sample sizes that are representative of typical practice, should there be a true ordering of hazard functions in the data, there is a reasonably high likelihood that this ordering will be detected (i.e., the null hypothesis of "no ordering" will be rejected), even when the magnitude of the ordering is reasonably small. In addition, it appears that, although there is some evidence for bias in the estimates (these being conservative), this bias is eliminated with increases in sample size. This small bias has positive implications for hypotheses regarding the magnitude of the ordering (see, in particular, Townsend & Nozawa, 1995), though such issues go well beyond the questions we seek to address in this chapter.

Figure 8.6: Magnitude of the difference between the true value of the proportionality parameter (β^*) and the value estimated from the data, as a function of the true value of the proportionality parameter and sample size, for the simulations involving the Weibull distribution with $\gamma = 1.8$ (see Equation 8.1).

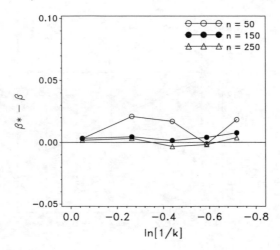

8.4.2   Simulating Aggregates of Observers

As noted at the beginning of this chapter, modal experimental practice in the RT literature is to collect a small number of observations from a large group of individuals, rather than (as was considered in the previous section) a large number of observations from a small set of observers. In such settings, data are typically aggregated across observers. When operating at the level of the mean, this aggregation does not pose any significant problems. However, the capacity hypotheses we wish to pursue are framed at the level of the RT distribution; here, aggregation across observers can pose serious problems (Thomas & Ross, 1980).

The most critical of these problems is referred to as unobserved heterogeneity (see, e.g., Allison, 1995). In situations in which multiple observations are taken on the individuals who contribute data to the overall sample, there can be assumed to be systematic differences among individuals. As discussed at the beginning of this chapter,

such individual differences are well acknowledged in the RT literature. In addition, there is the issue of within–observer dependencies,
with the relationship between any two RTs for one individual being
stronger than the relationship between one RT for one observer and
one RT for another observer.

There have been a number of suggestions for dealing with these
problems in the context of the use of proportional hazards models
(Allison, 1995; Klein, 1992; McGilchrist, 1993). The approach we
take here is to apply an extension to the proportional hazards model
known as fixed–effects partial likelihood models (Allison, 1995, 1996).
These models assume that the log–hazard function for each observer
i and each observation j can be written as

$$\ln[h_{ij}(t)] = \alpha_i(t) + \beta x_{ij}(t) + \epsilon_i,$$

in which $\alpha_i(t)$ is some unspecified hazard function particular to the
individual, $x_{ij}(t)$ represents one of the experimental factors as it im-
pacts the performance of one individual, and ϵ_i is the unobserved
heterogeneity attributable to one individual, which is absorbed into
the baseline log–hazard function $\alpha_i(t)$.

The basic structure of the aggregate simulations followed the
structure of the simulations of individual observers, with one critical
difference. To better simulate the problems associated with individual differences, we included two additional manipulations. First, we
allowed the overall sample of individuals to be composed of samples
drawn from each of the three shapes of the Weibull distribution, in
four different ratios. In the first, all three shapes were represented
with equal frequency and will be referred to as the "1:1:1" condition.
In the remaining three conditions, the frequency of individuals with
one of the three shape parameter values was allowed to be four times
that of the other two: The "4:1:1" condition was dominated by individuals simulated with $\gamma = 1.0$ (approximating the exponential distribution); the "1:4:1" condition was dominated by individuals simulated with $\gamma = 1.8$ (approximating the ex–Gaussian distribution);
and the "1:1:4" condition was dominated by individuals simulated
with $\gamma = 3.0$ (approximating the Gaussian distribution). The second
manipulation used to approximate the range of individual differences
commonly observed in RT studies involved allowing the median time
for each individual in each replication to vary. Median times for the

distributions were drawn from a uniform distribution on the interval running from 750 to 1500 ms. The number of samples per observer was set to one of three levels (10, 20, or 30 per observer), approximating the range of samples per observer commonly seen in aggregate RT studies. The total number of individuals in the sample was held constant at 30, a value that is consistent with standard experimental practice. Table 8.2 presents the parameters for the simulations of the aggregate data.

Table 8.2: Parameters for the Simulations of the Group RT Data

Parameter	Role	Values
	Lower bound, RT distribution	100
	Upper bound, RT distribution	3000
γ	Distributional shape	1.0, 1.8, 3.0
k	Proportionality	1.05, 1.30, 1.55, 1.80, 2.05
β	$\ln[1/k]$	-.05, -.26, -.44, -.59, -.72
N	Total individuals	10
n_γ	Obs/shape	1:1:1, 4:1:1, 1:4:1, 1:1:4
n	Trials/individual	15, 30
T_M	Median	[750, 1500], uniform

We begin our consideration of the results of these simulations by examining the likelihood of rejecting the null hypothesis (no ordering). Figure 8.7 presents these results, as a function of sample composition, number of observations per observer, and magnitude of the proportionality parameter. The results from the group data are very similar to those for the simulations of single observers, in spite of the variations intended to approximate individual differences. In all cases, once the proportionality constant was greater than 1.30, the probability of rejecting the null hypothesis was reasonably high, even with small numbers of observations per individual. There were no appreciable differences across the various mixtures of distributional shapes.

Figure 8.8 presents the mean values of the estimated parameters across the variations in sample size, magnitude of the proportionality parameter, and mixture of the three distributional forms. As before, error bars represent the 95% confidence intervals, estimated using the 2.5th and 97.5th percentiles on the obtained sampling distribu-

Figure 8.7: Estimated probability of rejecting the null hypothesis of equality in the hazards, as a function of the magnitude of the proportionality parameter, sample size, and composition of the overall sample for the group data simulations.

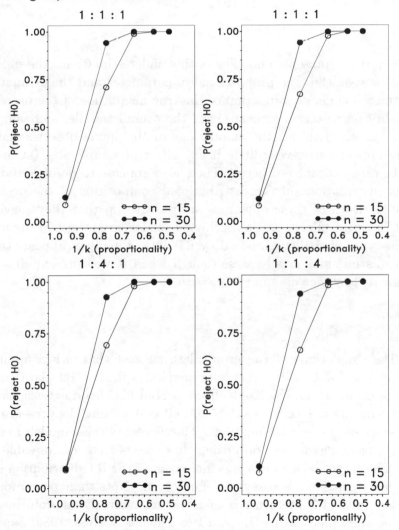

tions, and the solid line running from the origin to the lower right corner presents the true proportionality. As was true for the simulations of the single–observer data, the effects of sample size were minimal, as were the effects of distributional mixtures. In addition, there appeared to be little evidence for bias in the estimates of the true proportionality.

Figure 8.9 presents one view of this underestimation—the difference between the true proportionality parameter and the estimated parameter value, as a function of the true magnitude of the proportionality parameter, composition of the overall sample, and sample size. As was true for the simulations of the single–observer data, there appear to be very little if any effect of sample size (at least in the range considered here). There also appears to be little if any effect of variations in the distributional composition of the overall sample. Both of these outcomes are positive, in that they suggest that the fixed–effects partial likelihood models are robust in the face of the types of challenges posed by RT data. Finally, it appears that bias was minimal in all cases, though when it was present, it was modulated by increases in sample size.

The simulations of the group data suggest that, when applied to simulated data that possess properties typical of RT data from groups of observers, the fixed–effects partial likelihood extensions to the proportional hazards models do well in detecting the presence of orderings on the hazard functions. The success of these models in detecting orderings is very promising: It suggests that it is possible to test hypotheses regarding a specific aspect of the RT distribution using data aggregated across a set of observers. Note that conventional wisdom in the RT literature is that such an enterprise is problematic and possibly inadvisable (Luce, 1986; Thomas & Ross, 1980; Zandt, 2000). The outcomes documented here suggest that proportional hazards modeling, with its weak assumptions regarding the underlying distributions, may be an excellent solution to such problems.

Figure 8.8: Estimated parameters for the proportional hazards model, as a function of the actual proportionality parameter, sample size, and composition of the overall sample for the group data simulations. Error bars give the 95% confidence intervals for each of the sample sizes.

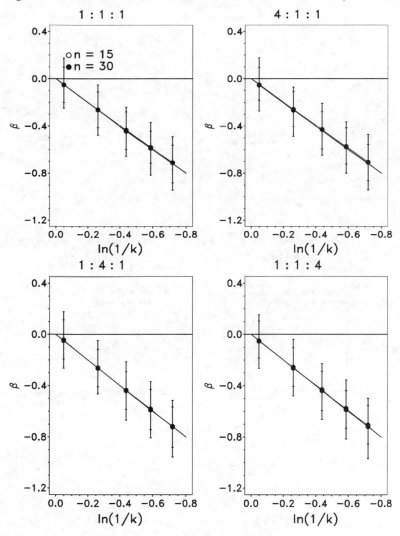

Figure 8.9: Magnitude of the difference between the true value of the proportionality relationship (β^*) and the value estimated from the data, as a function of the true value of the proportionality parameter, sample size, and composition of the overall sample for the group data simulations.

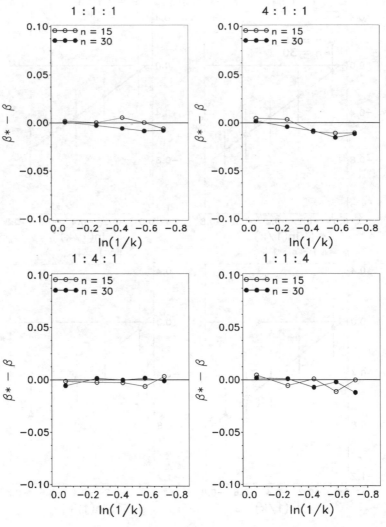

8.5   An Example Application: Recall Latencies in Older Adults

To illustrate the potential utility of the proportional hazards models, we consider a data set collected at the Mayo Clinic Alzheimer's Disease Research Center. These data were collected as a pilot project examining the characterization of the changes in memory performance associated with normal aging and mild cognitive impairment (see Petersen, 1995; Petersen et al., 1992, 1994, 1999). Previous work in this area has documented that performance on a task involving both free and cued recall (Bushke, 1984; Grober & Bushke, 1987) is one of a set of reliable indicators that may help distinguish the changes associated with normal aging from the changes involved in mild cognitive impairment (Petersen, 1995; Petersen et al., 1992). One particular aspect of performance tapped by this task is the ability to acquire, retain, and express memory for new information. This aspect of performance, particularly as it taps cognitive processes critical in the expression of recently acquired memory, can be characterized in terms of the real–time capacity for retrieving and expressing memory. To our knowledge, however, latencies in a free and cued recall task have never been analyzed with respect to hypotheses regarding capacity, particularly when framed in terms of the hazard function of the RT distribution.

Data were collected from a sample of 34 adults at the Mayo Clinic Alzheimer's Disease Research Center. There were 18 male and 16 female participants, with a mean age of 76.7 years and a mean education of 13.6 years. Thirty individuals were normal control participants, whereas three had the diagnosis of mild cognitive impairment, and one had very mild Alzheimer's disease. The mean Mini–Mental State Exam score for controls was 27.8 (max = 30), and the mean Dementia Rating Scale was 136.8 (max = 144). All were presented with a list of items to learn, in the form of a set of pictures of common objects (e.g., "hammer"). Each picture was accompanied by two words: a category label (e.g., "tool") and the name of an associated object within the same category (e.g., "saw"). Following presentation of the list, participants were first asked to freely recall as many of the items as possible. They were then cued for recall of any items not produced in free recall in one of three ways: with the category cue, with the associated item, or with both the category cue and the associated item. This procedure was repeated a total of five times.[5] Time to respond to the cue(s) was measured using a timer accurate to ±1 ms.

Our goals for this initial work were reasonably modest. First, we needed to determine if it was possible to collect a set of RT data in this task that could be analyzed in terms of hypotheses regarding retrieval capacity. Second, if we were able to collect RT data, we needed to determine the extent to which the distribution of latencies in this population could provide interpretable information when analyzed using proportional hazards models. Finally, if we were able to glean interpretable results from the analyses, we needed to ascertain the extent to which those results were consistent with earlier work. Specifically, we were interested in determining the extent to which the various cuing conditions impacted the retrieval capacity of participants.

Figure 8.10 presents a summary of overall performance on four measures—mean free recall, mean cued recall, mean free + cued recall, and mean latency to respond to the retrieval cue. Overall, participants increased their performance (as measured by the sum of free and cued recall) and decreased their mean latency to respond to cues with repeated testing. This outcome is generally consistent with prior work in the literature on aging effects in memory (e.g., Petersen et al., 1992) and with work on the general effects of repeated testing in college–aged observers (hypermnesia; Payne, 1987; Payne & Wenger, 1996; Roediger & Payne, 1982).

For present purposes, the analyses of central interest were those pertinent to the possibility that the various cuing conditions might affect the retrieval capacity of participants, as measured by the hazard function of the RT distribution. Prior to analysis, RTs that were shorter than 200 ms or greater than 3000 ms were removed from the data set. The remaining observations were analyzed using the fixed–effects partial likelihood extensions to the proportional hazards model. A set of models was specified using linearly independent subsets of the following variables: (a) the cuing condition (category cue, associated instance cue, both), (b) the pass (or iteration), (c) free

---

[5]Details of the basic task procedure can be found in Petersen et al. (1992), with related details in Bushke (1984) and Grober and Bushke (1987).

Figure 8.10: Descriptive statistics for recall performance, as a function of iteration, summarized in terms of mean free recall (upper left), mean cued recall (upper right), mean free + cued recall (lower left), and mean RT to the recall cues (lower right).

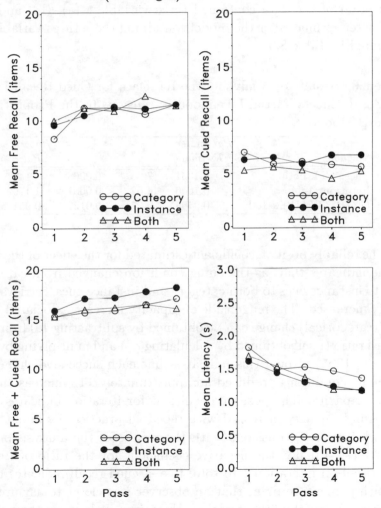

recall on each iteration, (d) cued recall on each iteration, (e) free +
cued recall on each iteration, (f) total free recall, (g) total cued recall,
(h) total free + cued recall, and (i) the ratio of free + cued recall on
iteration 1 to total free + cued recall (expressed as a percentage).
This last variable was included to assess the extent of improvement
across iterations: the higher the value, the lower the magnitude of
improvement across iterations. The model that provided the best
description of the data contained three variables: (a), (b), and (i).
Parameter estimates for the model containing these three variables is
presented in Table 8.3.

Table 8.3: Results of Analyzing the RT Data for Cued Recall Using
the Fixed–Effects Partial Likelihood Extensions to the Proportional
Hazards Model

Variable	Parameter Estimate	χ^2	p	Hazard Ratio
Cues: C, I, both	0.1331	7.33	0.0068	1.142
Iteration: 1-5	0.1646	44.62	< 0.0001	1.179
$(FCR_1/TFCR) \times 100$	-0.0498	6.27	0.0123	0.951

The reliably positive coefficient estimated for the effect of the type
of cue indicates that, as the cuing condition changed from category
cues to instance cues to both category and instance cues, retrieval capacity increased. The magnitude of capacity increase associated with
each (categorical) change can be obtained by subtracting 1.0 from the
hazard ratio (itself obtained by calculating e^β) and multiplying by 100
(Allison, 1995). Doing this indicates that each successive change in
the cuing conditions produced an approximately 14% increase in retrieval capacity. The positive coefficient for iteration indicates that
processing capacity increased with repeated practice, by about 18%
on each iteration, consistent with the results of the analysis of the
mean RTs. Finally, the negative coefficient for the ratio of free +
cued recall on interation 1 to total free + cued recall indicates that,
for each percentage point that an observer was closer to asymptotic
performance on the first iteration, there was little more than a 5%
decrease in capacity. In other words, lower retrieval capacity was
associated with lower levels of improvement across iterations, when
assessed using the free + cued recall. This latter point is important,

as the free + cued recall measure has been shown to be an important indicator in studying changes in memory performance associated with both normal aging and mild cognitive impairment (Petersen, 1995; Petersen et al., 1992).

8.6   Conclusions

RT data are extensively used in the study of cognitive processes and provide a central source of evidence for the testing of numerous hypotheses. Following the suggestion of Townsend and Ashby (1978), we have advanced the notion that one characterization of the RT distribution—specifically, the hazard function—naturally captures the construct of processing capacity and does so in a much more meaningful way than does either the mean or the median RT. Although conventional wisdom in the RT literature has suggested that it is potentially inadvisable to test hypotheses regarding hazard functions, we hope to have provided an initial demonstration that proportional hazards regression models are well suited to such a task. This is due in no small part to the fact that the distributional assumptions of the proportional hazards model are easily satisfied, giving the approach a great deal of flexibility. Simulations of individual observer and aggregate data sets, each constructed to mirror the typical properties of empirical RT distributions, demonstrated that proportional hazards models are reasonably powerful, even with generally small sample sizes. They do, however, possess a consistent conservative bias, in that they underestimate the actual proportionality that exists in the data. Thus, a necessary next step in our methodologial program will involve exploration of the use of procedures designed to correct the bias (Colosimo, Silva, & Cruz, 2000; Hughes, 1993).

Our approach to dealing with unobserved heterogeneity and repeated events was to use a class of extensions to the proportional hazards models known as fixed–effects partial likelihood models. These are but one type of adaptation to repeated events, with an important second class being frailty models (Klein, 1992; McGilchrist, 1993). We are currently examining the robustness of these frailty models with both simulated and actual RT data across variations in the magnitude of proportional relationships and sample sizes.

The results of our pilot study indicate that it is possible to collect RT data in a free and cued recall task and analyze those RTs with reference to hypotheses regarding retrieval capacity. The ability to do this suggests that analyses of retrieval capacity may provide an important and novel source of evidence regarding the changes in memory that are associated with normal aging and with mild cognitive impairment, and we are currently planning an effort that will examine the manner in which retrieval capacity may change across the life span.

References

Allison, P. D. (1995). *Survival analysis using the* SAS *system: A practical guide.* Cary, NC: SAS Institute.

Allison, P. D. (1996). Fixed-effects partial likelihood for repeated events. *Sociological Methods and Research, 25,* 207–222.

Ashby, F. G., & Townsend, J. T. (1980). Decomposing the reaction time distribution: Pure insertion and selective influence revisited. *Journal of Mathematical Psychology, 21,* 93–123.

Atkinson, R. C., & Shiffrin, R. M. (1968). Human memory: A proposed system and its control processes. In K. W. Spence & J. T. Spence (Eds.), *The psychology of learning and motivation* (Vol. 2, pp. 89–195). New York: Academic Press.

Bloxom, B. (1984). Estimating response time hazard functions: An exposition and extension. *Journal of Mathematical Psychology, 28,* 401–420.

Bloxom, B. (1985). A constrained spline estimator of a hazard function. *Psychometrika, 50,* 301–321.

Bushke, H. (1984). Cued recall in amnesia. *Journal of Clinical Neuropsychology, 6,* 433–440.

Cahan, D. (1993). *Hermann ludwig ferdinand von helmholtz and the foundations of nineteenth century science.* Los Angeles: University of California Press.

Collett, D. (1994). *Modeling survival data in medical research.* London: Chapman & Hall.

Colonius, H. (1990). A note on the stop-signal paradigm, or how to observe the unobservable. *Psychological Review, 97,* 309–312.

Colonius, H. (1995). The instance theory of automaticity: Why the Weibull? *Psychological Review, 102*, 744–750.

Colosimo, E. A., Silva, A. F., & Cruz, F. R. B. (2000). Bias evaluation in the proportional hazards model. *Journal of Statistical Computing and Simulation, 65*, 191–201.

Cooper, G. R., & McGillem, C. D. (1999). *Probabilistic methods of signal and system analysis.* New York: Oxford University Press.

Cox, D. R. (1972). Regression models and life tables (with discussion). *Journal of the Royal Statistical Society, B34*, 187–220.

Cox, D. R., & Hinkley, D. V. (1974). *Theoretical statistics.* London: Chapman & Hall.

Engle, R. W. (2001). What is working memory capacity? In H. L. Roediger & J. S. Nairne (Eds.), *The nature of remembering: Essays in honor of Robert G. Crowder* (pp. 297–314). Washington, DC: American Psychological Association.

Faust, M. E., Balota, D. A., & Spieler, D. H. (2001). Building episodic connections: Changes in episodic priming with age and dementia. *Neuropsychology, 15*, 626–637.

Ferster, C. B., & Skinner, B. F. (1957). *Schedules of reinforcement.* New York: Appleton-Century-Crofts.

Fisher, D. L., & Glaser, R. (1996). Molar and latent models of cognitive slowing: Implications for aging, dementia, depression, development and intelligence. *Psychonomic Bulletin & Review, 3*, 458–480.

Garfield, E. (1990, February 12). 100 most cited papers of all time. *Current Contents, February 12.*

Grober, E., & Bushke, H. (1987). Genuine memory deficits in dementia. *Developmental Neuropsychology, 3*, 13–36.

Hecht, S. A. (1999). Individual solution processes while solving addition and multiplication math facts in adults. *Memory & Cognition, 27*(6), 1097–1106.

Hughes, M. D. (1993). Regression dilution in the proportional hazards model. *Biometrics, 49*, 1056–1066.

Ingvalson, E. M., & Wenger, M. J. (2005). A strong test of the dual mode hypothesis. *Perception & Psychophysics, 67*, 14–35.

Jastrow, J. (1890). *The time relations of mental phenomena.* New York: Hodges.

Klein, J. P. (1992). Semiparametric estimation of random effects using the cox model based on the EM algorithm. *Biometrics*, *48*, 795–806.

Kornblum, S. (1969). Sequential determinants of information processing in serial and discrete choice reaction time. *Psychological Review*, *76*, 113–131.

Logan, G. D. (1988). Toward an instance theory of automatization. *Psychological Review*, *95*, 492–527.

Logan, G. D. (1992). Shapes of reaction time distributions and shapes of learning curves: A test of the instance theory of automaticity. *Journal of Experimental Psychology: Learning, Memory, and Cognition*, *18*, 883–914.

Logan, G. D. (1995). The Weibull distribution, the power law, and the instance theory of automaticity. *Psychological Review*, *102*, 751–756.

Luce, R. D. (1986). *Reaction times: Their role in inferring elementary mental organization*. New York: Oxford University Press.

Massaro, D. W., & Loftus, G. R. (1996). Sensory and perceptual storage: Data and theory. In E. L. Bjork & R. A. Bjork (Eds.), *Memory: Handbook of perception and cognition* (Vol. NONE, pp. 67–99). San Diego CA: Academic Press.

McGilchrist, C. A. (1993). REML estimation for survival models with frailty. *Biometrics*, *49*, 221–225.

Miller, D. R., & Singpurwalla, N. D. (1977). *Failure rate estimation using random smoothing* (Tech. Rep. No. AD-A040999/5ST). National Technical Information Service.

Pachella, R. (1974). The interpretation of reaction time in information processing research. In B. H. Kantowitz (Ed.), *Human information processing: Tutorials in performance and cognition* (pp. 41–82). Hillsdale, NJ: Lawrence Erlbaum Associates.

Papoulis, A. (1991). *Probability, random variables, and stochastic processes*. New York: McGraw-Hill.

Payne, D. G. (1987). Hypermnesia and reminiscence in recall: A historical and empirical review. *Psychological Bulletin*, *101*, 5–27.

Payne, D. G., & Wenger, M. J. (1996). Practice effects in memory: Data, theory, and unanswered questions. In D. Herrmann, C. McEvoy, C. Herzog, P. Hertel, & M. K. Johnson (Eds.), *Ba-*

sic and applied memory research: Practical applications (pp. 123–138). Mahwah, NJ: Lawrence Erlbaum Associates.

Payne, D. G., & Wenger, M. J. (1998). *Cognitive psychology*. Boston, MA: Houghton Mifflin.

Petersen, R. C. (1995). Normal aging, mild cognitive impairment, and early alzheimer's disease. *The Neurologist, 1*, 326–344.

Petersen, R. C., Smith, G., Kokmen, E., Ivnik, R. J., & Tangalos, E. G. (1992). Memory function in normal aging. *Neurology, 42*, 396–401.

Petersen, R. C., Smith, G., Kokmen, E., Ivnik, R. J., & Tangalos, E. G. (1994). Memory function in very early Alzheimer's disease. *Neurology, 44*, 867–872.

Petersen, R. C., Smith, G. E., Waring, S. C., Ivnik, R. J., Tangalos, E. G., & Komken, E. (1999). Mild cognitive impairment: Clinical characterization and outcome. *Archives of Neurology, 56*, 303–308.

Ratcliff, R. (1978). A theory of memory retrieval. *Psychological Review, 85*, 59–108.

Ratcliff, R. (1979). Group reaction time distributions and an analysis of distribution statistics. *Psychological Bulletin, 86*, 446–461.

Ratcliff, R., & Rouder, J. N. (1998). Modeling response times for two-choice decisions. *Psychological Science, 9*, 347–356.

Roediger, H. L., & Payne, D. G. (1982). Hypermnesia: The role of repeated testing. *Journal of Experimental Psychology: Learning, Memory, and Cognition, 8*, 66–72.

Ross, S. (1994). *A first course in probability*. New York: Macmillan.

Ross, S. M. (1997). *Introduction to probability models* (6th ed.). San Diego, CA: Academic Press.

Salthouse, T. A. (2000). Aging and measures of processing speed. *Biological Psychology, 54*, 35–54.

Shannon, C. E. (1948). A mathematical theory of communication. *The Bell System Technical Journal, 27*, 379–423.

Shannon, C. E., & Weaver, W. (1963). *The mathematical theory of communication*. Urbana: University of Illinois Press.

Shiffrin, R. M. (1975). The locus and role of attention in memory systems. In P. M. A. Rabbitt & S. Dornic (Eds.), *Attention and performance* V. New York: Academic Press.

Shiffrin, R. M. (1976). Capacity limitations in information processing, attention, and memory. In W. K. Estes (Ed.), *Handbook of learning and cognitive processes: Memory processes* (Vol. 4, pp. 25–68). Hillsdale, NJ: Lawrence Erlbaum Associates.

Spieler, D. H., & Balota, D. A. (1997). Bringing computational models of word naming down to the item level. *Psychological Science, 8*, 411–416.

Spieler, D. H., Balota, D. A., & Faust, M. E. (2000). Levels of selective attention revealed through analyses of reaction time distributions. *Journal of Experimental Psychology: Human Perception and Performance, 26*, 506–526.

Sternberg, S. (1966). High-speed scanning in human memory. *Science, 153*, 652–654.

Sternberg, S. (1969). Memory scanning: Mental processes revealed by reaction time experiments. *American Scientist, 4*, 421–457.

Theeuwes, J. (1994). Stimulus-driven capture and attentional set: Selective search for color and visual abrupt onsets. *Journal of Experimental Psychology: Human Perception and Performance, 20*, 799–806.

Thomas, E. A. C., & Ross, B. H. (1980). On appropriate procedures for combining probability distributions within the same family. *Journal of Mathematical Psychology, 21*, 136–152.

Townsend, J. T. (1974). Issues and models concerning the processing of a finite number of inputs. In B. H. Kantowitz (Ed.), *Human information processing: Tutorials in performance and cognition* (pp. 133–168). Hillsdale, NJ: Lawrence Erlbaum Associates.

Townsend, J. T. (1992). On the proper scales for reaction time. In H.-G. Geissler, S. W. Link, & J. T. Townsend (Eds.), *Cognition, information processing, and psychophysics: Basic issues* (pp. 105–120). Hillsdale, NJ: Lawrence Erlbaum Associates.

Townsend, J. T., & Ashby, F. G. (1978). Methods of modeling capacity in simple processing systems. In J. Castellan & F. Restle (Eds.), *Cognitive theory* (Vol. 3, pp. 200–239). Hillsdale, NJ: Lawrence Erlbaum Associates.

Townsend, J. T., & Ashby, F. G. (1983). *Stochastic modeling of elementary psychological processes*. Cambridge, UK: Cambridge University Press.

Townsend, J. T., & Nozawa, G. (1995). On the spatio-temporal properties of elementary perception: An investigation of parallel, serial, and coactive theories. *Journal of Mathematical Psychology*, *39*, 321–359.

Vincent, S. B. (1912). The function of the viborisse in the behavior of the white rat. *Behavioral Monographs*, *1*.

Weibull, W. (1951). A statistical distribution function of wide applicability. *Journal of Applied Mechanics*, *18*, 293–297.

Wenger, M. J., & McKinzie, D. L. (1996). Ontogenetic differences in variability on simple measures of learning: Theoretical and practical implications. *Developmenal Psychobiology*, *29*, 219–240.

Wenger, M. J., Schuster, C., & Townsend, J. T. (2002, June). *Testing capacity hypotheses: Applying proportional hazards and frailty models*. Miami University, Oxford OH.

Wenger, M. J., & Townsend, J. T. (2001). Faces as gestalt stimuli: Process characteristics. In M. J. Wenger & J. T. Townsend (Eds.), *Computational, geometric, and process perspectives on facial cognition* (pp. 229–284). Mahwah, NJ: Lawrence Erlbaum Associates.

Zandt, T. Van. (2000). How to fit a response time distribution. *Psychonomic Bulletin and Review*, *7*, 424–465.

Zandt, T. Van. (2002). Analysis of response time distributions. In J. T. Wixted (Ed.), *Stevens' handbook of experimental psychology* (3rd ed., pp. 461–516). San Diego, CA: Academic Press.

9

The Utility of Genetically Informative Data in the Study of Development

Michael C. Neale[1]
Virginia Commonwealth University

Steven M. Boker and Cindy S. Bergeman
University of Notre Dame

Hermine H. Maes
Virginia Commonwealth University

Data collected from groups of relatives, such as MZ and DZ twins, provide an opportunity to test alternative hypotheses about factor structure and the origins of covariation across time. Such data require multiple–group modeling and constraints to equate parameters across the family members, providing the opportunity to test various hypotheses about growth. One set of hypotheses addresses familial resemblance for growth curve components, and if so whether these patterns are consistent with genetic or environmental factors. A second set of hypotheses addresses whether variation in growth is associated with genetic factors and whether the residual variance in a growth curve model has reliable as well as unreliable components of variance. The full information maximum likelihood model–fitting framework provided by Mx is described. Genetic modeling of dynamical systems is also described and illustrated with application to twin data on blood pressure collected in a physical and mental stress experiment.

---

[1]Michael C. Neale is supported by PHS grants MH-65322, DA-11287, MH/AA49492, MH01458, and AG18384.

9.1   Introduction

Genetically informative research designs, such as the classical twin study of monozygotic (MZ) and dizygotic (DZ) twins, are used to assess genetic and environmental influences on individual differences. In their simplest form, these methods can address questions such as, "Why are some individuals more prone to heart attacks or high blood pressure?" or "Why do some elderly individuals recover easily from adverse life circumstances, whereas others do not?" At this simplest level, a genetically informative study partitions phenotypic variation into genetic and environmental variance components. In a multivariate context, these designs allow the covariation between traits to be partitioned in a similar way. That is, they can address questions such as, "Do the genetic influences on personality overlap with those that influence intellectual functioning?" Similarly, longitudinal behavioral genetic analyses can assess whether genes or environment contribute to continuity (or change) at different ages and answer questions such as, "Are the genes that affect measures of cognitive performance in young adulthood the same as those that affect cognition later in life?" From a molecular genetic vantage point, linkage and association analyses can assess whether particular regions of the genome or particular alleles at a locus confer risk to disorders such as Alzheimer's or Parkinson's disease, or whether they influence their age at onset.

The purpose of this chapter is to provide the reader with a brief background on methods in statistical genetics and to highlight some new analytical techniques that can be useful for fitting models of development using genetically informative data. For additional information on behavioral genetic methodologies, see M. C. Neale and Cardon (1992) and for an overview of the research in the area of aging, see Bergeman (1997).

For those less familiar with elementary statistical genetics, *heritability* is defined as the proportion of phenotypic variance in a population that is due to genetic variance. The genetic variance can also be partitioned into two types, additive and nonadditive. Additive genetic variance stems from the linear effects on the phenotype, whereas nonadditive genetic variance includes hereditary influences that are due to genetic dominance (interactions between alleles at a single locus), and due to interactions between two or more different loci, termed *epistasis*. Although heritability is a popular summary statistic, it suffers from limitations common to standardized statistics. For example, equal heritability at two stages of development can mask real changes in genetic variance that are matched by similar changes in the environmental variance. It is also very important to bear in mind that estimates of variance components are basically an average population statistic. They do not inform us about possible unmeasured heterogeneity in the population. Furthermore, they do not necessarily generalize to other populations or to other cohorts.

Obviously, different people are exposed to different environments; it is an empirical question whether these different exposures cause individual differences in a particular trait. The beauty of using genetically informative methods is that they provide one of the best ways to evaluate the impact of *environmental* factors on development. Broadly speaking, environmental influences may be separated into those that are shared among members of a family (referred to in a variety of ways, including *common, shared, within, E2*) and those that are not (termed *specific, nonshared, between, E1*). Common environmental factors contribute to resemblance between relatives, whereas specific environmental factors contribute to differences between family members. In many applications, measurement error and genotype × specific environment interaction also contribute to the estimate of specific environmental variance.

Figure 9.1 shows a simple path diagram for pairs of MZ or DZ twins. Path diagrams follow the convention that observed variables are shown in squares, and latent variables are shown in circles. In Fig. 9.1, PT1 represents the score of one member of the twin pair on the attribute of interest, and PT2 represents the score of their co–twin. *A* and *C* correspond to the genotypic and shared environmental variables, respectively. The model embodies a number of assumptions, which have been made on the basis of either genetic or statistical theory. The statistical assumptions are that both the latent and the observed variables are normally distributed. This reflects the "multifactorial" premise: that there are a very large number of genes and environmental factors that influence the trait and that these factors are of small and equal effect. The central limit theorem then predicts that variation in the population should be normally distributed. Although these assumptions appear rather drastic at the

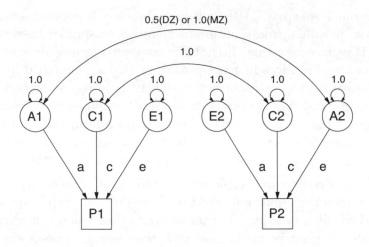

Figure 9.1: Univariate structural equation model for data collected from twins.

outset, it has been shown that very good approximations to normal distributions can be observed when there are as few as 10 factors (Kendler & Kidd, 1986). The double–headed arrows denote covariance paths, indicating that for some unspecified reason, a pair of variables may covary. Variation specific to a variable is shown as a small double–headed arrow (McArdle & Boker, 1990) attached to a variable. Linear regression paths are denoted by single–headed arrows, where the regression of Y on X would be drawn as an arrow from X to Y. These assumptions may seem unduly restrictive, and it is possible to make them more liberal, but this is a good starting point for the statistical modeling of relationships between variables.

Assumptions based on genetic theory are that the covariance between the additive genetic factors, r_a, is 1.0 for identical (MZ) twin pairs and 0.5 for fraternal (DZ) pairs. For genetic dominance, the correlation is fixed at $r_d = 1.0$ for MZ pairs and at $r_d = .25$ for DZ. The environmental correlation r_c is specified as 1.0 if the twins are reared together (T), and at zero if the twins are reared apart (A). This does not mean that the actual correlation between the twins is 1.0 for either genetic or environmental reasons; the model merely indicates that identical twins reared together (MZT) share all ge-

netic effects that influence the trait of interest, and they share all
environmental effects on the trait that occurs as a result of living
together. The latent variable labeled E represents nonshared environmental influences that do not contribute to twin similarity. In
other words, E represents environmental factors that generate differences between twins (or other family members), including error of
measurement. Multivariate model–fitting techniques allow the twin
design to be used to assess genetic and environmental factors me-
diating the covariation among measures (see Boomsma, Martin, &
Molenaar, 1989; Boomsma & Molenaar, 1986; M. C. Neale & Cardon, 1992, for details).

Developmental behavioral genetics merges developmental questions with behavior genetic research designs and methods. One of
the most basic developmental genetics questions is whether the impact of genetic factors differs with age. On the whole, it makes little sense to consider whether the heritability changes with age, because the impact of genetic factors might be identical at different
ages; however, due to a change of environmental variance, the proportion of variation accounted for by genetic factors would change.
Whether genetic variation changes with age is often assessed cross–
sectionally by comparing subjects of different ages within studies or
by comparing results across studies that focus on different age groups.
Reviews of behavioral genetic research indicate differences in the results of behavioral genetic analyses in infancy, childhood, adolescence,
adulthood, and old age. Because most of the work to date is cross–
sectional, however, it has addressed only the question of whether the
impact of genetic and environmental influences vary by age group.
Cross–sectional studies of this sort are not able to address whether
the same genetic or environmental factors influence the phenotype at
different ages.

Thus, cross–sectional research can provide information about age
differences, but not about age changes, in genetic variance. As a result, the comparison of individuals in different age groups may reflect
cohort differences rather than the developmental processes that occur
as individuals age. For example, characteristics associated with specific cohorts (e.g., epidemics) or factors related to historical change
(e.g., the development of antibiotics) can contribute to different estimates of genetic and environmental influence on health. These dif-

ferences occur because heritability is a statistic that describes the average effect in a population. As noted by Galton, who first published the idea of using twins to disentangle the effects of heredity and environment (Galton, 1869), estimates of the impact of genetic and environmental factors may change when the genetic and environmental factors vary.

9.1.1 Molecular Genetics

During the 20th century, the development of methods for studying the average effects of genetic and environmental factors in the population, such as the study of twins, proceeded in parallel with the development of methods to study the effects of individual genes. Initially, genetic markers such as the ABO and Rhesus blood groups were quite scarce and not evenly distributed along the human genome. The development of laboratory techniques that have made high throughput genotyping practical, especially with highly polymorphic genetic markers, that is, ones that have many (15+) alleles, has allowed researchers to assess whether individual differences in traits are likely to be affected by genetic factors in particular regions of the genome. Linkage studies of this type can provide an approximate localization[2] of single genetic factors that account for a substantial proportion of variation. Factors with very large effects (accounting for 10% or more of phenotypic variation) are often called "major genes" and they have somewhat different effects on a trait than the polygenic system espoused by the genetic epidemiologists using twin studies. To begin with, variation in a trait that is measured on a continuous scale may depart from normality and may even be multimodal.

Being able to measure variation in the human genome has the advantage of being able to show that genetic factors relate to a trait in a very direct fashion. For example, if cardiovascular function has a different mean in those individuals with one genotype (say AA) than with others (say Aa and aa), then this locus is said to be associated with the trait. This form of evidence for the involvement of genetic factors is more direct than that of the twin study, because

---

[2]The localization typically achieved is to within 5 to 30 centimorgans (cM) on one arm of a chromosome, where 1 cM is about a million base pairs, there being approximately 3 billion in the human genome.

it only involves comparison between first degree statistics, that is, the means. The term *associated with* is especially appropriate in this context, where the old adage "correlation does not imply causation" is especially applicable. Two limitations are particularly significant (Sullivan, Eaves, Kendler, & Neale, 2001). First, a locus that is very close to the candidate locus may be the true causal gene. Such a locus would said to be in linkage disequilibrium with the candidate locus. Second, it is possible that genotypes occur with different frequencies in different strata in the population and that these strata have different trait means for reasons quite unrelated to the gene in question. Studies of family members provide an excellent way to control for such effects, however, because they come from the same stratum in the population (Allison & Neale, 2002; Fulker, Cherny, Sham, & Hewitt, 1999; M. C. Neale et al., 1999).

9.1.2   Summary

Identical and fraternal twins, family members, and adopted siblings are pairs of relatives that differ in their average genetic relatedness. Family members may also have been reared together or apart (i.e., adopted into separate homes), which provides groups of individuals who differ in environmental similarity. We refer to research designs of this type as genetically informative. Data from genetically informative studies are typically analyzed via multiple group structural equation modeling, and they allow us to answer questions such as, "To what extent are health characteristics influenced by genetic factors, environmental factors, or both?" The purpose of this chapter is to provide a description of the methodological framework that has been devised to deal with the unwieldy data sets that occur as a result of assessing people from the same family. Methods include using different types of genetically informative data, linkage and association analysis using data from molecular biological studies, longitudinal models, and methodological developments in dynamical systems that can also be used in the context of twin studies. These methods can make the problem much more tractable and can take advantage of the extra information available from relatives. Indeed, these research designs offer a way to address fundamental issues in the measurement, nature, and development of all manner of human behavior.

9.2   General Issues in Model–Fitting

9.2.1   Maximum Likelihood Estimation

Maximum likelihood estimates (MLEs) have several desirable statistical properties. The advantages of MLEs include that they are asymptotically unbiased; that is, they give one the "right" answer if one has a large enough data set. Additionally, of all of the unbiased estimates, MLEs have the least variance (i.e., they have the least variation if the experiment is repeated multiple times). In the case of a small sample size, however, we would not necessarily want to use maximum likelihood; that is, there is a trade–off between estimation bias and variance. Typically, alternative estimators are used when MLEs are impractical to compute or when the sample size is too small to achieve the desirable asymptotic behavior. The good news is that improvements in both hardware and software continue to expand the set of problems in which maximum likelihood estimation is practical.

9.2.2   Normal Theory Maximum Likelihood

There are many excellent texts on maximum likelihood estimation. Edwards (1972) provides a basic introduction to the approach, with illustrations from elementary probability theory. In this section, we consider normal theory maximum likelihood estimation, because normal theory is the underlying assumption of the structural equation model for the twin data described earlier. Again, this theory has been described in many places: Bollen's *Structural equation modeling* (1989), Mardia et al.'s *Multivariate analysis* (1989), and Neale and Cardon's *Methodology for genetic studies of twins and families* (1992) are some examples. Normal theory likelihood is described in software manuals for most of the popular structural equation modeling programs (see Ed Rigdon's Structural Equation Modeling Web page, http://www.gsu.edu/~mkteer/).

Normal theory likelihood models are typically expressed in terms of predicted means and predicted covariances, as these are sufficient statistics to describe the likelihood. Thus, a basic structural equation model has one predicted mean vector and one predicted covariance structure, which is typically termed a *single–group analysis*. In twin research, researchers usually must deal with different covariance structures for different types of twins, which requires multiple–group analysis. Structural equation models dealing with non–twin data usually involve only one model, but tests for heterogeneity across populations, or between different strata are often accomplished using multiple groups. This is also the case for so–called multilevel contexts, in which different subjects have, for example, different predicted means.

The likelihood function and the probability density function are so closely related that they are very easily confused. The main point to remember is that the probability density function is used to compute the likelihood. For a univariate normal distribution, the density function (plotted on the y–axis) is given by

$$\frac{1}{\sigma\sqrt{2\pi}} e^{-\frac{(x-\mu)^2}{2\sigma^2}}, \tag{9.1}$$

which yields the familiar bell curve whose utility Carl Frederich Gauss (1777–1855) first developed. The density function of a particular value of x depends on two unknown parameters in Equation 9.1, the mean, μ, and the variance σ^2 (π and e are the mathematical constants 3.14159 and 2.71828, respectively). We can examine the likelihood curve, as a function of the value of these two parameters, by plotting the likelihood (the height of the probability density function, still on the y–axis) for different values of the parameters μ or σ plotted on the x–axis. Figure 9.2 illustrates this situation for two points, $x_1 = 1.3$ and $x_2 = -0.9$.

The usual situation is that a larger series of data points, for instance $\{x_1, x_2, \ldots, x_n\}$, have been observed. The joint likelihood of all the observed points can then be computed as the product of the individual likelihoods, as long as these observations are independent of one another. This multiplicative relationship is directly analogous to the situation in which two fair (p(heads)=.5) coins are tossed, and the probability of observing two heads is computed as .5 × .5 = .25. In practice, maximum likelihood analysis usually proceeds by maximizing the logarithm of the likelihood function. This transformation is performed for several reasons. First, it can be shown that the parameter estimates obtained by maximizing the log–likelihood are the same as those that would be obtained by maximizing the likeli-

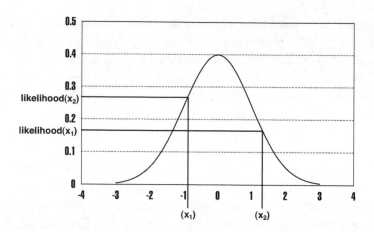

Figure 9.2: Geometric view of likelihood of two points, $x_1 = 1.25$ and $x_2 = -.9$, when the model is a univariate normal distribution with mean zero and variance one.

hood directly. Second, the product of many numbers, each of which may be between zero and one, can yield an extremely small number. Computers operate with finite number precision, so it is possible that the likelihood becomes so small that it is indistinguishable from zero, which can cause serious problems for numerical optimization. Third, it can be shown that, under certain regularity conditions, the difference in minus twice the log–likelihood of two nested models is asymptotically distributed as χ^2 with degrees of freedom equal to the difference in the number of parameters in the two models (Lehmann, 1998).

For a model (M_2) to be "nested" within another (M_1), it must be possible to apply one or more linear or nonlinear constraints to the parameters of model M_1 that will make it equivalent to model M_2. Examples of such constraints include fixing parameters to predetermined values, setting two parameters equal to each other, or specifying that one parameter is a linear or nonlinear function of other parameters of the model. The maximum likelihood approach therefore provides a very general apparatus with which we can test the statistical significance of parameters of the model.

Social scientists are often interested in measurements that are not normally distributed. Does this mean that normal theory maximum likelihood is inappropriate in these cases? The answer is "not necessarily," for several reasons. First, it has been shown that maximum likelihood estimation is quite robust to violations of normality (see, e.g., Allison et al., 1999, for an example involving data collected from relatives). Second, the normality assumption does not mean that the marginal distribution of the variables must be normal, nor does it mean that the joint distribution of two or more observed variables must be approximately multivariate normal. This is a common misconception, which becomes obvious when we consider a simple univariate example.

Suppose that two groups have been measured on a continuous trait, and that within each group the data are normally distributed. There is a substantial mean difference between the groups however, such that the joint distribution of the two groups is bimodal. Clearly, this joint distribution cannot be normal, but once the two groups have been distinguished from one another, the residual variation within each group is normally distributed, and the normal theory likelihood assumptions are met. In practice, the heterogeneity that gives rise to the bimodal distribution may not be associated with any observed variable. In such circumstances, it may be possible to fit a mixture distribution, that is, a simple mixture of two normal distributions, to the observed data. Indeed, it has long been recognized (Bauer & Curran, 2003; Pearson, 1894a, 1894b) that arbitrarily complex distributions can be approximated by a weighted mixture of normal distributions. Third, it is possible to model the situation in which binary or ordinal data, which can never be normally distributed, are supposed to arise by imprecise measurement of the underlying distribution, which is assumed to be normal. This threshold model has been used widely in genetic studies (Falconer, 1965; M. C. Neale & Cardon, 1992; Reich, James, & Morris, 1972; Reich, Rice, Cloninger, Wette, & James, 1979), among other areas. To accommodate this model, the likelihood is computed by integrating the multivariate normal probability density function over the region bounded by the thresholds on each of the variables.

One aspect of normal theory maximum likelihood methods that is particularly useful for longitudinal studies is that it provides a natural

framework for accounting for the effect of missing data. The basic
idea here is that the likelihood should be computed on the basis of
only those observations that have been made. An example will clarify
the approach. Suppose that we have a study in which observations of
magnetic resonance imaging (MRI) total brain volume and a measure
of cognitive ability (IQ) have been made. Unfortunately, the study
encounters financial problems and cannot complete the MRI scans on
many of the subjects. The goal here is simply to estimate the means
and variances of the MRI volumes and IQ scores, and their covariance.
The likelihood for the complete data vectors will be computed as

$$|2\pi\Sigma|^{-n/2} \exp\left\{-.5(\mathbf{x_i} - \mu)'\Sigma^{-1}(\mathbf{x_i} - \mu)\right\}, \qquad (9.2)$$

where Σ is the predicted covariance matrix and μ is the (column)
vector of predicted means of the variables, and $|\Sigma|$ and Σ^{-1} denote
the determinant and inverse of the matrix Σ, respectively. The vector $\mathbf{x_i}$ contains the observed scores (MRI, IQ) for subject i in the
sample. The likelihood of the data for particular values of Σ and μ is
simply calculated by Equation 9.2, which in geometrical terms gives
the height of the bivariate normal distribution at the values of the
observed MRI and IQ scores. For subjects whose MRI is missing,
only the likelihood of the IQ score is computed. The predicted variance of the IQ score is obtained from element (2,2) of the matrix Σ,
and the predicted mean is obtained from the second element of the
vector μ. Then Equation 9.1 is used to compute the likelihood. Note
that there is no imputation of the missing MRI data. The likelihood
is simply a function of the parameters of the model and the data we
have observed, nothing more and nothing less.

9.2.3   Missing Data

The treatment of missing data (presented in the previous section)
has some advantages for statistical purposes. First, being maximum
likelihood, the valuable general properties of MLEs (particularly the
asymptotic unbiasedness and minimum variance described earlier)
are in effect. Second, these properties are retained when the data are
missing due to either or both of two common mechanisms of missing
completely at random or missing at random. The first of these is missing completely at random (MCAR), in which the factors that cause

missingness are independent of all the variables being analyzed. In our example, what caused the MRI scores to be missing is presumed to have nothing to do with either the MRI scores or the IQ scores. A more general case, known as missing at random (MAR) is when the missingness is predicted by the other variables that have been measured. So, if the investigator had decided to collect MRI scans only on those subjects with IQ scores below some threshold (e.g., average IQ), and if this was the only reason for the MRI scores to be missing, they would be said to be MAR. In fact, the definition of MAR is a little more general, such that it includes cases of MCAR as well (Little & Rubin, 1987).

To summarize this introduction to normal likelihood theory, we can make a brief list of the requirements of a software program to compute the likelihood for a set of observed data. First, there must be some mechanism to read the data and to indicate whether the variables are to be treated as continuous, with normally distributed residuals, or whether they are ordinal. Second, it is necessary to supply a model in terms of (a) predicted means and (b) covariances. Third, in case we are fitting a mixture distribution, it will be necessary to supply weights for the components of the mixture, which may be parameters to be estimated or functions thereof. Finally, in some instances it may be advantageous to use frequencies, for example, to deal with sample weights or to make the coding of binary or ordinal data sets easier.

9.2.4 Implementation in Mx

Mx (M. Neale, Boker, Xie, & Maes, 2003) was designed to let the user specify models using matrix algebra formulae. Matrices may be declared to be of several special types (full, symmetric, lower triangular, identity, etc.), and individual elements of matrices may be specified as free parameters to be estimated. The program provides a built–in matrix algebra interpreter that allows the user to specify arbitrarily complex formulae to manipulate matrices. Thus, there are four types of formulae that may be supplied to specify a model: the means, the covariances, the weights, and the frequencies. To specify a mixture of m distributions for p variables, the user supplies one formula that is evaluated to give a vertically stacked set of predicted mean vectors (order $m \times p$), a second that yields the covariance matrix vertically stacked (order $mp \times p$), and a third for a vector of weights (order $m \times 1$).

One further feature of Mx dramatically increases the variety of types of models that may be fitted to the data. This is the concept of a data–defined model (M. C. Neale & Cardon, 1992) in which certain variables (called definition variables) are used to define the model. To take a trivial example, in the case of two groups in which we want to model different means on a single variable X, we could read in variables X and G, where G is scored 0 or 1. The variable G could then be assigned to a 1×1 matrix (say matrix **G**) and used to model the means. Thus, the mean vector might be declared as Means M + B*G, where **M** and **B** are matrices with free parameters to be estimated and **G** contains either 0 or 1 (on a record–by–record basis). The predicted mean for those with **G** $= 0$ would be M, whereas for cases with **G** $= 1$, the predicted mean would be M+B.

We are now in a position to write an expression for the general model for normal theory maximum likelihood model fitting that is implemented in Mx. For the vector of observation scores $\mathbf{x_i}$, the log–likelihood of a normal mixture with $j = 1 \ldots m$ components is

$$\ln L_i = f_i \ln \sum_{j=1}^{m} \left[w_{ij} g(\mathbf{x_i}, \mu_{\mathbf{ij}}, \mathbf{\Sigma_{ij}}) \right], \qquad (9.3)$$

in which $g(\mathbf{x_i}, \mu_{\mathbf{ij}}, \mathbf{\Sigma_{ij}})$ is the multivariate normal probability density function given in Equation 9.2 evaluated at the observed scores in $\mathbf{x_i}$, f_i is the frequency associated with this observed vector, w_{ij} is the weight for component j of the mixture, and $\mu_{\mathbf{ij}}$ and $\mathbf{\Sigma_{ij}}$ are the predicted mean and covariance matrix for model j corresponding to the observed vector i. The most important thing to note about this otherwise rather dull–looking expression is that it permits a different weight, mean, and covariance to be predicted for every subject in the sample. This is in stark contrast to the standard practice of structural equation modeling, in which there is relatively little opportunity to model the effects of measured covariates.

9.3   Brief introduction to Mx syntax

The program manual (available online at http://www.vcu.edu/mx)
gives a detailed description of the syntax for specifying model scripts.
In brief, the program allows the user to specify a job as a collection
of groups. These groups may be of one of three different types: Data,
Calculation, or Constraint. The first type reads observed data and is
designed to compute the likelihood function (or some other built–in
or user–defined fit function) of the data. The second, a calculation
group, is used purely to evaluate matrix algebra expressions, which
may be used in subsequent data, calculation, or constraint groups.
The third, a constraint group, is used to specify linear or nonlinear
equality or inequality constraints on the parameters. The structure
of an Mx job essentially has a preamble followed by one or more
groups. Additional commands may request further jobs to be run, or
modifications to an existing job to be made for the purposes of fitting
alternative models.

```
! Preamble
#define stuff 3        ! Sets the string 'stuff' to the
                       ! value 3 (optional)
#ngroups 1             ! Number of groups in this
                       ! job (mandatory)

! The one--group job itself
Group 1 Title          ! Title of first group (mandatory)
 Type of group         ! Data/Calculation/Constraint line
                       ! (mandatory)
  <read data>          ! Data reading commands (mandatory
                       ! for data groups)
  Declare matrices     ! Indicate name type & size of
                       ! matrices (mandatory)
  Put things in matrices                   ! optional
  <Do some matrix algebra>                 ! optional
  <Write formulae for means, covs, etc> ! mandatory for
                                           ! data groups
  <specify options>                        ! as expected,
                                           ! optional
End group                                  ! mandatory
```

In practice, therefore, a simple script to fit a two–factor model to eight continuous measures could be written as follows:

```
! Preamble
#ngroups 1          ! Number of groups
#define nfac 2      ! Number of factors
#define nvar 8      ! Number of observed variables

! The one--group job itself
Group 1 CFA         ! Title of first group (mandatory)
  Data NI=nvar      ! Data/Calculation/Constraint line
                    ! (mandatory)
  Rectangular file=mydata.rec
  Begin Matrices;
    L Full nvar nfac free ! Factor loadings
    E Diag nvar nvar free ! Specifics
    M Full 1 nvar free    ! Means
  End Matrices;

  Start 1 all ! starting values
  Drop L 1 2   ! set factor rotation

  Means M;
  Covariance L*L' + E ;

End
```

The file mydata.rec would be an ASCII flat file; in other words, with one row per subject and variables separated by one or more spaces. For example, here is a two row by eight column file

```
8.3 2.7 1.9 1.3 .   6.5 7.0 1.8
1.2 5.6 7.8 2.3 4.6 8.3 1.3 2.5
```

where the fifth variable is missing for the first subject. This missing observation is denoted using the default missing value code of a period (.).

9.4 Introduction to Modeling Data Collected from Relatives

One of the advantages of using matrix algebra to specify models is that it makes it very easy to maintain constraints that equate parameters across relatives. Why one should wish to do so is explained in this section. We begin with an illustrative elementary model for the mean and variance of a single variable.

9.4.1 Modeling Means and Variances

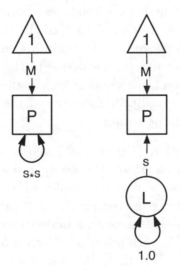

Figure 9.3: Alternative models for the mean and variance of a variable. Left (a): estimating the mean M and variance $s * s$; right (b) estimating mean M and standard deviation s.

Figure 9.3a shows a path diagram for a model for the mean and the variance of a single variable. The data for such a model would consist of one score per subject, for a sample of N subjects. In Mx, these data would be organized as a rectangular data file with N lines it, with one observed score per line. The graphical notation used in the figure may be only partly familiar to those accustomed to structural equation modeling. However, it can be argued that the graphical devices used are minimally sufficient to represent the model. Only two types of directional arrow are used, and only squares, circles, and triangles are used to denote variables. The square represents the observed score; the double–headed arrow is used to denote the variance of the observed score. The triangle is used to denote a constant variable with value 1.0 for every subject. The path to this constant variable is used to estimate the mean of the observed variable. There exists a set of rules to compute the variance and covariance between all objects in the diagram; these are standard for path analysis (Bollen, 1989; McArdle & Boker, 1990; M. C. Neale, 1994; Wright, 1934) and will not be repeated here. The estimation of means is carried out by a second, less familiar set of rules. As for covariances, paths are traced back to the triangles to form path chains. The coefficients on a path chain are multiplied together to obtain the contribution to the mean due to that chain. In the event that there is more than one chain from a variable to a triangle, the mean is influenced by multiple factors, and the contributions of the different chains are to be summed.

The second diagram (Figure 9.3b) shows an alternative representation of the model. Here, the variance path has been replaced by a causal path from a latent variable, whose variance is fixed at unity. The parameter s on the causal path estimates the standard deviation of the observed variable, because the rules of path analysis generate a predicted covariance of s^2. Both models will fit the data equally well. It turns out that[3] in both cases, the model estimates the variance to be equal to the average of the squared deviations of the observed scores from the mean, or $\hat{\sigma}^2 = \sum_{i=1}^{N}(x_i - \mu)^2/N$. This result differs from the usual "unbiased" estimate of the variance, $\sum_{i=1}^{N}(x_i - \mu)^2/(N - 1)$, but it can be seen that the two estimates of the variance converge as N approaches infinity, illustrating the asymptotic unbiased property of maximum likelihood estimates.

---

[3]This is shorthand for "if you take the partial derivatives of the likelihood with respect to the parameters and set them equal to zero you can show that..." which in turn is something that we won't do here (see, e.g., Edwards, 1972).

9.4.2   Modeling Means, Variances, and Covariances of Relatives

The elementary study of unrelated subjects measured on a single variable becomes more interesting if the measures are taken from pairs of relatives. First note that data collected from a pair of relatives cannot in general be considered independent observations; it frequently happens that relatives are positively correlated for some traits. At the very least, that relatives correlate is a hypothesis that we may wish to test. Therefore, the data from a pair of relatives become the unit of observation and would be supplied to Mx in the form of a single row of the data file.

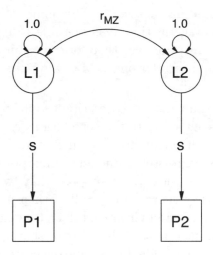

Figure 9.4: Path diagram for the covariance between relatives' phenotypes, $P1$ and $P2$, which are specified to have equal variances (s^2). Covariance is due to two standardized latent variables, $L1$ and $L2$, whose correlation is rMZ.

Figure 9.4 shows a path diagram for a pair of relatives, which is based on the latent factor model of Fig. 9.3b. Note how the same model is specified for relative 1 and relative 2; the main addition to this model is that we allow the latent factors of the relatives to covary.

In fact, since the latent variables are standardized to unit variance, the covariance path rMZ estimates the correlation between relatives.

This simple model could be repeated for different classes of relative, for example, MZ and DZ twin pairs. Estimates of the mean, the standard deviation, and the correlation could be obtained separately for each type of relative. We might infer that a greater correlation of MZ pairs suggests a role of genetic factors in the trait in question, since MZ twins share all their genes in common, whereas DZ twins share approximately one half. Such "eyeballing" of the data can yield insights, but even when supported by confidence intervals on the parameters in question, it provides only a rough–and–ready approach to testing hypotheses about the origin of individual differences. A more rigorous approach is to use multiple–group analysis, in which the data from the MZ twins are used in one group and those from the DZ twins are used in the second. This joint estimation approach has the great advantage in that it is possible to equate parameters across the groups. In principle, therefore, we can test whether the means, variances, and correlations of MZ twin pairs are equal to their counterparts in DZ pairs.

The multiple–group approach described so far permits some testing of hypotheses such as, "Are the correlations of MZ and DZ pairs equal?" or "Are both correlations equal to zero?" However, it has more potential once we revise the model to incorporate what we know from genetic theory. Basically, we suppose that twin pairs may correlate because (a) they share some or all of their genetic factors; (b) they share some of their environmental factors; and (c) there are some environmental factors that they do not share. It is a short step, therefore, to go from the model for estimating correlations to one that is specified entirely in terms of these three latent factors. This model, known as the ACE model, is shown in Fig. 9.1. Note that the correlation between the shared environmental factors C_1 and C_2 is set at 1.0 for both types of twin pairs. This specification reflects the equal environment assumption (EEA) of twin studies, meaning that it is assumed that MZ and DZ twin pairs share the environmental factors to an equal degree. Often this assumption is questioned (Winerman, 2004). However, both theoretical and empirical examinations of this assumption indicate that it is unlikely to be violated to any substantial degree. First, it is not a violation of the EEA if more similar environments are evoked by MZ twins on account of heritable characteristics such as their physical appearance. That is, if MZ twins receive more similar treatment because they look more similar, the effect of such treatment on their phenotypes is correctly identified as a genetic effect. The pathway from genes to phenotype in this case involves the external environment (i.e., the behavior of other people), but it is still ultimately an effect of genotype. Second, empirical investigations into the role of similarity of treatment (Hettema, Neale, & Kendler, 1995; Kendler, Neale, Kessler, Heath, & Eaves, 1994; Loehlin & Nichols, 1976; Plomin, Willerman, & Loehlin, 1976) have failed to find a relationship between phenotypic similarity and similarity of treatment for a variety of personality and psychopathology measures. Third, even if such relationships were found, they would not necessarily indicate EEA failure if twins select their own environments and do so for reasons to do with their genotype (L. Eaves, Foley, & Silberg, 2003).

The predictions of this simple ACE model for twin data are as follows:

1. Means will be equal (within sampling error) for Twin 1 and Twin 2 of a pair.

2. Means will be equal for MZ and DZ twin pairs.

3. The variances will be equal for Twin 1 and Twin 2 and for MZ and DZ pairs.

4. MZ and DZ correlations will be greater than or equal to zero.

5. The DZ correlation will be greater than or equal to one half of the MZ correlation.

6. The DZ correlation will not exceed the MZ correlation.

It is quite striking that in the immense body of twin research published to date that these predictions are often born out by the data. Certain phenotypes show a pattern of familial resemblance in which DZ pairs correlate less than one–half as much as MZ pairs, particularly parental ratings of activity (M. C. Neale, 1985; Rietveld, Hudziak, Bartels, Beijsterveldt, & Boomsma, 2003). These findings are consistent with nonadditive genetic variation, defined as inter-action between alleles at a single locus (dominance) or interaction between alleles at different loci (epistasis). For these phenotypes, however, there is also evidence of variance differences between MZ and DZ pairs, consistent with a rater contrast or sibling competi-tion effect (L. J. Eaves, Last, Young, & Martin, 1978). Variations of the ACE model have been developed that include these effects and therefore can predict reduced (and even negative) DZ correlations, and different MZ and DZ variances (M. C. Neale, 1985; M. C. Neale & Cardon, 1992; Rietveld et al., 2003), but it is relatively unusual for them to be needed to obtain an adequate fit to the data.

9.4.3   Multivariate Models for Data Collected from Relatives

It is relatively straightforward to convert the univariate ACE model described previously into a multivariate model suitable for the simul-taneous analysis of multiple traits. Such models have great potential for understanding why different phenotypes do or do not correlate with each other. They also form the basis of a variety of models for development. Indeed, developmental genetic data (repeated measures taken within a genetically informative design) can be viewed as a spe-cial form of multivariate genetic analysis in which regression paths cannot be drawn from later to earlier occasions of measurement. It is perhaps no accident that to regress means "to go backwards," since it is in this context that regression makes the most statistical sense.

Usually, it is important to establish a saturated model against which more restricted, hypothesis–driven models can be compared. For multivariate data, it is typically possible to estimate a large co-variance matrix for all variables on both members of the MZ twin pairs, and a second matrix for the DZ pairs. If there are m variables per twin, a total of $2m(2m + 1)$ parameters will be required.[4] The means are similarly allowed to differ between Twin 1 and Twin 2, and across zygosities (estimated as $4m$ free parameters). This en-tirely model–free approach has some advantages; it provides a base-

---

[4]Twin pairs may be further subdivided according to gender and possibly chori-onicity for this purpose, but consideration of these issues distracts from the pri-mary goals of this chapter.

line for overall goodness–of–fit, but it is also a computationally intensive model to fit if m is large, as it requires $2m(2m + 3)$ free parameters. In a cohort–sequential study (Bell, 1953), subjects are measured on a limited sequence of ages within a broader age range. For example, measurements may be taken once per year for five years from a sample of individuals aged between 21 and 61 years at the start of the project. In this case, the saturated model is underidentified because there are no subjects who have been measured at both ages 21 and 65. A fourth–order Markov chain model would be a better choice of saturated model for such designs, as would a banded covariance matrix in which elements $C_{i,j}$ are set to zero when $|i - j| > 4$. Likelihood ratio tests of models against such saturated models provide a test of global fit that is analogous to that which is obtained when models are fitted to summary statistics such as covariance matrices and vectors of means. Its convenient handling of numerous patterns of missing data and its additional flexibility in model specification, however, make the raw data approach more attractive than fitting models to summary statistics.

These fully saturated models are useful guides to whether the overall model fits well. In a genetic context, one of the first questions to be addressed is whether the overall covariance structure is adequately described by a multivariate ACE model consisting of three saturated models: one for each of the three components of covariance, A, C, and E. These covariance matrices are symmetric. The predicted phenotypic covariance matrix of an individual is the sum of the three components because it is an additive model: $P = A+C+E$. The covariance matrix for a pair of MZ twins is therefore predicted to be

$$\Sigma_{MZ} = \begin{pmatrix} A + C + E & A + C \\ A + C & A + C + E \end{pmatrix}$$

and for DZ pairs is

$$\Sigma_{DZ} = \begin{pmatrix} A + C + E & .5 \otimes A + C \\ .5 \otimes A + C & A + C + E \end{pmatrix},$$

where $\otimes$ denotes Kronecker product. In practice, we use a device called the lower triangular decomposition, also known as the Cholesky decomposition, to estimate the covariance matrices A, C, and E. Parameters estimated for each of these components are specified in lower triangular counterparts, such that $A = X * X', C = Y * Y'$ and $E = Z * Z'$. This approach is used to constrain the component matrices to be nonnegative definite in the case of matrices A and C, and to be strictly positive definite in the case of matrix E. In this last case, the diagonal of this matrix includes the effects of measurement error, so it is natural to specify some variable–specific variation. Taken together, these constraints will restrict the overall covariance matrices Σ_{MZ} and Σ_{DZ} to be positive definite. This is done by constraining the diagonal elements of matrix Z to be greater than zero.

The model with Cholesky decomposition of the three variance components is sometimes referred to as the triple Cholesky. There are three main advantages to its use. First, it provides a valuable reference point against which more restricted models, based for example on developmental theory, may be compared. Second, it is useful to compare its fit against that of the completely saturated model, to provide an index of how well any model based on these three components could possibly fit. Third, it provides estimates of the genetic and environment covariance matrices, so it is possible to apportion the variance of variables into the three components and to do the same with covariances between variables. When apportioning covariances in this way, we note that it is possible for one observed variable to have zero covariance with a second. For this independence to arise, it must be due to counterbalancing of, e.g., a positive genetic covariance and a negative specific environmental covariance. The implications of situations of this sort for scale construction or for the assessment of risk factors for a disorder are cause for concern, as not much research in these areas has been conducted with data collected from relatives.

Two further models are currently popular in the analysis of multivariate data collected from twins. Both are based on the factor model, in which covariation among variables is assumed to arise from the effects of one or more common factors that influence two or more of the measured variables. Residual variance components specific to each variable are also specified (see Fig. 9.5). A natural extension of this factor model to data collected from twins is shown, for one member of a twin pair, in Fig. 9.6. This model, known as a "latent

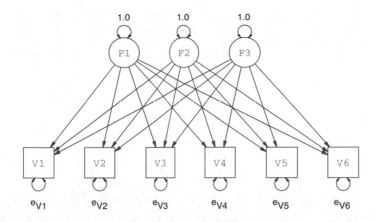

Figure 9.5: Path diagram of model with three factors and residuals.

phenotype" or common pathway model (Kendler, Heath, Martin, & Eaves, 1987; McArdle & Goldsmith, 1990), includes three latent phenotypes that influence all the observed measures. All the covariation between twins' measures occurs through correlations between the additive genetic (A) and common environment (C) latent variable in Twin 1 and their counterparts in Twin 2. These correlations are fixed, in accordance with genetic theory, at 1.0 for MZ twins for both A and C, and at .5 and 1.0 for A and C, respectively, in DZ twins. Note that residual or "variable–specific" covariation between twins may occur through the A and C paths at the bottom of the figure.

An important submodel of this three–factor model is one in which the factor coefficients a_{F2}, a_{F3}, c_{F1}, c_{F3}, e_{F1}, and e_{F2} are fixed to zero, and the remaining three coefficients are fixed to unity. This submodel, known as the "independent pathway" or "biometric factor" model (McArdle & Goldsmith, 1990), estimates loadings from variance components that are specified as having only one source of variation. Another important submodel is one in which only one latent phenotype is specified; that is, $F2$ and $F3$ are omitted. These models form the core of most multivariate genetic analyses.

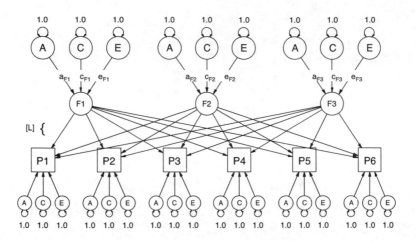

Figure 9.6: Three–factor latent phenotype model, shown for only one member of a pair of twins. Common environment factors (C) and residuals covary 1 with their counterpart in their co–twin. Additive genetic factors and residuals covary in the same way for MZ but .5 in DZ twins.

9.4.4   Specification of Multivariate Genetic Models

Specification of the general latent phenotype factor model is slightly more complex than for the triple Cholesky described earlier. First, we note that the common factor and the variable–specific parts of the model are independent of each other, which makes this a useful place to separate the components. The variable–specific part of the model can be specified in the same way as the triple Cholesky, but the lower triangular matrices X, Y, and Z are replaced with diagonal matrices. Therefore, these components contribute to the variance of the measured variables and to the diagonal of the block of covariances between Twin 1's variables and those of Twin 2.

At the factor level, a multivariate[5] ACE model can be devised to describe the covariance between the latent factors of the twins. For orthogonal factor analysis, a diagonal structure to the A, C, and E factors is appropriate. To estimate path coefficients (and to restrict

---

[5]In this case, *multifactor* may be a more appropriate term because the model directly generates covariance among the factors but only indirectly between the observed variables.

variance components to be nonnegative), we may specify $A_F = PP'$, $C_F = QQ'$, and $E_F = RR'$, in which P, Q, and R are diagonal matrices of path coefficients. The relationship between the factors and the observed measures may be specified in the usual way for a factor–loading matrix, namely, a full matrix L of order m variables by k factors. The same relationship of the observed measures to the latent factors is required for both Twin 1 and Twin 2, and there is no direct effect of Twin 1's factors on Twin 2's observed variables, nor vice versa. This patterning of the overall factor–loading matrix for the two twins can be obtained through the Kronecker product $I \otimes L$ where I is a 2×2 identity matrix. In sum, the specification of the general latent phenotype model can be written as

$$\boldsymbol{\Sigma}_{MZL} = (I \otimes L) \begin{pmatrix} A_F + C_F + E_F & A_F + C_F \\ A_F + C_F & A_F + C_F + E_F \end{pmatrix} (I \otimes L)' +$$

$$\begin{pmatrix} A + C + E & A + C \\ A + C & A + C + E \end{pmatrix}$$

and for DZ pairs as

$$\boldsymbol{\Sigma}_{DZL} = (I \otimes L) \begin{pmatrix} A_F + C_F + E_F & .5 \otimes A_F + C_F \\ .5 \otimes A_F + C_F & A_F + C_F + E_F \end{pmatrix} (I \otimes L)' +$$

$$\begin{pmatrix} A + C + E & .5 \otimes A + C \\ .5 \otimes A + C & A + C + E \end{pmatrix}.$$

9.5   Models for Longitudinal Genetically Informative Data

9.5.1   Biometric Simplex Model

Data that are measured repeatedly in time on the same participants are often characterized by a specific correlation structure among the measures at the different measurement occasions: The correlations are highest among adjacent occasions, and they fall away systematically as the distance between measurement occasions increases. This is referred to as a simplex structure, after Guttman (1954). Figure 9.7 depicts the simplex model for the genetic and environmental analysis of covariance structure for five occasions of measurement

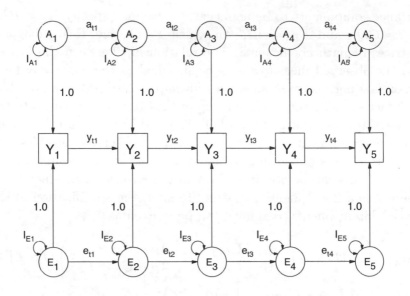

Figure 9.7: Simplex model for genetic and environmental transmission over time (see Eaves et al., 1986).

$\{Y_1, Y_2, \ldots, Y_5\}$. Models of this type have been described in detail elsewhere (Boomsma & Molenaar, 1987; L. J. Eaves, Hewitt, Meyer, & Neale, 1990; Hewitt, Eaves, Neale, & Meyer, 1988; M. C. Neale & Cardon, 1992). In brief, a simplex structure defines an autoregressive model in which latent variables at time i are causally related to variables at time $i-1$. Strictly speaking, this is a first–order simplex; higher (nth) orders are possible if variables at time i are allowed to be directly influenced by their counterparts at times $i-1, i-2, \ldots i-n$. Here we consider first–order simplex models.

In a classical twin study, simplex models for each of the three genetic and environmental components of variance can be fitted, which is why we refer to it as the biometric simplex model. In what follows, for simplicity, the common environment component C will be omitted, but this is for ease of presentation; ordinarily we would fit models with models for all three components, possibly substituting genetic dominance for common environment.

Let A_i and E_i represent the latent genetic and environmental factors at each occasion $i = 1 \ldots t$. The measurement model for occasion i is

$$Y_i = A_i + E_i.$$

At the first occasion, the equations for the latent (structural) part of the model are

$$A_1 = I_{A1} \tag{9.4}$$
$$E_1 = I_{E1},$$

and for all subsequent occasions they are

$$A_i = a_{t_{i-1}} A_{i-1} + I_{A_i} \tag{9.5}$$
$$E_i = e_{t_{i-1}} E_{i-1} + I_{E_i},$$

in which A_i and E_i are the latent genotype and environment at time i ($\forall i > 1$), respectively; $a_{t_{i-1}}$ and $e_{t_{i-1}}$ are the regressions of the latent genetic and environmental factors on the respective previous latent genetic and environmental factors; and I_A and I_E are random innovations that are uncorrelated with A_{i-1} or or E_{i-1}. In other words, the innovations are that part of the latent variable at time i not caused by the latent variable at time $i - 1$, but which forms part of the subsequent time point $i + 1$. (For a more detailed description, see e.g., Boomsma & Molenaar, 1987; L. J. Eaves, Long, & Heath, 1986; Hewitt et al., 1988; M. C. Neale & Cardon, 1992).

As indicated in Fig. 9.7, simplex models include causal pathways between effects at adjacent occasions (represented by the a_{t_i} paths). Thus, A_1 causes A_2, which in turn causes A_3; similarly, E_1 causes E_2, which causes E_3. The innovations (I_{A_i} and I_{E_i}) represent the residual genetic and environmental variances not accounted for by genetic or environmental factors operating at earlier occasions. It is therefore possible to calculate the proportion of genetic and environmental variations unique to each occasion, as well as proportion that is common with previous occasions (Pedersen, 1991). Results of these model–fitting analyses can be used in the assessment of three dimensions outlined by Pedersen (1991). First, the relative importance of genetic and environmental influences at each time point can be estimated (heritability and environmentality). Second, the portion of genetic and environmental variance that is due to the previous measurement occasion and that which is unique (innovative) can also be determined, indicating the extent to which there is continuity and change in the latent genetic and environmental influences longitudinally. Finally, the genetic and environmental contributions to phenotypic stability can be assessed using the genetic and environmental correlations (r_A and r_E) and the path coefficients. That is, the age–to–age phenotypic covariance can be partitioned into genetic (genetic mediation) and environmental (environmental mediation) components.

Alternatively, instead of genotypes at different occasions being a function of genotypes at previous occasions, we can specify that the genotype and environment combine to form the phenotype, and it is the phenotypic transmissions that predict future development at later time points. This model is equivalent to equating the transmission of the genetic and the environmental parts (both for shared and nonshared environment).

The model for development described here has advantages and disadvantages. Note that the causal paths from occasion i to $i + 1$ are allowed to be estimated as different values. The same is true of the innovation variances. This can be a good thing from the perspective of having a model that will fit many different data sets. There is no predicted monotonic change in the genetic variances or covariances over time, so it would be quite possible, for example, for the genetic variance to follow any pattern of increase or decrease from one occasion to the next. It should be noted, however, that this flexibility comes at a price. The model makes no predictions about what will happen on the next occasion in the series. A wide variety of possible observed variances and covariances of twins, and of covariances of scores at this new occasion with those of the twin and co–twin at prior occasions, may be absorbed by the model by suitable adjustments of the transmission parameter estimates and innovations variances. An even wider variety of such patterns of variance and covariance may be explained if a common factor is included in the model, representing genetic or environmental effects that are in operation at all time points (see Fig. 9.8; Hewitt et al., 1988). This ability to account for practically any observed pattern of covariances has been bought at the cost of an inability to predict future occasions. Furthermore, nothing is being predicted about the change in means across occasions.

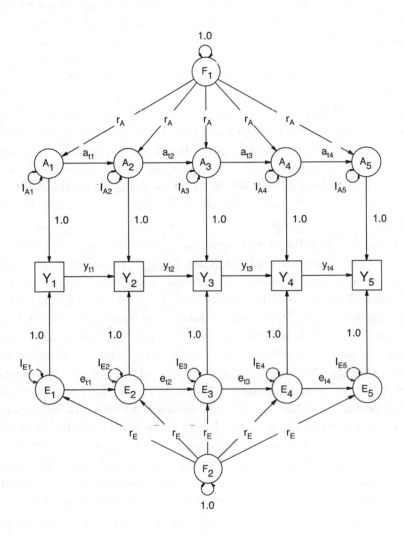

Figure 9.8: Simplex developmental genetic model including a common factor.

It might be argued that despite these shortcomings, the biometric simplex model (with or without a common factor) is valuable because it is appropriate for situations in which the intervals between measurement occasions are not uniform. Although this is true, there exist alternative approaches that are able to deal with data collection shortcomings when subjects are not measured at equally spaced intervals in time. One simple method would be to insert dummy ages as latent variables, to keep the intervals equal (McArdle, 1994). We should note, however, that these models, and their simpler counterparts for the analysis of data from genetically uninformative designs, are sensitive to variation in age within the measurement occasions. They would be appropriate if, for example, all the subjects are measured on their birthdays, so that there is negligible variation in age within occasions relative to the variation between occasions, but this is typically not the case.

Consider the following example. A sample of twins 8 to 11 years of age were to be measured annually for 3 years. To study development, it would be wise to combine all the first–wave assessments together, call them Time 1, and do the same for the second and third waves. This approach is really a study of waves of measurement, which might be useful for understanding the effects of practice but is likely to be relatively uninformative about development across this age range. Organizing the data set according to year of age, say 8– to 14–year–olds, would still be inadequate because, those aged 8 years 11 months would be more similar in age to those aged 9 years 1 month than to those aged 8 years 1 month. Although there would still be an average age difference of 1 year between these groups, the variation in age within a group can still be problematic. Mehta and West (2000) have shown that considerable bias can accrue in growth curve modeling even when the heterogeneity within wave is relatively modest.

The obvious solution to problems of this nature is to use the participant's actual age at testing to define the model. The definition variable approach available in Mx is a useful technique for handling such complications. If subjects' actual ages at different assessments are used to quantify precisely the amount of change that would be expected to have occurred according to the parameters of the model, then unbiased estimates of model parameters can be obtained. In addition, this conceptual orientation permits greater flexibility in research design. Those collecting data do not have to worry that the interval between successive assessments varies across subjects, because the actual intervals observed for each individual case are used to quantify the predictions of the model. This problem of trying to maintain equal intervals between assessments can be particularly acute in studies of twins and other relatives, in which greater concordance in the timing of interviews of MZ pairs than of DZ pairs could be misinterpreted as genetic factors influencing development. Analysis using actual ages at assessment would circumvent this problem. It would also make more practical the appropriate analysis of non–twin pairs of relatives, whose differences in age at assessment are likely to be both greater on average and more variable.

Another advantage of modeling observed age over grouped age ranges is that it should give greater statistical power. Furthermore, group size becomes immaterial, as models are specified in terms of actual age at assessment. Better still, it becomes possible to design developmental studies to have more frequent assessments during periods of rapid development (or changes in rate of development) and less frequent assessments when growth is more stable.

Of course, there is a downside to this general approach. The largest drawback (which has historically made such methods impractical) is that they are more computer intensive than using groups. This problem continues to dwindle, however, as Moore's law of approximate doubling of computer power every 18 months exerts its inexorable effects. A further consequence of adopting a definition variable approach to modeling development is that there is greater motivation to develop statistical models within this framework. It is to the specification of genetic models for continuous development that we now turn.

9.6   Linear and Nonlinear Growth Curves

Growth curve modeling has attracted considerable attention in the social sciences in recent years. The vast majority of work in this area has concerned linear growth curve[6] modeling. Possible reasons

---

[6]Although the application of the word *curve* to a straight line may appear a misnomer, if the definition of curve is taken to be "the trace of a point whose direction of motion changes," it is not inconsistent with the alternative definition

for this almost exclusive focus on linear growth are many, but likely
contributors include that simple models that account for data are,
ceteris paribus, to be preferred over more complex ones; the relative
ease with which linear growth models can be specified; the lack of
suitable software for fitting nonlinear growth curves; and for comparison with prior studies using the same methods.

In a linear growth curve model, it is supposed that an individual's
development follows a straight line but that individuals vary in their
initial value (*intercept*) and in the steepness of their development
(*slope*). The specification of such a model in a structural equation
modeling program is straightforward. Latent variables representing
the population variation in initial value (I), and in the slope (S)
are specified with their variances and covariance to be estimated.
Also specified are the means of these factors, μ_i and μ_s. Especially
simple are the loadings of the observed scores at each occasion of
measurement $(Y_1, Y_2, \ldots Y_K)$ on these latent factors. For the initial
value, the factor loadings are fixed at a constant 1.0 for all occasions.
The factor loading on the latent slope variable is fixed at 1.0 for the
first occasion and increases by 1 for each unit of elapsed time between
subsequent measurements (see Fig. 9.9).

This specification yields predicted means, predicted variances,
and predicted covariances across the occasions. Note that the means
may increase, decrease, or remain unchanged over time according
to whether μ_i is positive, negative, or zero, respectively. Also note
that changes in variance over time do not necessarily match this pattern, even when the residual variance components are set equal to
each other. Despite this model being linear, it predicts a quadratic
increase in variance over time. And despite its popularity, it seems
unlikely that individual growth follows a linear form in the long term.
If so, there would be some very tall/intelligent/(insert your favorite
adjective or developmental trait here) old people!

In early econometric work, Malthus (1798) suggested that the op-
timism of his father and others, who supposed that population growth
was invariably beneficial as it led to an increased labor force, could be
misplaced. Malthus' argument was that the population could grow
at a geometric rate that would outstrip the arithmetic growth of the
food supply. In mathematical terms, geometric growth can be rep-

---

"a line on a graph representing data."

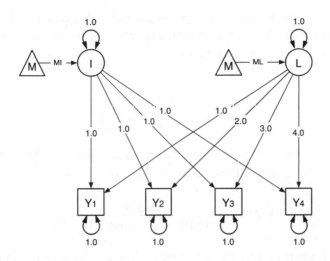

Figure 9.9: Latent growth curve model. Variation in initial value I and slope S affect means, variances, and covariances of the observed measures $Y_1 - Y_4$.

resented by a differential equation, which expresses the slope of the variable y, in terms of the current value of the variable y:

$$\frac{dy}{dt} = y(t)c,$$

where c is a constant and $y(t)$ is the size at time t. This differential equation involves both y and the derivative (or slope) of y with respect to time t. This differential equation can be solved to yield an expression for $y(t)$:

$$y(t) = y(0)e^{tc}.$$

This type of growth is, unsurprisingly, often called exponential. [7]

Exponential growth does not solve the problem of predicting ever–increasing values over time; in general, it makes it worse. We now have a more convenient mathematical framework, however, in which

---

[7]Unfortunately, the term *exponential growth* is frequently used in common parlance to indicate particularly rapid growth, instead of its more technical definition here, which concerns a specific change in the rate of growth over time.

models for growth (and changes in growth rate) can be specified. If
we suppose that growth is limited by the square of the current size
of the population, we can write:

$$\frac{dy}{dt} = ay(t) - by(t)^2$$
$$= y(t)(a - y(t)b),$$

in which a is the ultimate size or asymptote, and b is the initial level.
The solution of this differential equation is

$$y(t) = \frac{ay(0)}{by(0) + (a - by(0))e^{-at}},$$

which is known as the logistic curve. It has a sigmoidal shape characterized by growth that is initially slow, increases to its maximum
at the midpoint of the initial and asymptotic values, and decreases
as it approaches the asymptote.

There is, in principle, little additional complexity in specifying
structural equation models for nonlinear growth curves (Browne, 1993).
Many such curves are expressed in terms of only three parameters,
the initial value (I), the slope (S), and the asymptote (A). In the
linear growth curve model, the initial value and the slope are sufficient to describe the linear function; in the nonlinear case, at least
one further parameter, such as the asymptote, is needed. As in the
linear case, we suppose that there may be population variation in the
asymptote, as well as in the initial and slope values, and that these
three components may covary with each other. In a fashion precisely
analogous to the linear case, the partial derivatives of the growth
curve with respect to its parameters are used as fixed factor loadings
for the regressions of the observed variables $T_1, T_2, \ldots T_K$ on the factors. This last statement may come as a surprise to those familiar
with linear growth curve models, but who had not recognized that the
fixed values of the slope parameters were in fact partial derivatives
of the equation for the linear model $y = xt + i$:

$$\frac{dy}{dc} = 1 \tag{9.6}$$
$$\frac{dy}{dx} = t.$$

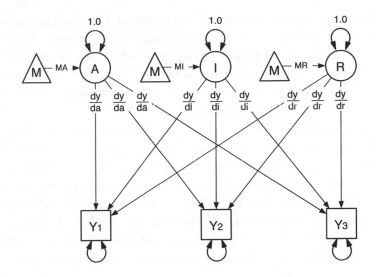

Figure 9.10: Path diagram of nonlinear latent growth curve model with three parameter curves.

The more general case, for the three–parameter curve, is shown as a path diagram in Fig. 9.10. As we have shown elsewhere (M. C. Neale & McArdle, 2000), it is a simple matter to extend such models to data collected from twins. The three latent variables corresponding to the parameters of the curve can be thought of as three variables in a multivariate genetic model. It is therefore natural to use the triple Cholesky model to estimate their covariance both within and between twins without imposing any special restrictions other than that the covariances within Twin 1 are the same as those within Twin 2.

A key feature of the growth curve approach is that it makes predictions about means and covariances. Note that it also predicts means, variances, and covariances for future time points that may have yet to be measured. Indeed, it does so with very few parameters. If the residual variances are assumed to be equal for all occasions, the number of parameters required to fit a growth curve model is constant, regardless of the number of occasions of measurement. A further advantage of this property is that it becomes easy to deal with incomplete data, whether they are either missing by design (sometimes called structured incomplete data) or missing at random due to subject dropout or other factors. The more difficult task when fitting these models to large numbers of occasions of measurements is to judge their overall fit against a saturated model, since the latter can be difficult to establish and specify.

One limitation of the nonlinear growth curve approach is that the model can yield biased estimates of certain parameters (such as the asymptote variance). This problem may arise because the first–order Taylor's series expansion of the growth curve, which is used to define the factors and the factor loadings in the model, is not sufficiently accurate to describe the predictions of the model. Possibly, using higher order terms of the Taylor series would yield greater precision in the estimates of the parameters of nonlinear growth curves.

9.6.1   Alternative Growth Models

The notion of using differential equations to model data collected from twins has been around for much longer than the treatment in 2000 by Neale and McArdle. Eaves et al. (1986) presented not only the simplex model described earlier in this chapter, but also a continuous time version of it. Although the simplex structural equation model of Eaves and colleagues has received much attention, and indeed has been the mainstay of modeling development in genetically informative studies, we know of no applications of the continuous time part of that article. The lack of suitable software for this purpose likely accounts for this neglect. It would seem relatively straightforward, however, to implement it in a package like Mx using definition variables. However, although this feature has been available for the past 10 years, a direct implementation has yet to emerge, but it may be equivalent to a variant of McArdle's (2003) model, which we now briefly describe.

Given a model specified to have equal intervals between time points, only a subset of which may have any observed data, it becomes more attractive to model development through restricted versions of the simplex model described earlier. This approach, pioneered by McArdle and Nesselroade (1994) and McArdle (2001), is known as the latent difference score approach. In its most fully parameterized form, the latent difference score model is specified as:

$$\delta y_t = \alpha y_s + \beta y_{t-1} + z_t, \tag{9.7}$$

in which δy_t is the latent variable representing the difference of time
t from time $t-1$, y_s is the individual slope or rate of change for each
subject, α and β are regression coefficients, and z_t is a residual term
(McArdle & Hamagami, 2003). This general expression is equivalent
to the latent growth curve model if the β and z terms are set to zero.

9.6.2 Summary

The saturated triple Cholesky model and the biometric simplex model
are parameterized separately for the three variance components (A,
C, and E) usually specified in a model for data collected from twins.
These models have the advantage that they typically fit the data very
well but have the disadvantage that they fail to predict the future of
the series. They also require a large number of parameters when
the time series is long. Growth curve models provide an alternative
framework that is more directly tied to the analysis of data collected
from non–twins. For this type of model, the advantages and disadvantages are the converse of those for the saturated Cholesky and
the biometric simplex. The partitioning of variation for latent growth
curve and difference score models occurs at a level more distal to the
observed phenotypes than is the case for the biometric simplex and
triple Cholesky models. This more remote partitioning of variation
into genetic and environment components creates a simpler model
that requires fewer parameters but that is less likely to fit the data
adequately. We should remember, however, that it is not the objective of a model to fit every set of observed data; such a model would
be tantamount to reporting either the data or a transformation of it.
Relying exclusively on unrestrictive models of this type would hinder
inference and prediction about other sets of data, and thus scientific
progress.

9.7 Dynamical Systems Models

There has been extensive research into dynamical systems in the
physical sciences. Models for the behavior of springs, oscillators,

thermostats, and so on are of substantial interest to physicists and engineers and form the foundation of research into such exotic areas as chaos theory and nonlinear dynamics (Beltrami, 1987). More recently, Boker and colleagues (Boker, 2002; Boker, Neale, & Rausch, 2004) have investigated the potential of dynamical systems models for psychological research. A natural extension of this work is to consider genetic models for dynamical systems. We focus on a simple linear dynamical system, commonly used to model the behavior of a damped oscillator. Given that physiological processes, such as the homeostatic regulation of body temperature and blood sugar concentrations, and, to some extent, the firing of neurons can be modeled in this way, it seems reasonable to suppose that the expression of genes over time, or the regulation of responses to environmental events, might be usefully modeled in this way.

The essence of the linear dynamical system for a damped oscillator is that it specifies certain relations between the level of a function and its first and second derivatives. The function is taken to be the trace of the level on the y–axis measured over time t on the x–axis. In this system, the second derivative of the function with respect to time is specified as a linear function of the level and the first derivative:

$$\frac{d^2 L}{dt^2} = \eta L + \zeta \frac{dL}{dt}$$

or using dot notation for derivatives with respect to time,

$$\ddot{L} = \eta L + \zeta \dot{L} \ .$$

The values of L and $\dot{L}$ are allowed to covary. This linear system models damping; that is, it tends toward an equilibrium value, or set point, when the values of η and ζ are negative. When η is negative and $\zeta^2 < -4\eta$, the system will exhibit oscillations about an equilibrium. When ζ is positive, the system will diverge from equilibrium; that is, rather than damping, it will exhibit amplification.

Structural equation modeling of individual differences in the parameters of dynamical systems has been described by Boker (2002). One readily implemented method is to precompute measures of the mean level and the first and second derivatives of a time series. This simple approach has the advantage of yielding quantities that are readily modeled as observed variables in standard genetic models. A

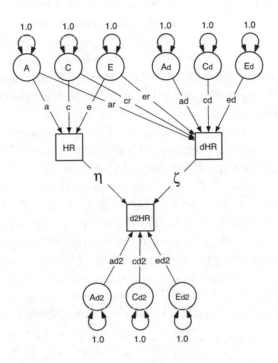

Figure 9.11: Path diagram of a psychodynamic model: a linear dynamic model specified as a psychometric factor model. Here HR, dHR, and $d2HR$ represent heart rate and its first and second derivatives, respectively.

structural equation model for this approach is shown in Fig. 9.11. This model is a straightforward extension of the structural equation model for data collected from unrelated persons, described by Boker (2002). In essence, the variances of the level and first and second derivatives are each partitioned into their respective additive genetic, common, and specific environment components. A Cholesky decomposition is used to allow the components of variance for level and first derivative to covary. As is usual with bivariate models of resemblance between twins, this method permits partitioning of the covariance between two variables, in this case L and $\dot{L}$, into genetic and environmental components. An empirical study might, for example, reveal that the covariation between these components is entirely environmental in origin.

A second approach to the analysis of these precomputed estimates of the level and first and second derivatives is to use the biometric factors, or independent pathway, model (Kendler et al., 1987; McArdle & Goldsmith, 1990; M. C. Neale & Cardon, 1992). In this case, the simple structure of the relations between $L, \dot{L}$, and $\ddot{L}$ of L and $\dot{L}$ covarying and causing $\ddot{L}$ may be shifted to the latent additive genetic, common environment, and specific environment components. This approach is analogous to the Eaves et al. (1987) approach to specifying simplex structures to the variation and covariation over time. This alternative model allows specification of variance components, each of which is hypothesized to behave as a damped oscillator.

9.7.1   Application to Cardiovascular Data

Sample

These methods were applied to a set of data collected in the Medical College of Virginia Study of Cardiovascular Health. Twin pairs living in the Commonwealth of Virginia were ascertained using school rosters for identification. Twin families were asked to participate in a longitudinal adolescent cardiovascular study. The sample for the present analyses consists of 106 MZ and 43 DZ male Caucasian twin pairs who participated in at least one of possibly six visits. The first visit was as close as possible to the twin's 11th birthday, with follow–up visits at 12.5, 14, 15.5, and 17 or to the twin's 9.5th with a follow–up 18 months later (at ages 11 and 12.5). The sample consisted of male and female MZ and DZ pairs. The protocol was approved by the institutional review committee, and all subjects gave informed consent. The data used here are from a single visit, close to the twins' 11th birthday.

Zygosity was assessed initially through a questionnaire and confirmed by testing of the twins and their parents for the ABO, MNS, Rh, Kell, Fy, Hp, Tf, Hb, PGM. AP, G-6-PD, Ct, and LDH systems. HLA typing was also performed. With this battery of polymorphisms, the probability that completely concordant pairs are MZ is typically > 0.999.

Systolic and diastolic blood pressure measures were taken 10 times, at the end of each minute in each of 5 consecutive 2–minute periods. Activities during these periods occurred in the following sequence: rest, hand grip, rest, mental arithmetic, rest. To illustrate the dynamic modeling approach, we used three consecutive measures: the second handgrip assessment and the two subsequent resting measures.

Data analysis

Two models are fitted. The first specifies the oscillator at the phenotypic level and uses the common pathway or psychometric factor model approach to specify the oscillator model directly on the observed level, first derivative, and second derivative $(BP, \dot{BP},$ and $\ddot{BP})$, and partition the variation into A, C, and E components. The second approach specifies a separate oscillator model for each of the A, C, and E components and is similar to the genetic simplex, independent pathways (biometric factor) model. Thus, in parallel to the distinction between the psychometric and the biometric, we can label these models psychodynamic and biodynamic, respectively.

Two options for model specification are possible. First, we could precompute estimates of the mean, the first derivative, and the second derivative using local linear approximation (Boker & Nesselroade, 2002):

$$
\begin{aligned}
L &= y_2 \\
\dot{L} &= (y_3 - y_1)/2t \\
\ddot{L} &= (y_3 + y_1) - 2y_2/t^2,
\end{aligned}
\tag{9.8}
$$

where y_1 is the manifest variable y at occasion 1 and t is the unit of time elapsed between occasions (in the following analysis assumed to be $t = 1$). One problem with this approach is that if, for example, y_2 is missing for one twin, then both L and $\ddot{L}$ become missing. An alternative, which retains all the information, is to respecify the model so that the derivatives are latent variables and the observed scores y_1, y_2, and y_3 are linear functions of these latent variables. The appropriate linear functions of the latent variables can be found with a little matrix algebra:

$$\begin{pmatrix} L \\ \dot{L} \\ \ddot{L} \end{pmatrix} = \begin{pmatrix} 0 & 1 & 0 \\ -.5 & 0 & .5 \\ 1 & -2 & 1 \end{pmatrix} \begin{pmatrix} y_1 \\ y_2 \\ y_3 \end{pmatrix}$$

or

$$\mathbf{L} = \mathbf{By}$$

so

$$\mathbf{B}^{-1}\mathbf{L} = \mathbf{y}.$$

In this case, we can specify fixed factor loadings that correspond to the elements of $\mathbf{B}^{-1}$, which are

$$\begin{pmatrix} 1 & -1 & .5 \\ 1 & 0 & 0 \\ 1 & 1 & .5 \end{pmatrix}.$$

We note that for this method to work, in general, the matrix $\mathbf{B}$ must be nonsingular, but this is normally the case because a singular matrix $\mathbf{B}$ would imply redundancy in the derived estimates of the derivatives.

Therefore, the biodynamic model for the covariance of twins scores on the three time points (y_1, y_2, y_3) can be written:

$$\left(\mathbf{J} \otimes \mathbf{B}^{-1}\right) \begin{pmatrix} \mathbf{A} + \mathbf{C} + \mathbf{E} & \alpha\mathbf{A} + \mathbf{C} \\ \alpha\mathbf{A} + \mathbf{C} & \mathbf{A} + \mathbf{C} + \mathbf{E} \end{pmatrix} \left(\mathbf{J} \otimes \mathbf{B}^{-1}\right)',$$

in which $\mathbf{J}$ is a 2×2 identity matrix, $\otimes$ denotes Kronecker product, and α is 1 for MZ twin pairs and .5 for DZ:

$$\begin{aligned} \mathbf{A} &= (\mathbf{I} - \mathbf{K})^{-1} * (\mathbf{X} * \mathbf{X}') * (\mathbf{I} - \mathbf{K})^{-1\prime} \\ \mathbf{C} &= (\mathbf{I} - \mathbf{L})^{-1} * (\mathbf{W} * \mathbf{W}') * (\mathbf{I} - \mathbf{L})^{-1\prime} \\ \mathbf{E} &= (\mathbf{I} - \mathbf{M})^{-1} * (\mathbf{Z} * \mathbf{Z}') * (\mathbf{I} - \mathbf{M})^{-1\prime}. \end{aligned} \qquad (9.9)$$

$\mathbf{I}$ is an identity matrix of order 3; $\mathbf{X}, \mathbf{W}$, and $\mathbf{Z}$ are lower triangular matrices with free parameters except elements $(3, 1)$ and $(3, 2)$ and elements i, j where $j > i$; and $\mathbf{K}, \mathbf{L}$, and $\mathbf{M}$ are (3×3) with free parameters in elements $3, 1$ and $3, 2$ (for η and ζ, respectively) and zero otherwise. The psychodynamic model has the same form, except that the matrices $\mathbf{K}, \mathbf{L}$, and $\mathbf{M}$ are equated, so that the same oscillator mechanism is specified for all components. This is equivalent to specifying oscillation operating at the phenotypic, instead of the biometric, factor level.

Results

To establish a baseline model against which the psychodynamic and biodynamic models can be compared, we fitted the triple Cholesky model to the raw three occasion twin data, using the male MZ and DZ pairs (N = 106 and N = 43, respectively). Very few subjects had missing data, and we assume that these observations are missing at random. Estimates of the variance components are shown in Table 9.1, along with the contributions to covariance computing by element–wise division of, for example, $\mathbf{A}/(\mathbf{A} + \mathbf{C} + \mathbf{E})$. These results show modest heritabilities for blood pressure on all three occasions (.30, .22, .11) and a somewhat reversed pattern for the proportion of variance due to shared environment (.13, .12, .25). There is fairly substantial phenotypic correlation between the occasions, which is largely due to genetic and specific environment factors; the shared environment contributes little to covariation between the first occasion (hand grip) and the two subsequent rest conditions. Minus twice the likelihood of the data under this model is 2054.88, with 21 parameters and 888 observed diastolic blood pressure (DBP) readings.

Results of fitting the biodynamic model are shown in Table 9.2. First, we note that this model yields exactly the same log–likelihood as the triple Cholesky model, and it has the same number of parameters. Therefore, the proportions of variation due to heritable factors, and so on, discussed earlier for the triple Cholesky apply here; the model, however, yields insights into the possible mechanisms controlling change over time. We now obtain estimates of the variation in and covariation between the level of DBP and its first and second

Table 9.1: Parameter estimates of additive genetic, common environment and specific environment components of variance and covariance from triple Cholesky analysis of diastolic blood pressure data obtained from 11 year old twin boys.

	Unstandardized			Standardized		
	Additive Genetic					
	HG	R1	R2	HG	R1	R2
HG	0.37	0.25	0.18	0.30	0.48	0.39
R1	0.25	0.17	0.12	0.47	0.22	0.22
R2	0.18	0.12	0.09	0.39	0.22	0.12
	Common Environment					
	HG	R1	R2	HG	R1	R2
HG	0.16	-0.02	0.02	0.13	-0.04	0.04
R1	-0.02	0.09	0.13	-0.04	0.12	0.23
R2	0.02	0.13	0.19	0.04	0.23	0.25
	Specific Environment					
	HG	R1	R2	HG	R1	R2
HG	0.71	0.29	0.27	0.57	0.56	0.57
R1	0.29	0.51	0.31	0.56	0.66	0.55
R2	0.27	0.31	0.49	0.57	0.55	0.63

Note: Measures were taken three times: during handgrip (HG), and two rest periods (R1 and R2)

Table 9.2: Parameter estimates of additive genetic, common environment and specific environment components of variance and covariance from fitting a biodynamic model to diastolic blood pressure data obtained from 11 year old twin boys.

	Unstandardized			Standardized		
			Additive Genetic			
	BP	dBP	d2BP	BP	dBP	d2BP
BP	0.17	-0.06	0.04	0.22	-2.77	-0.09
dBP	-0.06	0.02	-0.01	-2.77	0.09	0.05
d2BP	0.04	-0.01	0.01	-0.09	0.05	0.01
			Common Environment			
	BP	dBP	d2BP	BP	dBP	d2BP
BP	0.09	0.07	-0.08	0.12	3.32	0.16
dBP	0.07	0.08	-0.13	3.32	0.30	0.48
d2BP	-0.08	-0.13	0.33	0.16	0.48	0.19
			Specific Environment			
	BP	dBP	d2BP	BP	dBP	d2BP
BP	0.51	0.01	-0.42	0.66	0.45	0.92
dBP	0.01	0.16	-0.13	0.45	0.62	0.47
d2BP	-0.42	-0.13	1.39	0.92	0.47	0.80

Note: Measures were taken three times: during handgrip (HG), and two rest periods (R1 and R2), and estimates of latent level (BP), first (dBP) and second derivatives (d2BP) were partitioned into variance components.

derivatives, and the size of the η and ζ parameters of the oscillator. Also obtained are biometric decompositions of variation in these components, and the model provides for different oscillator parameters in these three sources of variation. These estimates are $\eta_A = -.36$ and $\zeta_A = -1.59$ for the additive component, $\eta_C = 2.23$ and $\zeta_C = -3.78$ for the common environment, and $\eta_E = -0.81$ and $\zeta_E = -0.73$ for the specific environment. It is most important to bear in mind that the estimates of variance components shown in Table 9.2 are for the genetic and environmental factors in the components of the dynamical system — the level and the first and second derivatives. There is modest influence of genetic factors (about 22%) on variation in level but negligible separate genetic influence on the derivatives. Indirectly, the genetic factors that influence DBP level affect variation in the derivatives, via parameters η and ζ. A rather less simple picture emerges for the common environment and specific environment components, where the level and the derivatives each have sizable direct contributions from these sources of variance.

Parameter estimates from the psychodynamic model are shown in Table 9.3 and they indicate a damped oscillator, with values of $\eta = -0.59$ and $\zeta = -0.97$. This model yields a broadly similar pattern of genetic contributions to variance, but the common environment variance appears to influence the two derivatives and not the level. This model fits somewhat worse than the two previous models (-2lnL = 2062.25) although not significantly so ($\delta\chi^2 = 7.36$, df $= 4$, $p = 0.12$). By Akaike's information criterion (AIC), it gives a slightly more parsimonious fit (AIC = -2lnL - 2df = 320.25 for the psychodynamic vs. 320.88 for the biodynamic and triple Cholesky).

Figure 9.12 shows plots of the behavior of the oscillator based on the parameters η and ζ estimated under the biodynamic (plots a, c, and e) and the psychodynamic (plot p) models. These plots show damped oscillator behavior for the additive genetic and the specific environment components, but approximately quadratic increasing behavior for the common environment variance over the intervals assessed here (1–3). The psychodynamic model shows quite stable behavior of a damped oscillator, which is what one would expect for a homeostatically regulated biological system such as diastolic blood pressure. In either case, the models have the nice property of making predictions about other occasions and about the effects of other

Table 9.3: Parameter estimates of additive genetic, common environment and specific environment components of variance and covariance from fitting a biodynamic model to diastolic blood pressure data obtained from 11 year old twin boys.

	Unstandardized			Standardized		
	Additive Genetic					
	BP	dBP	d2BP	BP	dBP	d2BP
BP	0.18	-0.06	-0.04	0.23	-2.72	0.09
dBP	-0.06	0.02	0.02	-2.72	0.08	-0.06
d2BP	-0.04	0.02	0.01	0.09	-0.06	0.01
	Common Environment					
	BP	dBP	d2BP	BP	dBP	d2BP
BP	0.08	0.08	-0.12	0.10	3.36	0.25
dBP	0.08	0.08	-0.12	3.36	0.30	0.45
d2BP	-0.12	-0.12	0.39	0.25	0.45	0.22
	Specific Environment					
	BP	dBP	d2BP	BP	dBP	d2BP
BP	0.52	0.01	-0.31	0.67	0.36	0.66
dBP	0.01	0.16	-0.16	0.36	0.62	0.61
d2BP	-0.31	-0.16	1.34	0.66	0.61	0.77

Note: Measures were taken three times: during handgrip (HG), and two rest periods (R1 and R2), and estimates of latent level (BP), first (dBP) and second derivatives (d2BP) were partitioned into variance components.

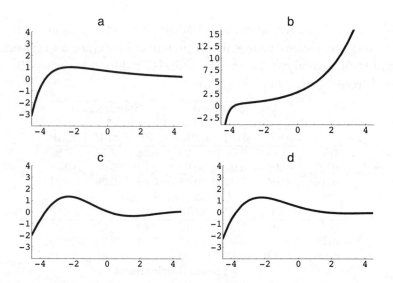

Figure 9.12: Plots of dynamic system behavior estimated from twin data on diastolic blood pressure. The parameter estimates η and ζ for the additive genetic, common environment, and specific environment dynamics were used to draw plots a, b, and c, respectively, while estimates from the psychodynamic model generated plot d.

perturbances (e.g., mental arithmetic) on DBP.

9.8 Conclusion

9.8.1 Likelihood–based Approach

The early part of this chapter describes the advantages of using a general model for the likelihood of observed data. This generalized approach allows for the specification of individual–specific models, in which the predicted means and covariances may differ for every subject in the sample. The likelihood may also be specified as a mixture distribution, with components weighted as an arbitrarily complex function of observed measures on the subjects and free parameters. A wide variety of statistical models are subsumed within this framework.

9.8.2 Strengths of Genetically Informative Research Designs

An important aspect of these models for genetic and environmental variances and covariances is that the biometric components are summed to provide the phenotype. This structuring is not what psychologists or psychometricians would typically use in their first effort to understand a phenomenon or process of interest. More typical approaches use factor analysis or item response theory (IRT) models that are based entirely on covariances within an individual. Studies of one type of family relative, such as siblings, extend the set of observed multivariate statistics in two ways: (a) covariances within variables across relatives and (b) correlations across variables across relatives. One class of relative allows partitioning of variation into familial versus individual specific. Two classes of relatives, such as MZ and DZ twins, may permit a further partitioning of the familial variance. The familial and nonfamilial components may counteract one another when generating covariance between observed phenotypes. It would be possible for the familial component to create a strong positive correlation between two traits or items, whereas the nonfamilial component generates a strong negative correlation, resulting in a zero phenotypic correlation. Yet, the joint assessment of these two

measures could prove very informative when we wish to obtain good
estimates of the latent factors. For this reason alone, it would make
sense to revisit the construction of all psychometric assessments using
data collected from groups of relatives.

In this chapter, we showed that the two primary multivariate
models used in multivariate twin research, the one psychometric factor and the one A, one C, and one E biometric factor model are
both submodels of the three–factor psychometric factor model. It
is a matter for empirical study to find out which of these models
provides the most parsimonious explanation for specific multivariate
assessments of twins. To date, the biometric factor model frequently
provides a substantially better fit than the one–factor psychometric
factor model. Whether this remains the case when two– or three–
factor psychometric factor models are used remains to be seen. An
interesting feature of the psychometric factor model, as applied to
data collected from twins, is that it is not invariant to factor rota-
tion. Orthogonal rotations of factor loadings in such a model yield
different fits to the observed data, due to the need to predict covariances across relatives, as well as within them. This is but one example
where data from relatives can be especially useful to psychology. As a
corollary to this, it should be noted that on the whole, behavioral geneticists are not just interested in estimating heritabilities or finding
genes. Rather, genetically informative studies provide ways to test
hypotheses about the measurement, the role of environmental risk
factors, comorbidity between disorders, and development and aging
across the life span.

Developmental and dynamic models

Following the description of a simple univariate model for data collected from twins, two popular models for multivariate analysis were
described in this chapter. The *psychometric factor model* partitions
variation in the latent variables of standard factor analysis models.
That is, the random components of the factor model — the latent
factors and the variable–specific residuals — are each partitioned into
components representing additive genetic, common environment, and
specific environment (A, C, and E) latent factors. The commonly
used *biometric factor model* specifies three latent factors and con-

strains the covariance of these factors across relatives to represent pure A, C, or E factors.

We discussed how growth curve models for twin data essentially partition components of the growth curve model in a way similar to that of the psychometric factor model. In the case of the linear growth curve model, level and slope are partitioned; in the case of certain nonlinear growth curves, initial value, asymptote, and rate are partitioned. More complex growth curve functions could be partitioned similarly. One aspect of growth curve modeling is that it makes predictions about both means and covariances, and indeed certain nonlinear growth curve models are not identified without information on the means. This restriction limits the partitioning of growth curves into genetic versus environmental growth curves because there is only a vector of observed phenotypic means. Observed genetic means might be observable in future studies of measured genetic factors, but to date, identification of these factors has proved difficult.

A model for twin data based on a simple dynamic model for oscillator was presented. Because these models are not tied to the means, it was possible to distinguish between genetic and environmental dynamic components. In our application to diastolic blood pressure in male twins, we found marginally better support for the psychometric version of the dynamic model.

Psychogenetics

All the modeling described in this chapter is possible simply by obtaining measures from related individuals. The collection of tissue samples to obtain specific genetic markers, such as is commonly done in linkage or association studies, is not required. However, as we have shown elsewhere (Allison & Neale, 2002; M. C. Neale et al., 1999; M. C. Neale, 2000, 2001), linkage and association analyses can also be considered from within the likelihood framework outlined here, and if available, they too can prove valuable in solving psychometric and etiological issues of interest to psychologists rather than geneticists. Perhaps a little Aristotelian logic would help to encourage psychologists to consider genetically informative designs in their research:

1. Psychologists know a lot about structural equation models.

2. Genetic models are just structural equation models.

3. Therefore, psychometricians know a lot about genetic models.

More seriously, studies of relatives continue to provide excellent opportunities to test hypotheses that are close to the hearts — and minds — of psychologists.

References

Allison, D. B., & Neale, M. C. (2002). Joint tests of linkage and association for quantitative traits. *Theoretical Population Biology*, *60*, 239–251.

Allison, D. B., Neale, M. C., Zannolli, R., Schork, N. J., Amos, C. I., & Blangero, J. (1999, Aug). Testing the robustness of the likelihood-ratio test in a variance-component quantitative-trait loci-mapping procedure. *American Journal of Human Genetics*, *65*(2), 531–544.

Bauer, D. B., & Curran, P. J. (2003). Distributional assumptions of growth mixture models: Implications for overextraction of latent trajectory classes. *Psychological Methods*, *8*, 338–363.

Bell, R. Q. (1953). Convergence: An accelerated longitudinal approach. *Child Development*, *24*, 145–152.

Beltrami, E. J. (1987). *Mathematics for dynamic modeling*. San Diego, CA: Academic Press.

Bergeman, C. S. (1997). *Aging: Genetic and environmental influences*. Thousand Oaks, CA: Sage.

Boker, S. M. (2002). Consequences of continuity: The hunt for intrinsic properties within parameters of dynamics in psychological processes. *Multivariate Behavioral Research*, *37*, 405–422.

Boker, S. M., Neale, M. C., & Rausch, J. (2004). Latent differential equation modeling with multivariate multi-occasion indicators. In K. van Montfort, H. Oud, & A. Satorra (Eds.), *Recent developments on structural equation models: Theory and applications* (pp. 151–174). Dordrecht, Netherlands: Kluwer Academic.

Boker, S. M., & Nesselroade, J. R. (2002). A method for modeling the intrinsic dynamics of intraindividual variability: Recovering the parameters of simulated oscillators in multi-wave panel data. *Multivariate Behavioral Research, 37*, 127–160.

Bollen, K. A. (1989). *Structural equations with latent variables.* New York: Wiley.

Boomsma, D. I., Martin, N. G., & Molenaar, P. C. M. (1989). Factor and simplex models for repeated measures: Application to two psychomotor measures of alcohol sensitivity in twins. *Behavioral Genetics, 19*, 79–96.

Boomsma, D. I., & Molenaar, P. C. M. (1986). Using lisrel to analyze genetic and environmental covariance structure. *Behavioral Genetics, 16*, 237–250.

Boomsma, D. I., & Molenaar, P. C. M. (1987). The genetic analysis of repeated measures. *Behavioral Genetics, 17*, 111–123.

Browne, M. W. (1993). Structured latent curve models. In C. M. Cuadras & C. R. Rao (Eds.), *Multivariate analysis: Future directions* (pp. 171–197). Amsterdam, Netherlands: Elsevier Science.

Eaves, L., Foley, D., & Silberg, J. (2003, Dec). Has the "equal environments" assumption been tested in twin studies? *Twin Research, 6*(6), 486–489.

Eaves, L. J., Hewitt, J. K., Meyer, J. M., & Neale, M. C. (1990). Approaches to quantitative genetic modeling of development and age-related changes. In M. E. Hahn, J. K. Hewitt, N. D. Henderson, & R. Benno (Eds.), *Developmental behavior genetics: Neural, biometrical and evolutionary approaches* (pp. 266–277). Oxford, UK: Oxford University Press.

Eaves, L. J., Last, K., Young, P. A., & Martin, N. G. (1978). Model fitting approaches to the analysis of human behavior. *Heredity, 41*, 249–320.

Eaves, L. J., Long, J., & Heath, A. C. (1986). A theory of developmental change in quantitative phenotypes applied to cognitive development. *Behavior Genetics, 16*, 143–162.

Edwards, A. W. F. (1972). *Likelihood.* London: Cambridge University Press.

Falconer, D. (1965). The inheritance of liability to certain diseases, estimated from the incidence among relatives. *Annals of Human Genetics, 29*, 51–76.

Fulker, D. W., Cherny, S. S., Sham, P. C., & Hewitt, J. K. (1999).

Combined linkage and association sib pair analysis for quantitative traits. *American Journal of Human Genetics, 64*, 259–267.

Galton, F. (1869). *Hereditary genius: An inquiry into its laws and consequences*. Macmillan.

Guttman, L. (1954). A new approach to factor analysis: The radex. In P. F. Lazarsfeld (Ed.), *Mathematical thinking in the social sciences* (pp. 258–349). Glencoe, IL.: Free Press.

Hettema, J. M., Neale, M. C., & Kendler, K. S. (1995). Physical similarity and the equal environment assumption in twin studies of psychiatric disorders. *Behavioral Genetics, 25*, 327–335.

Hewitt, J. K., Eaves, L. J., Neale, M. C., & Meyer, J. M. (1988). Resolving the causes of developmental continuity or "tracking." i. longitudinal twin studies during growth. *Behavioral Genetics, 18*, 133–151.

Kendler, K. S., Heath, A. C., Martin, N. G., & Eaves, L. J. (1987). Symptoms of anxiety and symptoms of depression: same genes, different environments? *Archives of General Psychiatry, 44*, 451–457.

Kendler, K. S., & Kidd, K. K. (1986). Recurrence risks in an oligogenic threshold model: the effect of alterations in allele frequency. *Annals of Human Genetics, 50*, 83–91.

Kendler, K. S., Neale, M. C., Kessler, R. C., Heath, A. C., & Eaves, L. J. (1994). Parental treatment and the equal environment assumption in twin studies of psychiatric illness. *Psychological Medicine, 24*, 579–590.

Lehmann, E. L. (1998). *Elements of large-sample theory*. New York: Springer.

Little, R. J. A., & Rubin, D. B. (1987). *Statistical analysis with missing data*. New York: Wiley and Son.

Lochlin, J. C., & Nichols, R. C. (1976). *Heredity, environment and personality: A study of 850 sets of twins*. Austin, TX: University of Texas Press.

Malthus, T. R. (1798). *An essay on the principle of population as it affects the future improvement of society, with remarks on the speculations of Mr. Godwin, M. Condorcet, and other writers* (First ed.). London: Johnson.

Mardia, K. V., Kent, J. T., & Bibby, J. M. (1989). *Multivariate analysis (probability and mathematical statistics)*. London, U.K.:

Academic Press, Harcourt Brace Jovanovich.

McArdle, J. J. (1994). Structural factor analysis experiments with incomplete data. *Multivariate Behavioral Research, 29*, 409–454.

McArdle, J. J. (2001). A latent difference score approach to longitudinal dynamic structural analyses. In S. R. Cudeck, S. du Toit, & D. Sorbom (Eds.), *Structural equation modeling: Present and future* (pp. 342–380). Lincolnwood, IL: Scientific Software International.

McArdle, J. J., & Boker, S. M. (1990). *Rampath path diagram software*. Denver, CO: Data Transforms.

McArdle, J. J., & Goldsmith, H. H. (1990). Alternative common-factor models for multivariate biometric analyses. *Behavioral Genetics, 20*, 569–608.

McArdle, J. J., & Hamagami, F. (2003). Structural equation models for evaluating dynamic concepts within longitudinal twin analyses. *Behavioral Genetics, 33*(2), 137–159.

McArdle, J. J., & Nesselroade, J. R. (1994). Structuring data to study development and change. In S. H. Cohen & H. W. Reese (Eds.), *Life-span developmental psychology: Methodological innovations* (pp. 223–268). Hillsdale, NJ: Lawrence Erlbaum Associates.

Mehta, P. D., & West, S. G. (2000). Putting the individual back into growth curves. *Psychological Methods, 5*(1), 23–43.

Neale, M., Boker, S., Xie, G., & Maes, H. (2003). *Mx: Statistical modeling* (6th ed.). Richmond, VA: Department of Psychiatry, Virginia Commonwealth University.

Neale, M. C. (1985). *Biometrical genetic analysis of human individual differences*. Unpublished doctoral dissertation, University of London, London, UK.

Neale, M. C. (1994). *Mx: Statistical modeling* (2nd ed.). Richmond, VA: Department of Psychiatry, Medical College of Virginia.

Neale, M. C. (2000). QTL mapping with sib pairs: The flexibility of Mx. In T. D. Spector, H. Snieder, & A. J. MacGregor (Eds.), *Advances in twin and sib-pair analysis* (pp. 220–243). London: Greenwich Medical Media.

Neale, M. C. (2001). The use of Mx for association and linkage analysis. *Genescreen, 1*, 107–111.

Neale, M. C., & Cardon, L. R. (1992). *Methodology for genetic studies of twins and families*. Dordrecht, Netherlands: Kluwer Academic.

Neale, M. C., Cherny, S. S., Sham, P., Whitfield, J., Heath, A. C., Birley, A. C., et al. (1999). Distinguishing population stratification from genuine allelic effects with Mx: Association of ADH2 with alcohol consumption. *Behavioral Genetics, 29*, 233–244.

Neale, M. C., & McArdle, J. J. (2000). Structured latent growth curves for twin data. *Twin Research, 3*, 165–77.

Pearson, K. (1894a). Contributions to the mathematical theory of evolution. *Philosophical Transactions of the Royal Society of London. A, 185*, 71–110.

Pearson, K. (1894b). Contributions to the mathematical theory of evolution. II. Skew variation in homogeneous material. *Philosophical Transactions of the Royal Society of London A, 186*, 343–414.

Pedersen, N. L., McClearn, G. E., Plomin, R., Nesselroade, J. R., Berg, S., & deFaire, U. (1991). The Swedish adoption twin study of aging: An update. *Acta Geneticae et Medicae Gemellologiae: Twin Research, 40*, 7–20.

Plomin, R., Willerman, L., & Loehlin, J. C. (1976). Resemblance in appearance and the equal environments assumption in twin studies of personality traits. *Behavioral Genetics, 6*, 43–52.

Reich, T., James, J. W., & Morris, C. A. (1972). The use of multiple thresholds in determining the mode of transmission of semi-continuous traits. *Annals of Human Genetics, 36*, 163–184.

Reich, T., Rice, J., Cloninger, R., Wette, R., & James, J. (1979). The use of multiple thresholds and segregation analysis in analyzing the phenotypic heterogeniety of multifactorial traits. *Annals of Human Genetics, 42*, 371–389.

Rietveld, M. J., Hudziak, J. J., Bartels, M., Beijsterveldt, C. E. van, & Boomsma, D. I. (2003, Feb). Heritability of attention problems in children: I. Cross-sectional results from a study of twins, age 3-12 years. *American Journal of Medical Genetics. Part B: Neuropsychiatric Genetics, 117B*(1), 102–113.

Sullivan, P. F., Eaves, L. J., Kendler, K. S., & Neale, M. C. (2001, Nov). Genetic case-control association studies in neuropsychiatry. *Archives of Genernal Psychiatry, 58*(11), 1015–1024.

Winerman, L. (2004). A second look at twin studies. *Monitor on Psychology, 35*(4), 46–47.

Wright, S. (1934). The method of path coefficients. *Annals of Mathematical Statistics, 5*, 161–215.